FROM FANTASY TO FAITH

From Fantasy to Faith

The Philosophy of Religion and Twentieth-Century Literature

D. Z. Phillips

Professor of Philosophy
University College of Swansea

MACMILLAN

First edition 1991

Phototypeset by Input Typesetting Ltd, London
Printed in Great Britain by
Billings of Worcester

Published by
MACMILLAN EDUCATION LTD
Houndmills, Basingstoke, Hampshire RG21 2XS
and London
Companies and representatives
throughout the world

British Library Cataloguing in Publication Data
Phillips, D. Z. (Dewi Zephaniah), 1934–
From Fantasy to Faith: The Philosophy of Religion and
Twentieth-Century Literature.
1. English literature. Special themes: Religion – Critical
studies
I. Title
820.9′382

ISBN 0–333–52956–1
ISBN 0–333–52957-X pbk

To
Valerie Gabe
Secretary of the Department of Philosophy
University College of Swansea
1970–88

Contents

Preface

In these essays, you are invited to explore central issues concerning religion through twentieth-century literature. These issues are often stated more directly in literature than they are in contemporary philosophy of religion. The literary voices I engage with simply happen to be those which entered my reflections. They are not meant to represent any kind of survey. On the other hand, my interest in them is not purely personal, since the questions the works occasion are likely to occur to anyone who reflects at all seriously about religion.

In Part I, I discuss the view that, at this stage of civilisation, we should have put aside the childishness of religion. But what is to take the place of empty heaven? Art? Perhaps we are not as self-sufficient as we think, and religion is simply one of those charitable untruths we need to get through life. In Part II, I discuss the view that, having put religion aside, man must make his own moral rules unaided. But what gives such rules their authority? It may be said that the status of the rules depends on the way of life of which they are a part. But, if that is so, that way of life may be invaded by the same idle dreams which can infect religion. Morality, like religion, may degenerate into a vulgar prudence. In Part III, I argue that, just as critics of religion need to recognise religious possibilities which fall outside their criticisms, so religious apologists need to recognise that there are moral perspectives which are independent of religion. In Part IV, I discuss religious perspectives which many philosophical attackers and defenders of religion tend to ignore. These perspectives do not ignore human suffering, but grow out of an experience of it. It is from an awareness of the limits of human existence that people have come to speak of their lives as being in the hands of God. In our dealings with nature, and other human beings, rain falls on the just and the unjust. Recognition of the will of God involves acceptance of this fact,

and loving God involves accepting that nothing is ours by right
and that everything is a gift of grace. This is so, even when love
of God and goodness is silent in face of great human suffering.
God has no omnipotence other than the omnipotence of love.

The idea of writing these brief essays originated in a series I
wrote for Radio Wales and Radio Four in 1985. I am grateful to
David Peat of Radio Wales for his support for the six-part series.

Selections from the essays were given as the 1986 Riddell Memorial Lectures at the University of Newcastle. Selections were also
given as Open Lectures on Religion and Literature at Yale University in the Fall Semester of 1985, and in a course of lectures at
Claremont Graduate School in the Spring of 1986, during my
tenure of visiting professorships at those institutions. I am grateful
to Peter Hawkins at Yale for making the lecture series possible,
and Alfred Louch for facilitating my visit to Claremont. I am also
grateful for the opportunity to deliver two of the lectures as a
Millercomm Lecture at the University of Illinois, Champaign/
Urbana in 1986. At Newcastle, Yale, Claremont and Illinois I ben-
efited from discussions of the lectures.

I am indebted to S. W. Dawson for a seminar on Tennyson at
Swansea, and to many conversations on literature with David
Sims, particularly to conversations about Lucretius, Horace, Eliot
and Larkin. Needless to say, those to whom I am indebted are
not responsible for the conclusions I reach.

I am grateful to Mrs Glynis Storey, Secretary of the Department
of Philosophy at Swansea, for typing the radical revisions I made
to an earlier manuscript, and for the readiness of my colleague,
R. W. Beardsmore, in helping me with the proof reading. The
original typescript was prepared by Mrs Valerie Gabe, to whom,
as Secretary to the Department of Philosophy from 1970 to 1988,
I have been enormously indebted.

DZP

Acknowledgements

The author and publishers wish to thank the following, who have kindly given permission for the use of copyright material.

Faber and Faber Ltd, and Alfred A. Knopf, Inc., for the extracts from *The Collected Poems of Wallace Stevens*.

Martin Secker & Warburg, and Schocken Books, published by Pantheon Books, a division of Random House, Inc., for the extracts from *The Castle* by Franz Kafka, translated by Willa and Edwin Muir with additional materials translated by Eithne Wilkins and Ernst Kaiser © 1930, 1941, 1954 by Alfred A. Knopf, Inc. Copyright renewed 1958 by Alfred A. Knopf, Inc.

Metheun Drama, a division of Octopus Publishing Group, for the extracts from *Three Plays* by Luigi Pirandello.

R. S. Thomas, for the extracts from *Selected Poems 1946–63* by R. S. Thomas, and Gwydion Thomas for the extracts from *Between Here and Now* and *Later Poems 1972–82* by R. S. Thomas.

Faber and Faber Ltd, and Farrar, Straus and Giroux, Inc., for the extracts from 'This be the Verse', 'Annus Mirabilis' and *'High Windows'* by Philip Larkin, © 1974 by Philip Larkin.

Faber and Faber Ltd, for the extracts from *The Whitsun Weddings* by Philip Larkin.

George Hartley and The Marvell Press, for the extracts from 'Next Please', 'Myxomatosis','Reasons for Attendance','Places', 'Loved Ones' and 'Church Going' from *The Less Deceived* by Philip Larkin.

Metheun London, a division of Octopus Publishing Group, and S. G. Phillips, Inc., for the extracts from 'After the Battle' from *The Collected Stories of Isaac Babel* by Isaac Babel , © 1955 by 11S. G. Phillips, Inc.

Harcourt Brace Jovanovich, Inc., and Harold Matson Company, Inc., for the extracts from 'The Artificial Nigger' from *A Good Man is Hard to Find and Other Stories*, by Flannery O'Connor, © 1955 by Flannery O'Connor and renewed 1983 by Regina O'Connor

Penguin Books Ltd, and Virginia Barber Literary Agency, for the extracts from *Something I've Been Meaning to Tell You* by Alice Munro, © 1974 by Alice Munro. Originally published by McGraw-Hill Ryerson Ltd.

Georges Borchardt, Inc., and Farrar, Straus and Giroux, Inc., for the extracts from *The Accident* by Elie Wiesel, © 1962 by Elie Wiesel, originally published in French by Editions du Seuil, 1961, renewal of copyright 1990 by Elie Wiesel; the extracts from *Dawn* by Elie Wiesel, © 1961 by Elie Wiesel, originally published in French by Editions du Seuil, 1960, renewal of © 1989 by Elie Wiesel; the extracts from *Night* by Elie Wiesel, © 1960 by MacGibbon and Kee, originally published in French by Les Editions du Minuit, 1958, renewal of © 1988 by The Collins Publishing Group.

1

Introduction: Marches of Vocabulary

Wither shall I go from thy spirit? or wither shall I flee from thy presence?

If I ascend up into heaven, thou art there; if I make my bed in hell, behold thou art there.

If I take the wings of the morning, and dwell in the uttermost parts of the sea;

Even there shall thy hand lead me, and thy right hand shall hold me.

If I say, Surely the darkness shall cover me; even the night shall be light about me.

Yea, the darkness hideth not from thee; but the night shineth as the day; the darkness and the light are both alike to thee.

For thou hast possessed my reins; thou hast covered me in my mother's womb.

I will praise thee: for I am fearfully and wonderfully made: marvellous are thy works; and that my soul knoweth right well.

What if you had to comment on these words of Psalm 139? I should be very surprised if you were not struck by the certainty they exemplify. The psalmist is talking about the inescapable reality of God. Wherever he goes, heaven, hell, the most distant horizon, the depths of the sea, he cannot escape from God. The psalmist's language is confident. He takes his audience for granted. They, too, he thinks, would acknowledge God's inescapable reality.

Inescapable? What about the evidence? What about the reasons? It has to be admitted that it never occurred to any prophet, or writer in the Old Testament, to seek evidence for the existance of God, let alone prove it. For them, this would be quite pointless, even senseless. The movement of thought in the Old Testament is not from the world to God, but from God to the world. The whole world declared God's presence, not because it gave excellent evidence for God's existence, but because it was seen, from the start, as God's world.

> . . . the hills are girded with joy
> The pastures are clothed with flocks:
>> The valleys also are covered with grain:
>> They shout for joy, they also sing.
>
> Let the floods clap their hands;
> Let the hills sing for joy together.
>
> O Jehovah, how manifold are thy works!
> In wisdom hast thou made them all:
>> The earth is full of thy riches.

How far away that seems! That world is not our world. It hasn't been our world for quite some time. Ever since the Renaissance, and through the Enlightenment, the view of the world as God's world had been under attack. As a result, it has become natural for us to look on religious belief as a conjecture, a hypothesis, and we look for evidence to justify it. Philosophers who write on such matters are busy weighing the probabilities. Some say the probability is that there is a God. Others say that the probability is that there is no God. Despite allegedly weighing the same probabilities, they never agree. How odd! In this scientific age one would at least expect people to be able to calculate! Has the psalmist miscalculated?

But is that our problem — a difficulty in weighing probabilities? Surely not. Our difficulty is that the majority of us no longer naturally see the world as God's world. It is all too easy to escape from God's presence. If we ascend into the heavens, even bishops tell us he is not there. If we descend into the depths, psychoanalysts tell us he is not there either. Our problem is not how to escape from God, but how to find him. We all too easily rise in the morning and lie down in darkness without him. The heavens no longer declare his glory for us, and the hills no longer sing for joy. For us, as T. S. Eliot pointed out, prophetically, the confidence of the psalmist is not available:

We can only say that it appears likely that poets in our civilization, as it exists at present, must be *difficult*. Our civilization comprehends great variety and complexity, and this variety and complexity, playing upon a refined sensibility, must produce varied and complex results. The poet must become more and more comprehensive, more allusive, more indirect, in order to force, to dislocate if necessary, language into his meaning. [1]

This complexity with which we are faced is recognised by the poet in *Ash Wednesday* (1930). He realises that the issue cannot be forced, that it may be important simply to recognise the difficulty we have in speaking confidently about religious belief:

> Because those wings are no longer wings to fly
> But merely vans to beat the air
> The air which is now thoroughly small and dry
> Smaller and dryer than the will
> Teach us to care and not to care
> Teach us to be still. [2]

It is in Eliot's *Four Quartets* that the poet shows what is involved in the struggle to mediate religious sense. He sees, clearsightedly, that the past, present and future have innumerable bearings on each other. We cannot understand our present circumstances without taking account of those which led up to them. The past and the present influence and determine what lies before us. What happens in the future my shift the aspect under which we view the past.

> Time present and time past
> And both perhaps present in time future
> And time future contained in time past
> (*Burnt Norton*, 1935)

If we try to cut off the moment from what precedes and follows it, we rob it of the surroundings in which it can be itself. We become hopelessly entangled in what philosophers have called 'the problem of the specious present'. Eliot is aware of the difficulty:

> If all time is eternally present
> All time is unredeemable.

Religion claims to offer 'an abiding sense'. But how is that sense to be related to past, present and future?

> Time past and time future
> What might have been and what has been
> Point to one end, which is always present.

But how is this possible? The temptation is to think that what we need to find is a religious sense which transcends the contingencies of the world of coming to be and passing away. In *Burnt Norton*, Eliot succumbs to this temptation. He looks for a kind of religious experience which is complete, timeless, immune to any threat. He calls the experience 'mystical', whereas, in fact, it is 'magical' in character:

> At the still point of the turning world. Neither flesh
>   nor fleshless;
> Neither from nor towards; at the still point, there the
>   dance is,
> But neither arrest nor movement. And do not call it
>   fixity,
> Where past and future are gathered. Neither movement from
>   nor towards,
> Neither ascent nor decline. Except for the point, the
>   still point,
> There could be no dance, and there is only the dance.
> I can only say, *there* we have been; but I cannot say
>   where.
> And I cannot say, how long, for that is to place it in
>   time.

But does this concept of religious experience mean anything? How does it avoid the difficulties we have mentioned? Eliot, as we have seen, said that if time is eternally present, it is unredeemable. But isn't his conception of religious experience unredeemble too, cut off as it is from all that precedes and follows it? Little wonder that the poet has to conclude that we cannot hold on to this so-called experience for long in our daily lives:

> Time past and time future
> Allow but a little consciousness
> To be conscious is not to be in time

But what on earth does that mean? Eliot himself is aware of the obvious difficulties, and says immediately:

> But only in time can the moment in the rose-garden,
> The moment in the arbour where the rain beat,
> The moment in the draughty church at smokefall
> Be remembered; involved with past and future.
> Only through time is time conquered.

The poet seeks for analogues of the religious experience he is struggling to convey:

> . . . Words, after speech, reach
> In the silence. Only by the form, the pattern,
> Can words or music reach
> The stillness, as a Chinese jar still
> Moves perpetually in the silence.

But, once again, do the forms or patterns of religious sense have their status or retain it quite independently of circumstances, of what is happening in language and the culture? Eliot, of course, is all too aware that they cannot:

> . . . Words strain,
> Crack and sometimes break, under the burden,
> Under the tension, slip, slide, perish,
> Decay with imprecision, will not stay in place
> Will not stay still . . .

These formidable difficulties are stated in *Burnt Norton*, but they are not resolved. On the one hand, he wants religious experience to be 'timeless', complete, given once-and-for-all. On the other hand, he recognises that the content of religious belief has to be expressed in a language which is not static, which is forever changing:

> Caught in the form of limitation
> Between un-being and being.

The difficulties Eliot wrestles with are our difficulties too. It is unsurprising, therefore, that the ways in which Eliot sets about tackling these issues in verse, captures, prophetically, the alternatives which have faced us with regard to religious belief. Five years separate *East Coker* (1940) from *Burnt Norton*. Eliot's struggle with the mediation of religious sense continues, but his understanding of the conditions and circumstances of the struggle has deepened considerably. Instead of the expression of timeless truths, immune to surrounding change, Eliot is now convinced that there is no deep appreciation of one's surroundings without an appreciation of the changes which have brought them about, and the further changes which may or may not threaten them.

> . . . In succession
> Houses rise and fall, crumble, are extended,
> Are removed, destroyed, restored, or in their place
> Is an open field, or a factory, or a by-pass.
> Old stone to new building, old timber to new fires,
> Old fires to ashes, and ashes to the earth
> Which is already flesh, fur and faeces,
> Bone of men and beast, cornstalk and leaf.

At a time of extremely rapid change, a time when a materialistic optimism had come to a dead-end, what kind of sense does religion have? Eliot reiterates the insight, expressed in *Ash Wednesday*, that the matter cannot be forced. Worse, we may not even be sure of what the matter is which needs to be conveyed. We may not know what hope, love or faith amount to. We cannot take it for granted that we do.

> I said to my soul, be still, and wait without hope
> For hope would be hope for the wrong thing; wait without
>   love
> For love would be love of the wrong thing: there is yet
>   faith
> But the faith and the love and the hope are all in the
>   waiting.

But the waiting is not without style. It appreciates the importance

of what is at stake, and realises, only too well, the futile results
of premature and inadequate efforts to right matters:

> . . . And so each venture
> Is a new beginning, a raid on the inarticulate
> With shabby equipment always deteriorating
> In the general mass of imprecision of feeling,
> Undisciplined squads of emotion . . .

Eliot no longer thinks that the meaning of religious belief can
be secured by invoking self-authenticating moments of intuition,
immune from all that surrounds them. If religious sense is to be
mediated, connections have to be shown between the richness of
religious tradition and the particularity of the present:

> Home is where one starts from. As we grow older
> The world becomes stranger, the pattern more complicated
> Of dead and living. Not the intense moment
> Isolated, with no before or after,
> But a lifetime burning in every moment
> And not the lifetime of one man only
> But of old stones that cannot be deciphered.

Without such contexts as these, the search for religious experience
becomes a search for the vacuous, for 'instant uplift'. Looking
back at such a search, Eliot says in *The Dry Salvages* (1941), 'We
had the experience, but missed the meaning'. Now and again,
however, even in circumstances as unpropitious as these, a saint
will break through despite it all:

> . . . But to apprehend
> The point of intersection of the timeless
> With time, is an occupation for the saint —
> No occupation either, but something given
> And taken, in a lifetime's death in love,
> Ardour and selflessness and self-surrender.

But what of the rest of us?

> . . . There are only hints and guesses.
> Hints followed by guesses; and the rest
> Is prayer, observance, discipline, thought and action.

Sometimes, we can do little more than to hold on to the regularity of religious observances. Doing so is not to be despised.

> We are only undefeated
> Because we have gone on trying;

What this trying may involve for us is brought to poetic culmination by Eliot in *Little Gidding* (1942). The poem's title is taken from the village in Huntingdon where, in the seventeenth century, Nicholas Ferrar established a monastic-like Protestant community. Yet no verification of this fact, no accumulation of facts about it, will, of itself, show us how religion is to mean something for us now. Our sense of what is required of us may be deepened when we contemplate the efforts in the past:

> . . . You are not here to verify,
> Instruct yourself, or inform curiosity
> Or carry report. You are here to kneel
> Where prayer has been valid . . .

We can even learn from those whom religion divided deeply, as in the Civil War. We are deeply confused if we think that their struggles and solutions can simply be reduplicated for us. But we can learn from the way in which both victors and vanquished responded to what was asked of them in their time.

> We cannot revive old factions
> We cannot restore old policies
> Or follow an antique drum.
> These men, and those who opposed them
> And those whom they opposed
> Accept the constitution of silence
> And are folded in a single party.

We, along with the poet, have to struggle, in our own day, to find what an authentic religious voice might be. To arrive at any-

thing worthwhile, the voice must be our own. Imitating the voices
of others will be worthless.

> For last year's words belong to last year's language
> And next year's words await another voice.

But how is this new voice to be found? Eliot has come a long
way from his conviction that religious sense depends on the
intrusion of magical moments in time, each carrying its own atom-
istic significance. If religion has redeeming sense, it will have to
be expressed in a pattern of meaning which informs everyday life.
Only in this way can a timeless truth be said again effectively.

> We shall not cease from exploration
> And the end of all our exploring
> Will be to arrive where we started
> And know the place for the first time.

Eliot is under no illusion about the unpropitious circumstances
for the mediation of religious sense in our century. He is certainly
not optimistic about such mediation. Some have thought otherwise because, at the end of his poem, he says:

> And all shall be well and
> All manner of things shall be well.

But this is not a prediction. It is a prayer. He is not the first to
utter it. Socrates, who said as plainly as any man could, 'Only a
fool would deny, Callicles, that anything can happen to me in this
city', bewildered Callicles by going on to say, nevertheless, 'All
will be well'. Socrates meant that no matter what people did to
him, he would face death with equanimity if he had loved truth
and goodness. The difference between the Socratic declaration and
Eliot's prayer, is the reliance on grace in the latter. The genius of
The Four Quartets is in the poetic right it establishes for Eliot to
utter that prayer.

When we look at attempts to mediate religious sense in our
century, it is easy to see the centrality of Eliot's poetic voice. Many
seek to deny what he shows so clearly. The essays which follow
will show why this should be so. Certainly, where religion is

concerned, the need is to go on from the point at which he left
us. For that, too, there is no formula.

In *Little Gidding*, Eliot gives magnificent expression to the conditions of authentic speech:

> . . . And every phrase
> And sentence that is right (where every word is at home,
> Taking it's place to support the others,
> The word neither diffident nor ostentatious,
> An easy commerce of the old and the new,
> The common word exact without vulgarity,
> The formal word precise but not pedantic,
> The complete consort dancing together)
> Every phrase and every sentence is an end and a beginning,
> Every poem an epitaph . . .

But the conditions are formidable. Who would presume that
many have gone on to express religious belief of a kind which
fulfils them? If one were asked to say what religion meant to one,
would one presume to reply? Might one not feel, harried by those
who offer precise philosophical formulations of religious belief,
much like Eliot's J Alfred Prufrock:

> And I have known the eyes already, known them all —
> The eyes that fix you in a formulated phrase,
> And when I am formulated, sprawling on a pin,
> When I am pinned and wriggling on the wall,
> Then how should I begin
> To spit out all the butt-ends of my days and ways?
>   And how should I presume?

But, in the end, one will work through to *some* account of
religious belief, sympathetic or unsympathetic. We shall be considering a number of such accounts in the essays which follow.
In the absence of complete indifference to religion, such accounts
continue to exert their influence and to exact their price. But the
accounts themselves are also subject to scrutiny. Where belief in
God is concerned, we have to ask whether we are justifiably
confident of any account we offer of it.

Greater glory in the sun,
An evening chill upon the air,
Bid imagination run
Much on the Great Questioner;
What He can question, what if questioned I
Can with a fitting confidence reply. [3]

Notes

1. T.S. Eliot, 'The Metaphysical Poets' in *Selected Essays* (Faber & Faber 1980), p. 289.
2. All quotations from Eliot's poetry are taken from *The Complete Poems and Plays of T S Eliot* (Faber & Faber, 1973).
3. W.B. Yeats, *At Algeciras — A Meditation upon Death*.

Part I
Somewhere Over the Rainbow

Somewhere, over the rainbow, way up high
There's a land that I heard of once in a lullaby.
Somewhere, over the rainbow, skies are blue
And the dreams that we dare to dream, there really do come true.

2

Down the Yellow Brick Road

Religion, in our century, is on the defensive. Why should this be so? Intellectually, it has not been respectable to believe in God. If most intellectuals were asked whether they believe in God, they would reply with the confidence of Iris Murdoch's Antagoras, 'No, of course not! That's all fable, superstitious belief in the supernatural, mythology, suitable for childish primitives'.[1] When Socrates points out to him that many educated people still have religious beliefs, he replies, 'Yes, but fewer and fewer, it's all going out. This is a time of transition. Our civilisation is growing up, we're scientific and factual, we can analyse the old superstitions and see how they arose. God is not the measure of all things, man is the measure of all things. We invented the gods' (pp. 72–3).

Notice the kind of accusation which is made against religion. It is equated with superstition, a superstition that man has seen through, now that he has come of age. Science has rescued us from superstition. Notice, not from false hypotheses, but from superstition. This is an important distinction. When we are confronted by two people, one of whom believes in God and one of whom does not, it is tempting to treat their disagreement as similar to a disagreement between two people who differ, say, about the existence of unicorns. One person insists that there are no unicorns, that they are fictional creatures. The other person knows that most people believe this, but he has a sneaking suspicion that, somewhere, creatures like unicorns exist. One day, he expects someone to come across one. If we look at this disagreement, there are certain important features of it which need to be noted. Both parties to the disagreement agree that the existence of unicorns is conceivable, their existence certainly makes sense. We can all imagine unicorns existing. They would be, perhaps, creatures akin to Welsh ponies with a horn on their foreheads. One person

15

believes that there are such creatures, while the other denies it. Both agree on the criteria which would have to be satisfied in order for it to be true that unicorns exist. The statement 'There are unicorns' and the statement 'There are no unicorns' are genuine contradictories. They contradict each other because the disagreement takes place within a common agreement about what it means to speak of the existence of unicorns.

But things are different where the existence of God is concerned. What are the criteria for determining whether God exists? Are these shared by the person who asserts and the person who denies the existence of God? Is 'God' some kind of object? If so, how can we find out whether it exists? Can we verify God's existence? We know, roughly, how we would go about verifying the existence of a chair, a mountain, a gas, a planet, a rainbow. But none of these procedures seem to be relevant where the existence of God is concerned. We cannot point at an object and say, 'That's God'. This is no trivial matter. It bears importantly on the kind of dispute we take a dispute between a believer and an unbeliever to be. What I mean is this: someone who says that there is no God, may feel that there ought to be some object he *can* point to. It ought to be possible to find it out, and identify it. On the other hand, the person who says that there is a God may reject this way of talking. He does not think God is an object among objects. Indeed, any object you come across, just because it is an object, could not be God. It doesn't matter how impressive the object is, how dramatic or impressive its appearance, it cannot be God. No matter how strange the object, it would be another object which one might succeed in explaining or fail to explain. But that's what it would be — an additional object among objects, and any such object could not be God.

So we see a strange feature emerging concerning the disagreement over God's existence. The atheist says that he does not believe that there is any object corresponding to the word 'God', and the believer says, 'Of course not!' The atheist insists that God's existence should be verifiable in some way akin to those ways in which we verify the existence of other objects, whereas the believer insists that anything which could be verified in this way could not be God. Unlike the dispute about the existence of unicorns, the atheist and the believer do not share common criteria for the existence of God. Their disagreement does not take place within an agreement about the *meaning* of what they are disputing over. That being the case, atheism and belief are not genuine contradictories. 'There is a God' — 'There is no God' is not like 'There are unicorns' — 'There are no unicorns'.

The atheist is not simply saying that belief in the existence of God is false. If he says it is false, he must admit that it *could* be true. 'There are unicorns' is a false proposition, but it could be true. I know what it would be like for it to be true. But when the atheist says, 'There is no God', he does not know what it would be like for the proposition to be true. No object can satisfy what the believer wants to say about God. Objects come into existence, they exist for a certain length of time and then cease to exist. We can distinguish one object from another. It gets its identity from such comparisons and contrasts. But God did not come into existence. We cannot ask how long God has existed and it makes no sense to speak of God ceasing to exist. Think of the words of the psalmist in the previous essay. No object could satisfy such talk of God. But, then, for the atheist, if God is not an object, he is nothing at all. So when someone tries to say that God exists, for the atheist, he is not saying something false, but something meaningless. He wants to speak of God's existence while ignoring the conditions for talking of the existence of things. The believer, the atheist claims, is trying to say something that cannot be said.

On this view, there is no point in the atheist treating the believer as someone who entertains false beliefs. If he entertains false beliefs, they are beliefs which could be true. What the believer entertains, according to the atheist, are not false beliefs, but meaningless beliefs. Once we appreciate this, we do not look for evidence against them, as though they were false hypotheses. What we need to do is to look for explanations of them: we need to ask how meaningless beliefs come to exercise such a hold on people, even people in the twentieth century. Why did man invent the gods?

Our century has become familiar with a certain kind of answer to this question. Primitive man, we are told, found himself in a world he did not understand. He feared nature, feared the thunder and the lightning. In order to make nature more manageable, primitive man personalises it. He hears the voice of the gods in the thunder. Nature, being the expression of the will of the gods, can be influenced by prayer and ritual. But, of course, when men become more and more interested in science, they come of age, and put away their childish ways.

In fact, it is suggested, religious believers seem to be like little children. The world of the small child is a world of magic. The child does not ask how it comes to be clothed and fed. The food and clothes appear, as if by magic. They seem to be gifts for which the child has to do nothing. Yet, all the time, of course, there are perfectly good explanations for the presence of food and clothing. Once the child comes of age, he comes to realise that the world's favours do not come to him by magic. Similarly, primitive man thinks that the gods are angry when it thunders, that the sun is the smile of the gods. Nature's favours are in the hands of the gods. But, like the child, man comes of age. He comes to understand, through science, the coming of thunder and the sun. As a result, he empties the heavens of the gods. The gods become outmoded concepts, part of the childishness which man puts aside when he comes of age.

But getting rid of superstition in our lives is not easy. After all, aren't these tendencies still in ourselves? Don't we fool ourselves if we think we are free of them? Let me give you an example from my own experience. When I sat my first honours examination — in philosophy, of all things — I thought it had gone reasonably well. I happened to be wearing a certain coat and tie. I continued to wear that same coat and tie for the remainder of the examinations. Now, if you ask me whether wearing a certain coat and tie can affect the course of the examination, I should reply, 'Of course not'. I do not mean the suggestion is false. It is utterly meaningless. Yet, I believed it. What does that mean? Well, not that I could tell you what the belief means. Believing is simply acting in the way I did. We call the belief 'superstitious' because it does not fit in with our causal expectations. Yet, it exerts its hold on us. We can all think of plenty of other examples: we touch wood, just in case; we're afraid of the dark; we travel with a St Christopher; and so on.

So we are not free of superstitions. How much more susceptible primitive man must have been. Isn't the cry for God like a child's cry in the dark? When the world does not smile on us, isn't it tempting to invent a god who does? There is a great desire in us for some comfort which is beyond what we see about us. We postulate an order of beings beyond the skies, a dispensation beyond the visible dealings we have with each other. It is this postulation which, increasingly, has come under attack.

If we had to pick a song which sums up the form of attacks on

religion since the Enlightenment, we could do no better than
the song made famous in the 1939 MGM film, *The Wizard of Oz*:
'Somewhere over the rainbow'. *The Wizard of Oz* was written by
L. Frank Baum in 1900,[2] the first of 14 Oz books written by him.
It reflects well, as we have seen, the way early anthropologists,
sociologists and psychoanalysts tried to explain religious belief.
Primitive man creates a 'something over the rainbow' to fulfil his
unfulfilled wishes. Ludwig Feuerbach said that religious belief is
a product of projection. He said: 'If there were no wishes, there
would be no gods'. God is created in man's image. To rid ourselves
of the confusions of religion, we must retrace the steps which led
to them. You'll remember Dorothy's last words in the MGM film
which are also the last words of Baum's novel: 'There's no place
like home'.

Do you remember the three characters Dorothy meets on the
Yellow Brick Road which the Munchkins have said will lead them
to the Emerald City — the Scarecrow who wants a brain, the Tin
Man who wants a heart and the Lion who wants courage? They
want to go to the Emerald City because they have been told that
the Wizard lives there, the Wizard who can grant all their wishes.
But they can only reach the Wizard if they are prepared to follow
the Yellow Brick Road. So off they go to see the Wizard, the
wonderful Wizard of Oz, because of the wonderful things he does.
'Because of the wonderful things he does' — but, as we all know,
the Wizard turns out to be a fraud, a humbug, a little old man
shouting hard into a megaphone in an attempt to sound supernatural. When he is discovered, the Wizard says, 'How can I help
being a humbug when all these people make me do things that
everybody knows can't be done'. The Wizard's tests simply show
that the Scarecrow had brains, the Tin Man a heart, and the Lion
courage, all along. The message seems to be: we must develop
our own abilities and not look for supernatural help. Gore Vidal,
writing about the Oz legend, sees the Emerald City as an alternative, a dream to contrast with the drabness of much of human
life. Vidal says that, like the Scarecrow, he cannot understand
why Dorothy, or anyone else, for that matter, would want to
return to Kansas.[3] But Vidal has forgotten Dorothy's response
when the Scarecrow suggests that she should stay in Oz: 'That's
because you have no brains'. Whatever the harsh realities of
Kansas, it is real, at least, whereas Oz is pure fantasy. We lose
nothing if we give up Oz, any more than Dorothy did. Oz, para-

dise, is a mere projection from our familiar surroundings. The Scarecrow, the Tin Man, the Lion and even the Wizard were all projections based on real characters she knew in Kansas, home on the farm.

'There's no place like home' — that could be the motto of atheistic humanism. Man's natural home is not a 'somewhere else', a fantasy beyond the sky. Rather, it is here, on earth, in a human society which does not need the supernatural to explain it. True, we are tempted, for various reasons, to dream of a somewhere over the rainbow, but these reasons are confused and lead us astray. They lead us down the yellow brick road. If we have taken this wrong turning, it is the work of philosophers, sociologists, anthropologists and psychoanalysts to show us where we have gone wrong. They will help us to retrace our steps, unravel our confusions, bring us back to this our one and only world. Once we have our feet on the ground, freed from flights of fancy, we will learn to cope with our lives without invoking a country, a being, or a helper, beyond the sky. This is how Freud expressed the vision:

> And, as for the necessities of Fate, against which there is no help, they will learn to endure with resignation. Of what use to them is the mirage of wide acres in the moon, whose harvest no one has ever seen? As honest smallholders on this earth they will know how to cultivate their plot in such a way that it supports them.[4]

Notes

1. Iris Murdoch, 'Above the Gods' in *Acastos* (Penguin, 1987), p. 72.
2. L. Frank Baum, *The Wizard of Oz* (Puffin, 1984).
3. Gore Vidal, 'The Oz Books' in *Pink Triangle and Yellow Star and Other Essays 1976–1982* (Granada, 1983).
4. Sigmund Freud, *The Future of an Illusion* (Hogarth Press, 1962), p. 46.

3

Emptying Heaven

The conclusion of the previous essay was that in losing heaven, we gain the earth. We are freed from supernatural fantasy and given a chance to become naturally self-sufficient. But don't we lose the most precious thing of all without religion, namely, the hope of immortality? But what kind of hope is this? Does it mean anything, or is it just another projected fantasy?

When immortality is discussed today, either it is taken for granted that we are assessing the probabilities of survival after death, a quasi-empirical enquiry, or else testing the authenticity of alleged attempts by the dead to get in touch with us. Science or seance — that seems to be the choice. Little wonder that many refuse that choice entirely; they will have nothing to do with it. Are not the very hopes behind the choice a product of illusion and confusion? Man is so afraid to die, longs to survive so much, that he projects a heaven from his emotions, a heaven which consoles him. This is why Feuerbach claimed that man's grave is the birthplace of the gods. We need to be rescued from religious illusions. This can only be done by emptying heaven, dismantling it, so that we may have a true view of the earth, and ourselves, once again.

Many philosophers and theologians who discuss immortality or resurrection today, would have a shock if they re-read T. S. Eliot's 1936 essay on Tennyson's *In Memoriam*. Eliot asserts that the faith expressed in the poem is a poor thing. The irony is that nowadays, in the circles I have mentioned, Tennyson's faith in immortality is considered ideal and passes for orthodoxy. What Eliot said in 1936 is even truer today as far as religion is concerned: the age which has succeeded Tennyson's surpasses it in shallowness.

So is this the choice facing us — a heaven created by our fears, or an empty heaven with a true view of the earth? As we shall see, this is a false choice. It may turn out to be just as urgent for religion that believers, too, should dismantle Tennyson's heaven, not simply in order to see earth again, but so that a different, lost

heaven might be reclaimed and seen again too. But in this essay
I shall be concerned with views, such as those of the American
poet, Wallace Stevens, who think that when a heaven, such as
Tennyson's is rendered empty, religion of any kind is shown to
be empty at the same time. Both Tennyson and Stevens fail to see
any possibilities outside the false choice I have mentioned. Here
is Tennyson:

> Thou wilt not leave us in the dust:
> Thou madest man, he knows not why:
> He thinks he was not made to die;
> And thou hast made him: thou art just.[1]

But, now, Wallace Stevens:

> The earth, for us, is flat and bare.
> There are no shadows. Poetry
> Exceeding music must take the place
> Of empty heaven and its hymns.[2]

Tennyson's poem, written after the death of his friend, Arthur
Hallam, was regarded by his contemporaries as an assertion of
faith, an assertion born of a marriage between the Darwinism of
his day, and formal adherence to the Christian creeds. On the one
hand, nature testifies that every living thing ends in death. On
the other hand, there is in man, an instinct, a cry from the heart,
which makes him fly in the face of nature's testimony, and hope
for survival after death.

> If e'er when faith had fall'n asleep,
> I heard a voice 'believe no more',
> And heard an ever-breaking shore
> That trembled in the Godless deep;
>
> A warmth within the breast would melt
> The freezing reason's colder part,
> And like a man in wrath the heart
> Stood up and answer'd 'I have felt',

How are reason and feeling to be reconciled? For Tennyson, by
postulating that human development does not cease at death, but

continues after it. Thus he brought about an unlikely marriage between Christianity and human perfectability:

> No longer half-akin to brute,
> For all we thought, and loved and did
> And hoped, and suffer'd, is but seed
> Of what in them is flower and fruit;
>
> Whereof the man, that with me trod
> This planet, was a noble type
> Appearing ere the times were ripe,
> That friend of mine who lives in God,
>
> That God, which ever lives, and loves,
> One God, one law, one element,
> And one far-off divine event,
> To which the whole creation moves.

Already, we can see, in these lines, the tensions Tennyson's enterprise creates. As Eliot says, 'his feelings were more honest than his mind'.[3] He is not content to place his noble dead friend on a Darwinian evolutionary ladder, and so he has to say that he was born before his time; hardly a happy resolution of the problem for either friendship or evolution. In his critical study, *Tennyson*, published in 1899, Stephen Gwynn says of the poet's attempted synthesis of religion and science:

'The more one thinks of this conception, the more apparent is its vagueness and want of outline. That, I think, did not trouble the poet. He was content to convince himself that we were put here with a purpose, and that we had a life to live beyond the grave; for the scope and range of this threescore years and ten pinned down to a point in limitless space seemed to him in itself a mockery of insignificance.'[4]

Gwyn sees Tennyson as untroubled. Eliot sees him as deeply troubled:

In Memoriam can, I think, justly be called a religious poem, but for another reason than that which made it seem religious to his contemporaries. It is not religious because of the quality of its faith, but because of the quality of its doubt. Its faith is a poor thing, but its doubt is a very intense experience. *In Memoriam* is a poem of despair, but of despair of a religious kind.[5]

When Tennyson despairs at the death of his friend, we have, as Eliot says, 'great poetry, economical of words, a universal emotion related to a particular place':

> Dark house, by which once more I stand
> Here in the long unlovely street,
> Doors, where my heart was used to beat
> So quickly, waiting for a hand,
>
> A hand that can be clasp'd no more —
> Behold me, for I cannot sleep,
> And like a guilty thing I creep
> At earliest morning to the door.
>
> He is not here; but far away
> The noise of life begins again
> And ghastly thro' the drizzling rain
> On the bald street breaks the blank day.

But this is not all we have. Tennyson is convinced, or better, tries to convince himself, that his friend has survived death, and is now living in some other realm, in some heaven. Eliot's assessment of this aspect of *In Memoriam* is exactly right:

> . . . he is naturally, in lamenting his friend, teased by the hope of immortality and reunion beyond death. Yet the renewal craved for seems at best a continuance, or a substitute for the joys of friendship upon earth. His desire for immortality never is quite the desire for Eternal Life; his concern is for the loss of man rather than for the gain of God.[6]

For example, Tennyson begins to worry about the company Hallam is keeping in heaven. Will he not be mingling with the great? Their friendship may seem small fry compared with such communings. Tennyson is hurt at these thoughts and warns the soul of his dead friend against them:

Yet turn thee to the doubtful shore,
Where thy first form was made a man;
I loved thee Spirit, and love, nor can
The soul of Shakespeare love thee more.

These lines are far removed from the expression of despair I
quoted earlier. So are lines in which Tennyson wishes, somehow,
that Hallam would get in touch with him; lines which smack more
of a seance than of spirituality:

Descend, and touch and enter; hear
The wish too strong for words to name;
That in the blindness of the frame
My Ghost may feel that thine is near.

For Wallace Stevens, this is an attempt to turn Hallam into an
ethereal being; into an angel, almost. We have lost sight of Hallam
as he really was. The angel Stevens offers in his poetry is, he says,
an angel of reality:

I am one of you and being one of you
Is being and knowing what I am and know.

Yet I am the necessary angel of earth,
Since, in my sight, you see the earth again.[7]

We see the earth again. Why, then, had we lost sight of it? Yes,
in the very act of creating a heaven out of our own fears. Yet,
Tennyson was not unaware of these dangers and doubts. On the
contrary, he gives powerful expression to them:

What profit lies in barren faith,
A vacant yearning, tho' with might
To scale the heaven's highest height,
Or dive below the wells of Death?

What find I in the highest place,
But mine own phantom chanting hymns?
And on the depth of death there swims
The reflex of a human face.

Does not that express Stevens' sentiments perfectly? The big difference is that Tennyson's despair is a religious one. He wants, somehow, to fulfil his religious desires by transcending the doubts. Stevens, on the other hand, sees the doubts as liberating us from desires we should not have in the first place. He does not call life incomplete, awaiting completion in some other realm. We see human beings die; we see, in nature, its fruit ripen and rot. We try to make permanent these creatures and things of change. But in thinking we can make them permanent, we change their character, since their character is inextricably bound up with coming to be and passing away. Thinking we can hold fast to changing things, we crush the very life out of them in our meta-physical grasp. They cease to be the things we loved and cher-ished. This is why, for Wallace Stevens, a changeless heaven, so conceived, is not a place to be desired, but a grotesque parody of the earth we love.

> Is there no change of death in paradise?
> Does ripe fruit never fall? Or do the boughs
> Hang always heavy in that perfect sky,
> Unchanging, yet so like our perishing earth,
> With rivers like our own that seek for seas
> They never find, the same receding shores
> That never touch with inarticulate pang?
> Why set the pear upon those river banks
> Or spice the shore with odours of the plum?
> Alas, that they should wear our colours there,
> The silken weavings of our afternoons,
> And pick the strings of our insipid lutes!
> Death is the mother of beauty, mystical,
> Within whose burning bosom we devise
> Our earthly mothers waiting, sleeplessly.[8]

Such a heaven has to be emptied in order that we may see the earth again. We must not be beguiled by siren voices. Those voices sometimes ask us questions like this: 'Think of a loved one — wife, husband, parent, child, friend. Do you want that loved one to die today?' What a grotesque question! We answer, 'Of course not'. The questioner continues, 'Do you want the loved one to die tomorrow, or the day after, then?' Again we answer, 'Of course not'. 'Ah', the siren voice concludes, 'it follows that you do not

want him to die at all. You wish that he could live for ever.' In
that conclusion we lose sight of the earth. If I do not want an
apple to rot before I eat it, does it follow that what I really want
to eat is an apple which could not rot? Since I do not want loved
ones to die, does it follow that what I really want is to love human
beings who could not die? Of course, it is not true that in all
circumstances death is not welcome. And just suppose that we
were told that we were to go on and on and on! Take away change,
take away death, and we take away, at the same time, what is
wonderful and terrible in love and life.

For Tennyson, the contingency of things, their finitude, seems
to rob them of their point:

> My own dim life should teach me this,
> That life shall live for evermore,
> Else earth is darkness at the core,
> And dust and ashes all there is;
>
> This round of green, this orb of flame,
> Fantastic beauty; such as lurks
> In some wild Poet, when he works
> Without a conscience or an aim.
>
> What then were God to such as I?
> 'Twere hardly worth my life to choose
> Of things all mortal, or to use
> A little patience ere I die;
>
> 'Twere best at once to sink to peace,
> Like birds the charming serpent draws,
> To drop head-foremost in the jaws
> Of vacant darkness and to cease.

For Wallace Stevens, on the other hand, this very same contingency and finitude are seen as essential parts of the wonder of
the world. The descent to death is not, for him, a plunge into
vacant darkness, but a dignified descent which is, in itself, a
victory:

> We live in an old chaos of the sun,
> Or old dependancy of day and night

Of island solitude, unsponsored, free,
Of that wide water, inescapable,
Deer walk upon our mountains, and the quail
Whistle about us their spontaneous cries;
Sweet berries ripen in the wilderness;
And, in the isolation of the sky,
At evening, casual flocks of pigeons make
Ambiguous undulations as they sink
Downward to darkness, on extended wings.[9]

Wallace Stevens is a poet of acceptance. Tennyson is not. He sees life as incomplete, existence as a riddle. As far as Stevens is concerned, the completion, the order, provided by religion is illusory. But the illusion he takes religion to be depends on confining religion within his linguistic parameters. Religion's hopes, fears and religion's heaven are all defined by those parameters. Yet, the irony is that it is these same parameters which limit Tennyson's expressions of faith. Those expressions are desperate, and no sooner does Tennyson utter them than he begins to worry about them. He worries about the language at his disposal:

Behold, we know not anything;
I can but trust that good shall fall
At last — far off — at last, to all,
And every winter change to spring.

So runs my dream: but what am I?
An infant crying in the night:
An infant crying for the light:
And with no language but a cry.

This was precisely the trouble. Tennyson had no language at his disposal to express the faith he yearned for. He yearned for it in an age which, Eliot says 'had, for the most part, no hold on permanent things, on permanent truths about man and God and life and death'. When he tried to speak of faith, he himself feared that he had 'darken'd sanctities with song'. For Stevens, those songs of so-called faith also darken the earth, clouding from us those things which, of necessity, come to be and pass away. For him, when we have emptied heaven, old terrors and fears will be exorcised:

> . . . And shall the earth
> Seem all of paradise that we shall know?
> The sky will be much friendlier then than now,
> A part of labour and a part of pain,
> And next in glory to enduring love,
> Not this dividing and indifferent blue.[10]

At the end of his poetic pilgrimage, Wallace Stevens has shown, powerfully, the need to empty heaven, the false heaven he attacks so well. There may be another heaven, however, one which can only be seen when that attack has had its due. *That* heaven lies outside the parameters of Stevens' verse, as does the God who dwells there.

Notes

1. Tennyson, all quotations from *In Memoriam* in *The English Parnassus* (Clarendon Press, 1952).
2. Wallace Stevens, *The Man with the Blue Guitar* in *Selected Poems* (Faber & Faber, 1965).
3. T. S. Eliot, 'In Memoriam' in *Selected Essays* (Faber & Faber, 1980), p. 336.
4. Stephen Gwynn. *Tennyson* (Blackie, 1899), p. 85.
5. Op. cit., p. 336.
6. Ibid, p. 334.
7. Wallace Stevens, *Angel Surrounded by Paysans* in *Selected Poems*.
8. Wallace Stevens, *Sunday Morning* in *Selected Poems*.
9. Ibid.
10. Ibid.

4

Priests of Our Time

For Wallace Stevens, as we have seen in the previous essay, once
we have emptied heaven of the gods, the sky will seem friendlier.
It will become part of the human story, 'a part of labour and a
part of pain', not 'the indifferent and dividing blue' which religion
makes of it. Religions cut us off from the human in their very
attempts to make sense of human life. The God above the sky,
who is supposed to be responsible for what happens to mankind,
would, if weighed in the decent scales of human justice, be found
guilty of the most monstrous crime — the unalleviated sufferings
of his creatures.

When we look at these sufferings, what kind of description can
we give of the will of the Creator? What kind of script has he
devised for us? In Dennis Potter's 1972 television play, *Follow the
Yellow Brick Road*, Jack Black, a 35-year-old TV actor, now
employed only in commercials, has been driven to seek psychiatric
help in his desperation at contemplating this question. He has
come to the conclusion that we are all in a dirty play, written by
an author who has put filthy words into our mouths. He is convinced that a camera records his every movement. He talks to his
psychiatrist:

> When I was a boy I — When I was little. I thought God was
> watching me all the time, every minute of the day. I could never
> escape his attention, not in the lavatory, not on the football
> field, not eating my dinner. He was there all the time . . . For
> years and years I hadn't thought about it, hadn't considered it.
> I just — assumed — somehow — that he — it — was there, still
> there, still watching, still *present*.[1]

But, then, one morning, at first light, he finds himself forced to
his knees:

> (Rush) I got down on my knees and closed my eyes and I put

my hands together and I said to myself I won't ask for anything, won't ask, *won't ask*, not even for . . . (*Stop*) I'll just let *you* come. I'll just see if you are there if you are still there still there — I'll wait. I'll wait for (*Gets it out*) — *the word*.

But what word came? What word, in his opinion, summed up his surroundings?

That was the word! Slime. That was the message I got. No God. On my knees with my eyes shut I got this one word or feeling or impression or — I don't know — but there it was, long slippery strands of it — slime — nothing else but slime. (*Chokes*) And dirt and — stinking slime contaminating everything. All over my hands. All over my face. In my mouth. In my eyes. (*Shuddering with revulsion*)

The psychiatrist has his own solution to offer:

The crucial thing to realise is that there is absolutely no need to walk around burdened with a sense of disgust. No man should carry *that* sort of cross nowadays . . . If Megabrium had been available two thousand years ago — well, I can think of at least one wild man who would have stuck to carpentry . . . Disgust is a purely medical phenomenon.

But Jack cannot accept this rationalistic explanation. Although no God will come for him, he still longs for purity. But what kind of purity is he looking for? The answer is: a spurious, well-rounded, complete purity, independent of, and unmediated through, that which surrounds it. He finds such a purity in the simple immediacy of television commercials. Dennis Potter comments:

It was, of course, a metaphor both for paranoia and for a world without a loving God. The actor found his Holy City not in any of the traditional images for grace and salvation, but in the television commercials . . . And these polished little dramas do indeed fill the 'natural breaks' on commercial television with penny-off perfection, where families are ideally happy with just one meat cube crumbled into their stew, girls become beautiful with one squirt from an aerosol can and raw pain itself disappears in a stream of glistening, laboratory-tested bubbles. 'Bring me my bow of burning gold.'[2]

These television commercials cannot inform real life. On the contrary, they blind us to the realities, the slime, which surrounds us. But do not religious stories of a happy land, far, far away, have the same effect? This is Potter's verdict: 'I don't think this is so very different from some of the ways "religion" is used to promise us New and Improved Pie in the sky'.[3] These are the grotesque answers religion gives to the world's afflictions.

Such answers are treated in Potter's 1974 play, *Joe's Ark*.[4] Joe, the Welsh keeper of a pet shop, finds that his evangelical religion cannot sustain him when he has to face the fact that his daughter is dying slowly in the upstairs room. When his minister, in Zion Chapel, says in his sermon, 'We all of us lack the holy imagination that could see life as the thrilling wondrous gift that it really is'. Joe can't stand the lie. He stands up and shouts, 'No! That's not true! Not true!' For Joe, a vengeful God, who can let his daughter die, is like someone who first neglects and then tortures the animals in their cages. As for the girl, she simply wants to die in peace. Her bleak, matter of fact realism, a form of atheism, is extremely powerful compared with the religious illusions on offer.

In Potter's 1977 play, *Brimstone and Treacle*, inexcusably banned by the BBC, the yellow brick road offered by religion is considerably more sinister. It turns out to be a road, not simply to illusion but to revulsion. This play, too, concerns a suffering girl, the victim of a road accident which has all but reduced her to a vegetable. Her father is realistic about her condition, but her mother finds solace in a lush, treacly sanctimoniousness. A young man, a demonic figure, intrudes into their lives. He rapes the girl, but plays up to the mother. He offers, and the mother accepts, a terrifying solace. He convinces her that her daughter's terrible plight is not pointless, purposeless or meaningless. Her suffering serves the purpose of calling forth a great love in the young man's care for her; a love which would not otherwise have been forthcoming. This is shocking enough when we come across it in fiction, but I have to tell you that there are influential contemporary philosophers of religion who argue that God allows people to suffer so that others may have the opportunity to develop morally in helping them. It is as if the Good Samaritan, on seeing the victim

of the thieves, said 'Thank you, God, for another opportunity of
developing morally'!

In the three dramas, *Follow the Yellow Brick Road*, *Joe's Ark*, and
Brimstone and Treacle, religion is criticised for dividing man off from
the realities of life. The bandage it offers cannot heal human
wounds. What Dennis Potter says of *Brimstone and Treacle*, can be
said of the other two plays too: 'The play tries to mock sanctimoniousness, which has too become the substitute for, or the last sickly
residue of, religious feelings'.[5] It is not enough to say that what
religion offers is idle language. It does too much damage for that.
It is a language which, once appropriated, divides a man off from
common decencies.

It is this language which breaks Nathanael West's Miss Lonelyhearts. Further, it is the way in which Miss Lonelyhearts tries to
come to terms with this language, which led West to say, 'Miss
Lonelyhearts became the portrait of a priest of our time who has
a religious experience'.[6]

Miss Lonelyhearts is the male writer of the New York Post
Dispatch advice column. Here is his account of how he came to
take the job, and of what it has done to him:

A man is hired to give advice to the readers of a newspaper.
The job is a circulation stunt and the whole staff considers it a
joke. He welcomes the job, for it might lead to a gossip column,
and anyway he's tired of being a leg man. He too considers the
job a joke, but after several months at it, the joke begins to
escape him. He sees that the majority of the letters are pro-
foundly humble pleas for moral and spiritual advice, that they
are inarticulate expressions of genuine suffering. He also discovers that his correspondents take him seriously. For the first
time in his life, he is forced to examine the values by which he
lives. This examination shows him that he is the victim of the
joke and not its perpetrator.[7]

Letters from 'Sick-of-it-all', 'Desperate', 'Broad Shoulders' and
others, plunge Miss Lonelyhearts into depression. He believes
that Christ is the answer, but, at the same time, wants to keep
away from what he calls, the Christ business. He is pursued by
Shrike, the features editor, who mercilessly exposes the sentimental rubbish Miss Lonelyhearts writes in his column; rubbish which
he cannot bring himself to write any longer:' 'Life is worth while,

for it is full of dreams and peace, gentleness and ecstasy, and faith that burns like a clear white flame on a grim dark altar."But he found it impossible to continue. The letters were no longer funny.'

Miss Lonelyhearts' girlfriend, Betty, thinks that his depression is morbid, a sign of sickness. She offers him a simple-minded pattern of country life, but he knows it cannot work. He cannot forget the letter writers. Miss Lonelyhearts drifts into situations from which he hopes, somehow, some kind of redeeming sense will emerge. He tries to have an affair with Shrike's wife, Mary, who, for all her coquettishness, cannot really give herself to him or her husband. When he meets Fay Doyle, a correspondent who has written about her problems with her crippled husband, he is quickly, and somewhat passively, seduced by her. When Doyle himself contacts Miss Lonelyhearts, there are moments when he feels genuine pity for the cripple. However, his attempts at reconciling the cripple and his wife are a disaster, and he just manages to escape another attempt at seduction by Fay Doyle. Miss Lonelyhearts comes to a faith which he thinks can transcend all the storms of life. He experiences what he takes to be union with God. Doyle's arrival seems a heaven-sent opportunity to put his new found love to the test. Actually, Doyle, believing that Miss Lonelyhearts has tried to seduce his wife, has come to shoot him. Panicking at Miss Lonelyhearts' attempts to embrace him, the cripple tries to escape, only to find the stairs blocked by Betty, who is pregnant by Miss Lonelyhearts. In the ensuing struggle, Miss Lonelyhearts is shot. He and the cripple tumble down the stairs together.

Miss Lonelyhearts — a priest of our time! What *can* that description mean? Critics have given wildly different answers to this question; answers which distort one aspect or another of West's description. In these answers, we see our own struggles to mediate religious sense.

At one extreme, there are critics who see *Miss Lonelyhearts* as an exposure, by West, of the illusion religion necessarily is. Josephine Herbst sees the novel as an allegory which has this purpose:

Miss Lonelyhearts stricken with the suffering of the underdog, seeks an answer. Flagellating himself with suffering, he in turn incurs suffering. His sadism breeds back upon himself and in bewilderment he turns to God, symbol of crucifixion and death . . . Let anyone who thinks this implies a grotesqueness out of line with the strictest contemporary reality pick up any newspaper. Terror accompanied by the great wash of indifference is in every line . . . That Miss Lonelyhearts in his great need clutches at nothing better than God is symptomatic also. As he goes down in his bad luck, the unsolved problems of Abandoned, Expectant and Despair must await some other deliverance.[8]

Stephen J. Gerkey argues in a similar way. He argues that the love of God and man which Miss Lonelyhearts seeks, is impossible, not only for him, but, by implication, for all men.

West's structural parody projects a plot designed to depict man's search for religious renewal in an orderly universe ruled by divine plan against the backdrop of an absurd world where God is either dead or irrelevant. Designed to explode the conventions of the traditional quest, *Miss Lonelyhearts* shows that for modern man, the search for spiritual enlightenment leads only to isolation and destruction.[9]

Both critics present a general thesis: West exposes the necessarily illusory character of religious belief. He certainly portrays the destructive language which religion often offers for public consumption. But is that all West is doing? If so, why call Miss Lonelyhearts a *priest* of our time? Why not, simply, a deceived child of our time? If West's sole aim is the exposure of illusion, his central character would not be Miss Lonelyhearts, but Shrike. Just as the shrike bird impales its prey on thorns or barbed wire in order to peck at it, so Shrike, with ruthless cynicism, impales on the logic of his arguments all attempts to understand human afflictions in terms of a divine plan.

Shrike mocks, not only the religious vulgarities of Miss Lonelyhearts' column, but all the alternatives offered once religious belief is put aside: a Thoreau-like celebration of the soil of the kind Miss Lonelyhearts' girlfriend tries to force on him; a Gauguin-like retreat to the South Seas; an aesthetic hedonism – all ignore the realities of human affliction. All these attempts seek to impose a false order on human life. In this judgement, Miss Lonelyhearts and Shrike are as one. Shrike would endorse Miss Lonelyhearts' judgement of the simple-minded order his girlfriend, Betty, sees in rural life; a judgement which could be extended to all the other false orders on offer: 'Her world was not the world and could never include the readers of his column. Her sureness was based on the power to limit experience arbitrarily. Moreover, his confusion was significant, while her order was not.'

Here we have West's final verdict on religion's fake consolations, the postulation of a divine planner above the sky: this order is not significant. On the other hand, in face of disorder, Miss Lonelyhearts cannot embrace Shrike's cynicism:

> Miss Lonelyhearts, my friend, I advise you to give your readers stones. When they ask for bread don't give them crackers as does the Church, and don't, like the State, tell them to eat cake. Explain that man cannot live by bread alone and give them stones. Teach them to pray each morning: 'Give us this day our daily stone.'

West, however, wants to do more than expose religion's false consolations. There is even more to Shrike than that. He knows that Miss Lonelyhearts is trying to have an affair with his wife. In an off-guard moment, he confesses to Miss Lonelyhearts that he suffers too. Even though his love is of the flesh, and devoid of the spiritual, he says he is driven to womanise by his wife's failure to give herself to him. Even in Shrike, the cynic, there is a longing for something more, something different. He is not content with the disorder, and the desperate character of his cynicism reveals this. This longing for something different obsesses Miss Lonelyhearts. It is in the way he tries to appease this longing that we find out why West called Miss Lonelyhearts a priest of our time.

This will never be appreciated, however, if we react to the novel in the way critics, at the other extreme from those we have considered, have done. Embarrassingly, they see the novel as an unqualified celebration of religion! James Light sees in Miss Lonelyhearts a 'Christlike man who perceives that love and faith are the only answers in a universe he cannot understand'.[10] This really is embarrassing, since Light is actually identifying West's parody of faith, the Christ complex, with genuine faith. Instead of seeing Miss Lonelyhearts as a priest *of* our time, the critic has made him a priest *to* our time — the last thing West is suggesting. For West, Miss Lonelyhearts is not a prophet *in* our age, but a product of our age.

Other critics, such as Arthur Cohen, see, in Miss Lonelyhearts, a holy fool, who cannot be heard by the society in which he finds himself:

> The holy fool is ultimately defeated. The saint can communicate only when there is a community to address, when people are at least bound by common affections and belief, when they share the sources of feeling and devotion. The saint cannot speak when absolutely nobody listens. He may live and die known to God, but such secret sanctity will not allow us to praise, witness, or follow him in his way . . . West's conclusion is that the holy fool will always be misapprehended and destroyed as long as the values of the industrial American world prevail. Success, money, power – all conspire to cast out love, to freeze the heart, to dull sensibility.[11]

But *is* Miss Lonelyhearts a holy fool, an unsung saint? It is hard to see how his behaviour in the story can sustain such a view. Not being able to make much of this behaviour, religiously, other critics accuse those who want to make Miss Lonelyhearts a saint, of not being able to distinguish between religious zeal and psychoneurosis. After all, isn't Miss Lonelyhearts sick for three days before having his so-called religious experience, and doesn't he say that what he has is a Christ complex? True enough, but Nathanael West is trying to show us a religious phenomenon. His primary interest is not in abnormal psychology.

Miss Lonelyhearts — an exposure of the illusion of religion, a celebration of religion, a depiction of a holy fool, a study in psychoneurosis: none of these characterisations will do. They all miss the essence of West's description of Miss Lonelyhearts as a priest of our time who has a religious experience.

Flannery O'Connor said that even if the South was not Christ-centred, it was certainly Christ-haunted. The same can be said of Miss Lonelyhearts. We must take him at his word. What he has is not a belief in Christ, but a Christ complex, a fixation on him from which he cannot free himself. This fixation has been with him since his early days. At college, he and some of his friends had tried to sacrifice a lamb in a mock ritual: 'While they held the lamb, Miss Lonelyhearts crouched over it and began to chant. "Christ, Christ, Jesus Christ. Christ, Christ, Jesus Christ."

Having whipped themselves into a frenzy, Miss Lonelyhearts brings down the knife, but botches it. They flee, covered in blood.

'After some time had passed, Miss Lonelyhearts begged them to go back and put the lamb out of its misery. They refused to go. He went back alone and found it under a bush. He crushed its head with a stone and left the carcass to the flies that swarmed around the bloody alter flowers.'

In relation to Christ, his whole life can be seen as a series of botched sacrifices. Miss Lonelyhearts stares at the crucifix on his wall as if, by unmediated magic, it can force its sense upon him. His favourite reading is Dostoyevsky. He turns to the chapter devoted to Father Zossima in *The Brothers Karamazov*:

> Love a man even in his sin, for that is the semblance of Divine Love and the highest love on earth. Love all God's creation, the whole and every grain of sand in it. Love the animals, love the plants, love everything. If you love everything, you will perceive the divine mystery in things. Once you perceive it, you will begin to comprehend it better every day. And you will come at last to love the whole world with an all-embracing love.

Miss Lonelyhearts cannot mediate the sense of these words in the world he finds himself in. This is because the words live for him only in a romantic, indulgent, way. He is described as a New England puritan, with a bony chin, shaped and cleft like a hoof. That cleft is the symbol of a deeper one that runs all through his life — the romantic cleft between word and action. This cleft, this divide, takes a religious form in Miss Lonelyhearts, but non-religious analogues of it can be seen in how the other characters talk and behave.

We have already mentioned attempts to divorce artistic beauty from the harsh realities of life, and the attempts of Betty, Miss Lonelyhearts' girlfriend, to separate an idyllic, romanticised view of life in the country, from the rest of life. But it is in this idyllic setting that Miss Lonelyhearts makes her pregnant. Shrike's wife, Mary, cannot move from the teasing play of sexuality, to actually giving herself to anyone. Shrike himself cannot transform his ruthless cynicism into an expression of the love he longs for in an inarticulate way. Fay Doyle, the most superficial character in the novel, plays with moral words when seducing Miss Lonelyhearts. When he suggests they go to his place, she asks, 'Ought I?', but is already on her way, not waiting for an answer. After the seduction, she says, 'I'm ashamed of myself . . . You must think

I'm a bad woman', but the words are mere decoration. Here, the
gap between word and deed is at its widest. In Miss Lonelyhearts
himself, the gap is born of romanticism. His haunt is the speakeasy
where, with drink and women, he hopes some sense will somehow emerge. He drifts into being seduced by Fay Doyle. He cannot
mediate the sense of religious words in conduct. He says that if
only he could believe in Christ, adultery would be a sin, but, of
course, he can't.

When he tries to reconcile the cripple and his wife by preaching
love to them, the love he offers is supposed to be immediate,
effective as if by magic. The effect is comic:

> She was too astonished to laugh, and the cripple turned his
> face away as though embarrassed.
> With the first few words Miss Lonelyhearts had known that
> he would be ridiculous. By avoiding God, he had failed to tap
> the force in his heart and had merely written a column for his
> paper.

But what is the force in his heart? Shrike gives a perfect diag-
nosis of it:

> Even if he were to have a religious experience, it would be so
> personal and so meaningless, except to a psychologist.

> The trouble with him, the trouble with all of us, is that we
> have no outer life, only an inner one, and that by necessity . . .
> We can't all believe in Christ, and what does the farmer care
> about art? He takes his shoes off to get the warm feel of the rich
> earth between his toes. You can't take your shoes off in church.

Shrike calls Miss Lonelyhearts an escapist. That is what he is.
His feet don't touch the ground. His religious complex is unmediated in the detail of human life. When he is sick for three days,
Miss Lonelyhearts convinces himself that he has achieved a calm
rock-like faith which can transcend life's storms. When Shrike
taunts him in a party with his inability to answer the letters sent
to the newspaper, he is unmoved: 'Miss Lonelyhearts stood it
with the utmost serenity; he was not even interested. What goes
on in the sea is of no interest to the rock.'

When Betty comes to see him after the party, he promises to

marry her, telling her everything she wants to hear. Again, the rock has withstood the test. But what sort of test is it, when the rock is not even interested in what goes on in the sea? Embarrassingly, James Light sees in all this, and the religious experience which follows it, a classic Christian experience:

> Following Christ's injunction that whosoever would find his life must first lose it, Miss Lonelyhearts can now attain a mystical union with God. Transcending the fevered sickness of his body through a transforming grace of light and perfumed cleanliness, he becomes 'conscious of two rhythms that were slowly becoming one'. When they became one, his identification with God was complete. His heart was the one heart, the heart of God. And his brain was likewise God's.[12]

True, the crucifix in Miss Lonelyhearts' room begins to dance before his eyes and the room seems full of light. But this is no instance of dying to the self, let alone the rare experience of mystical union. Dying to the self involves caring for others, not cutting oneself off from them. Miss Lonelyhearts' strange experience is simply a sensory extension of his romantic and indulgent pseudo-religious rapture. The true quality of it can be assessed from Miss Lonelyhearts' own view of it: 'He immediately began to plan a new life and his future conduct as Miss Lonelyhearts. He submitted drafts of his column to God and God approved them. God approved his every thought.'

Again, James Light grotesquely misrepresents the final scene between Miss Lonelyhearts and Doyle, the cripple.

> Dramatically West pictorializes the division of man from man when Miss Lonelyhearts runs towards Doyle with love in his heart, while the cripple filled with hatred, makes his way up the stairs. In the ironic lack of communication, Doyle's gun, the symbol of a mechanical, loveless world, goes off and the two men roll down the stairs together.[13]

The critic has the same condescending view of the cripple as Miss Lonelyhearts, who sees in his arrival a God-sent opportunity to perform a miracle to confirm his conversion. But what he wants to perform is indeed a miracle! It is the old instant, magical, unmediated, pseudo-solution to all things' 'He would embrace the cripple and the cripple would be made whole again, even as he, a spiritual cripple had been made whole'.

But Miss Lonelyhearts has not been made whole. On the one hand, he cannot stomach the lush sanctimoniousness he had to dish out in his column. The words do not address anything. But his only alternative is the instant embrace. To the last, his Christ complex retains its hold on him. He wants to get to Christ directly, without the patient mediation of salvation in the detail of human life. He is not the last to peddle instant salvation. Such magical solutions are still offered in abundance. That is why Miss Lonelyhearts became, and remains, as West said, 'a portrait of a priest of our time.'

Notes

1. All quotations from Dennis Potter, *Follow the Yellow Brick Road* in Robert Muller (ed.) *The Television Dramatist* (Paul Elek, 1973).
2. Dennis Potter, introduction in *Brimstone and Treacle* (Methuen, 1983).
3. Ibid.
4. Dennis Potter, *Joe's Ark* in *Waiting for the Boat* (Faber & Faber, 1984).
5. Dennis Potter, introduction in *Brimstone and Treacle*.
6. Nathanael West, 'Some Notes on Miss Lonelyhearts', *Contempo*, 15 May 1933.
7. All quotations are from Nathanael West, *Miss Lonelyhearts* in *The Day of the Locust and His Other Novels* (Secker & Warburg, 1957).
8. Josephine Herbst, 'Miss Lonelyhearts: An Allegory', in Thomas H. Jackson (ed.), *Twentieth Century Interpretations of Miss Lonelyhearts* (Prentice-Hall, 1971), p. 97.
9. Stephen J. Gerkey, *You only Have Time to Explode: Technique and Structure in Nathanael West's Narratives* (University Microfilms International, Ann Arbor, 1979), pp. 96–7.
10. James Light, 'The Christ Dream', in *Twentieth Century Interpretations of Miss Lonelyhearts*, p. 29.
11. Arthur Cohen, 'The Possibility of Belief: Nathanael West's Holy Fool' in *Twentieth Century Interpretations of Miss Lonelyhearts*, p. 48.
12. Op. cit., p. 29.
13. Ibid.

5

After Empty Heaven

Many have concluded, as a result of the attacks on religion we have considered in the previous essays, that the heavens have been successfully emptied of the gods. But if this has been achieved, what then? Even those who have been prominent in their attacks recognise that a dangerous void has been created which must be filled. There is no general agreement about how this is to be done. In Iris Murdoch's dialogue, *Above the Gods*, Antagoras takes an outrightly cynical view of how the situation is to be dealt with:

> We intellectuals, we understand the situation, we can bear the burden — of freedom and value and a responsible unaided morality. But considered simply as a social phenomenon religion can be a useful stabilising factor. We're living in a period of intellectual and psychological *shock*, a time of deep change, an interregnum, a *dangerous interim*. Public morality would break down, some would say it *is* breaking down.[1]

So even if there were a tyrant with absolute power at his disposal, Antagoras argues, he would not abolish religion before a suitable substitute can be found:

> Of course as you know I detest tyrants. But if people worshipped the gods and kept quiet this might save the state from worse things. So long as there is an uneducated mob, there's a place for something like religion. Personally, I don't like the smell of it, religiosity is in bad taste, 'religious experience' is infantile fantasy; it's a matter of style. But this doesn't mean one should disrupt society to put people right. Religious sanctions, even rather vague ones, support popular morality and social order. Let's face it, ordinary morals are full of superstitions, fear of the gods, fear of your neighbour, fear of the state. When young people lose that fear and become fearless,

when they lose all respect for authority, things can really fall apart. It's a dangerous time. Religion is ritual and ritual is a symbol of order. Religion carries moral tradition. It's dying a natural and inevitable death, but the majority of people are slow in growing up. Meanwhile the state may have to take the place of the gods. It's this *transition* that we intellectuals must try to *think* about. And we mustn't let sentimental modern political attitudes stop us from thinking.[2]

Timonax, who has supported Antagoras' attacks on religion, hitherto, exclaims, 'This is cynicism, it's elitism — !' That state cynicism and elitism has reached its zenith in Aldous Huxley's *Brave New World*, in the religion of Orgy-Porgy. The Second Solidarity Hymn reads:

> Come, Greater Being, Social Friend,
> Annihilating Twelve-in-One!
> We long to die, for when we end,
> Our larger life has but begun.[3]

Wallace Stevens is certainly not guilty of such cynicism. On the other hand, he too is mindful of the dangerous interregnum which follows the demise of religion. With the decline of religious authority and the growth of democratic tendencies, where is any authoritative direction for development to be found? Things are happening too quickly, and people may not be ready for such rapid changes. The poet expresses his worries:

> There is order in neither sea nor sun.
> The shapes have lost their glistening.
> There are these sudden mobs of men,
>
> These sudden clouds of faces and arms,
> An immense suppression, freed
> These voices crying without knowing for what,
>
> Except to be happy, without knowing how,
> Imposing forms they cannot describe,
> Requiring order beyond their speech.

Stevens' hope, however, is that poetry will address this new situation men find themselves in:

Too many waltzes have ended. Yet the shapes
For which the voices cry, these, too, may be
Modes of desire, modes of revealing desire.

Too many waltzes — The epic of disbelief
Blares oftner and soon, will soon be constant.
Some harmonious sceptic soon in a sceptical music

Will write these figures of men and their shapes
Will glisten again with motion, the music
Will be motion and full of shadows.[4]

Out of this poetic music, Stevens hopes, there will emerge new possibilities of union and accord between human beings:

> . . . out of the central mind,
> We make a dwelling in the evening air,
> In which being there together is enough.[5]

But have subsequent events shown the emergence of a mode of existence in which 'being there together' becomes enough? Only a blind optimist could answer this question in the affirmative. In fact, there is also reason to doubt Stevens' claim that poetry can take the place of empty heaven. This reason was ruthlessly expressed by Shrike in Nathanael West's *Miss Lonelyhearts*. He has little time for those who seek salvation in art when religion fails. Shrike pretends to offer Miss Lonelyhearts art as a substitute for the usual religious drivel in his advice column. But he offers it in a way which makes the deficiencies of art's pretensions all too obvious:

> Do not let life overwhelm you. When the old paths are choked with the debris of failure, look for newer and fresher paths. Art is just such a path. Art is distilled from suffering . . .
> Art is One of Life's Richest Offerings.
> For those who have not the talent to create, there is appreciation. For those . . .
> Go on from there.

After writing *Follow the Yellow Brick Road*, *Joe's Ark* and *Brimstone and Treacle*, Dennis Potter changed the emphasis of the plays which followed them. Potter said, 'The sort of "religious drama" that I want to write will not necessarily mention the word "God" at all. Perhaps, too, it will be based on the feeling that religion is not the bandage, but the wound.'[6] As we have seen, he like others, had attacked the efforts often made in the name of religion to bandage the injuries of life. The language offered turned out to be the language of false consolation. But even when we turn from this language, religion has, nevertheless, created a wound, a wound caused by the longing for some kind of perfection, for something more than the merely human. The difficulty, as Stevens says, is that, so often people long for an order which is 'beyond their speech'. The longing is then likely to take the form of those sentiments which dominate popular culture, no matter how trite they may be. This is the situation Potter explored in his 1978 television series, published as a novel in 1981, *Pennies from Heaven*.

People have often thought of this world as a place of exile, and they long for a somewhere else, a better place. They reach out for a quasi-religious perfection, but, for that very reason, can never really grasp it. Such is the case with Arthur, a song sheet salesman in *Pennies from Heaven*. Arthur feels that there must be somewhere where the songs are true. What he longed for, we are told, is what writers of fairy tales and the singer of the psalms longed for, except that it had degenerated into the language of the trite lyrics of his day. The songs have captured him:

> Somewhere the sun is shining
> So baby don't you cry.
> Look for the silver lining
> The clouds will soon roll by.

The longing cannot transcend sentimentality. In Potter's 1979 play, *Blue Remembered Hills*, it cannot transcend nostalgia. In the play, which concerns children, all the parts are, in fact, played by adults. In it, the longing is not for a somewhere over the rainbow but for the supposed lost innocence of childhood. But in the games the children play, the spite, cruelty, guile and pettiness they exhibit, we see that such innocence is a myth, and that our sins are indeed original. The games end with one of the children being burnt alive, and all the others denying any knowledge or responsibility concerning it. These facts concerning childhood are not unknown to us, and yet we find it easy to give ourselves to a nostalgia for a lost innocence. But to fall foul of this nostalgia is to fall foul of the dangerous and possibly poisonous longing Houseman expresses in his poem:

> Into my heart, an air that kills
> From yon far country blows.
> What are those blue remembered hills?
> What spires, what farms are those?
> That is the land of lost content,
> I see it shining plain.
> The happy highways where I went
> And cannot come again.[7]

Nostalgia for the past can paralyse us in the present. A longing for the better place beyond the rainbow can have the same effect. Such longings, in this way, can actually deepen human wounds. This is the case with the married couple we meet in Potter's 1980 play, *Cream in My Coffee*. In old age, they return to the south-coast hotel 41 years after they had first gone there for an illicit liaison. In the flashbacks and comparisons with the present, realities are forever being compared with unrealisable romantic dreams. Locked in the gap between dream and reality, they continue to wound each other, as they have done over the years, in a slow, inevitable mutual destruction. In the terrible last scene, the old man, as he pretends to get rid of a wasp from his wife's shoulder, finds memories, nostalgia, realities and unrealistic longings flooding in on him. His swatting becomes a frantic hitting of her, a hitting which precipitates a fatal heart attack for him.

Earlier in the play, wrapped against a stiff sea-breeze, the old couple look out to sea. He says that they are waiting for a boat, one he is likely to board first. She does not understand that he is talking about death. Dennis Potter has included *Joe's Ark*, *Blue Remembered Hills* and *Cream in My Coffee* in a collection to which he has given the title, *Waiting for the Boat*. But what does the waiting reveal? That oblivion awaits all? And do not our expectations for something which transcends the limits of human existence, warp our apprehensions of what human life does have to offer? I think that much of what Potter's plays shows, is expressed in Philip Larkin's poem, *Next Please*:

Always too eager for the future, we
Pick up bad habits of expectancy,
Something is always approaching;
Every day *till then* we say,

Watching from a bluff, the tiny, clear
Sparkling armada of promises draw near.
How slow they are! And how much time they waste,
Refusing to make haste!

Yet still they leave us holding wretched stalks
Of disappointment, for, though nothing balks
Each big approach, leaving with brasswork prinked,
Each rope distinct,

Flagged, and the figurehead with golden tits
Arching our way, it never anchors; it's
No sooner present than it turns to past.
Right to the last.

We think each one will heave to and unload
All good into our lives, all we are owed
For waiting so devoutly and so long.
But we are wrong:

Only one ship is seeking us, a black–
Sailed unfamiliar, towing at her back
A huge and birdless silence. In her wake
No waters breed or break.[8]

The expectation of future compensation goes deep with us. We
feel that something *must* turn up, to rectify matters, to balance
the books. Things may not seem to make much sense from the
perspective we are locked into here on earth. But there is a higher
perspective, one which will make everything all right in the end.
We are sustained by this hope against hope; by this transcendental
superstition. Even when more specific superstitions such as touch-
ing wood, kissing a rabbit's foot and crossing ourselves do not
sustain us, this transcendental superstition holds firm. It has a
dream-like quality which places it beyond disproof — someday,
somehow, everything will be all right. That expectation is a

wounding illusion. Death is the only boat that awaits us, but it has no compensating cargo.

The figure of the boat plays an essential role in the last of Potter's plays I want to mention, the 1983 play, *Sufficient Carbohydrate*.[9] Jack Barker, a failed English businessman in his mid-forties, is on holiday. With him is his wife, his American boss and his wife, and his boss' young son by a former marriage. Jack's family firm has been taken over by an American firm. The new firm, instead of producing quality food as his family's had done, now produces fast, junk food. Jack's wife is having an affair with his boss. Everything in his life seems to be disintegrating. Like the old man in *Cream in My Coffee*, he is locked in a nostalgia for a lost purity and a longing for what cannot be.

There are moments, rare moments early in the morning, when Jack thinks there is a hope for something better on the horizon. The figure which symbolises this hope is a cargo boat which moves very slowly across the horizon. But it is a figure fraught by doubt. There are times when he wonders whether the boat is real at all: 'Actually the bloody ship probably isn't there. A ship of fools. I probably didn't even see it. It was only a speck. A smudge on the horizon — or on the back of my eyelids.'

But, at other times, Jack is sure that he does see it. He tries to tell his boss' young son about it:

Trouble is, it reminds me of something else, too. Something delicious or terrible – which I've either forgotten or haven't yet had. Something gone for ever or awaiting one for ever . . . When it passes, the ship, the light is more opaque than it is now. Sort of — marbled. And cool. There are a few wisps of smoke curling about an inch from the top of the sea, and yet the water is still that impossible blue — It's all like when the world began, and God Saw That It Was Good — (*Bitter little laugh*) . . . And an uncertain smudge which sort of *solidifies* out of the ache in the mind and very slowly becomes a black freighter dragging itself across the edge of the world — For a moment — a whole minute — it's all so perfect you want to reach out — pull it into your soul. You want to pick it all up — and *eat it* (He turns) Do you understand?'

The boy responds, 'That would be quite a mouthful'.

The attempt to see the world as God sees it, the reaching for a religious vision. But what is it to seek? What is it to find? Does belief in God offer food for the soul? What kind of food is it? Junk food? These questions cannot be avoided. When we try to answer them, we may find that we have gone down a yellow brick road. That road may lead to a religion of revulsion. Alternatively, wrestling with such questions may bring us to see what is involved in seeing the world as God sees it. Such an exploration still lies before us. But whatever the outcome, if it is religiously penetrating, it is likely to be quite a mouthful.

Notes

1. Iris Murdoch, *Aceastas*, p. 76.
2. Ibid., pp. 76–7.
3. Aldous Huxley, *Brave New World* (Penguin Books, 1955), p. 71.
4. Wallace Stevens, 'Sad Strains of a Gay Waltz' in *Selected Poems*.
5. Wallace Stevens, 'Final Soliloquy of the Interior Paramour' in *Selected Poems*.
6. Dennis Potter, introduction in *Brimstone and Treacle*.
7. A. E. Housman, 'A Shropshire Lad' in *Collected Poems* (London: Penguin, 1956).
8. Philip Larkin, *Next Please* in *The Less Deceived* (Marvell Press, 1977).
9. All quotations are from Dennis Potter, *Sufficient Carbohydrate* (Faber & Faber, 1983).

6

Charitable Untruths

In a collection of essays by admirers of the poet Philip Larkin, a collection published in 1982 to celebrate his sixtieth birthday, two of the contributions have the titles, 'Nothing to Be Said' and 'Like Something almost Being Said'. For many, Larkin was the most honest of our recent poets; the one who spoke most directly to them. How can this be? How can a poet who speaks eloquently to his audience, have nothing to say, or, at best, give them poems which are like something almost being said?

What is meant by saying that Larkin believes that there is nothing to be said? The beginnings of an answer can be found in a poem called *Myxomatosis*, where Larkin finds he has nothing to say when confronted by a rabbit in a trap.

> Caught in the centre of a soundless field
> While hot inexplicable hours go by
> *What trap is this? Where are its teeth concealed?*
> You seem to ask.

He kills him quickly with his stick.

> I make a sharp reply
> Then clean my stick. I'm glad I can't explain
> You may have thought things would come right again
> If you could only keep quite still and wait.[1]

'I'm glad I can't explain' — that response is the mark of Larkin's honesty, not only about the plight of animals, but about the traps that lie in wait for human beings too. His failure to explain, to offer large, sweeping, answers to the ills and misfortunes of life, is not simply a personal failure on his part. He is saying that such explanations, religious or otherwise, are no longer possible for us. Sometimes he seems to go further, to say that such explanations have never been possible.

Notice, he is *glad* that he cannot explain. To think there is an explanation, a remedy, is to indulge in a lie and a deception. Such lies and deceptions do not always take a religious form. Familiar secular surrogates for religion attempt to force promises of perfection on us. We find them, for example, in the vast advertisement-hoardings with their pictures of perfect health and happiness, hoardings which 'Reflect none of the rained-on streets and squares / They dominate outdoors'.

> Rather they rise
> Serenely to proclaim pure crust, pure foam,
> Pure coldness to our live imperfect eyes
> That stare beyond this world, where nothing's made
> As new or washed quite clean, seeking the home
> All such inhabit.[2]

It is often said, with an unearned easiness, that we must pass from the imperfections of this life, to the perfection which informs it. Larkin, on the other hand, asserts that what we have had too much of, is not the imperfections of life, for, at least, they are real, but the delusion of timeless essences, transcendental absolutes, which poison us with false expectations. Such essences and absolutes deserve to be attacked just as Titch Thomas defaces the poster featuring the ideal girl and place in the poem, *Sunny Prestatyn*. I suspect Larkin would ask of any account of perfection the four questions he says he asks of novels: 'Could I read it? If I could read it, did I believe it? If I believed it, did I care about it? And if I cared about it, what was the quality of my caring, and would it last?'[3] Commendable questions, but it must be remembered that they, too, operate within certain conditions. What one is able to accept as a reading, what one is able to believe or care about, all depend on what one takes the limits of reality to be. The determination of these limits in Larkin's verse is a complex and complicated matter.

Does religion lie outside these limits for Larkin? Obviously, it does. Early, in his schooldays, during a history lesson, he passed a book under the table to his schoolfellow, Noel Hughes, pointed to paragraph and hissed, 'get out of that'. Hughes says: 'I believe the book to have been an early Joad and the paragraph set out the clear illogicality of any belief in God'.[4] But, once again, everything depends on what one takes to be the parameters of logic. Hughes says that, where religion is concerned, Larkin has 'always kept his cards tight to his chest, suspecting, probably without looking, that any God that might exist would have dealt him a Yarborough'.[5] It is assumed, without examination, that if there were a God, he would deal us good cards, see to it that things go well rather than badly.

Once these assumptions are made, religion will appear, necessarily, to be a delusion. It is condemned by the all too obvious reality of human affliction. Sometimes, struck by the difficulties parents create for their children, and the children create for their children Larkin makes recommendations too cynical for most people:

> Man hands on misery to man.
> It deepens like a coastal shelf.
> Get out as quickly as you can,
> And don't have any kids yourself.[6]

On this showing, if one asked what Larkin is alienated from, cut off from, one would have to answer. 'The whole of life'. On the other hand, there are incidents which show Larkin ready to mock such *a priori* bleakness. He describes a meeting with Auden in which Auden asked him if he liked living in Hull. 'I said "I don't suppose I'm unhappier there than I should be anywhere else", to which he replied, "Naughty, naughty". I thought that was very funny.'[7]

Even so, such incidents are not enough to shift the overall impression of the bleak view of human life revealed in his verses, a bleakness not to be consoled by the false promises of religion. Larkin has said that the most difficult thing to learn about life is that there are no absolutes, religious or otherwise. For example, he challenges the popular view that real happiness can only be found by couples. Larkin says, 'sheer / Inaccuracy, as far as I'm concerned' and prefers his individual relationship to art. Watching the couples on the dance-hall, he is content to stay outside.

> . . . Therefore I stay outside
> Believing this: and they maul to and fro,
> Believing that; and both are satisfied,
> If no one has misjudged himself. Or lied.[8]

Despite the apparent tolerance in these lines, there is more than a suggestion that the couples do not have what they think they have. Notice how their dancing is described: 'they maul to and fro'. The suggestion becomes explicit statement in *Love Songs in Age*. A widow takes out the romantic records she had played in youth; records which told of 'that much-mentioned brilliance, love . . . promising to solve, and satisfy, / And set unchangeably in order'. Mature now, she admits that the love these records tried to tell of could never fulfil its promises:

> . . . So
> To pile them back, to cry
> Was hard, without lamely admitting how
> It had not done so then, and could not now.[9]

In *Places, Loved Ones*, Larkin's admission is as frank as it could be:

> No, I have never found
> The place where I could say
> *This is my proper ground,*
> *Here I shall stay;*
> Nor met that special one
> Who has an instant claim
> On everything I own
> Down to my name;[10]

George Hartley has said that Larkin is 'outside all the main emotional entanglements of most people's lives — love, marriage, children'.[11] Defending Larkin, Anthony Thwaite replies: 'The fact that he has never married and has no children doesn't entail ignorance of, or contempt for, the institution or its usual result. As for love, "that much-mentioned brilliance", even to feel outside it one must know what it is; and he does.'[12]

Our only business is with Larkin's verse. There, Thwaite's defence is difficult to maintain. While it is true that you can know what it is you feel excluded from, it is also true that you may feel excluded because what confronts you is a puzzle. Larkin finds love a puzzling phenomenon. In *Love* he characterises it as the readiness to be selfish enough: 'To upset an existence / Just for your own sake'. The unselfish side of love is said to be, 'Putting someone else first / So that you come off worst'. There is little doubt about his conclusion: 'My life is for me. / As well ignore gravity'. In *Self's the Man*, Larkin advances the view that a married man, attentive to his wife and children, must be less selfish than he is. But, then, he says:

> But wait, not so fast:
> Is there such a contrast?
> He was out for his own ends
> Not just pleasing his friends;
>
> And if it was such a mistake
> He still did it for his own sake,
> Playing his own game,
> So he and I are the same,
>
> Only I'm a better hand
> At knowing what I can stand
> Without them sending a van —
> Or suppose I can.[13]

These lines are severely honest, but also severely limited. We have only to compare them with the following lines by E.E. Cummings:

> 　　　　　　　　you only will create
> (who are so perfectly alive) my shame:
> lady through whose profound and fragile lips
> the sweet small clumsy feet of April came
> into the ragged meadow of my soul.[14]

That is the language of love.

If that language is unavailable to Larkin, if absolutes divine and human have no place in his vocabulary, this does not mean that he embraces the permissiveness which, in the 1960s, celebrated the apparent demise of such authorities. On the contrary, he feels as cut off from that as from anything else:

> Sexual intercourse began
> In nineteen sixty-three
> (Which was rather late for me)
> Between the end of the *Chatterley* ban
> And the Beatles' first L P[15]

He does not envy the drop-outs in the park who, one way or another, avoid old toad, Larkin's symbol for work. The discipline of the ordinary round is necessary, and not to be despised.

> No, give me my in-tray,
> My loaf-haired secretary,
> My shall-I-keep-the-call-in-Sir:
> What else can I answer,
>
> When the lights come on at four
> At the end of another year?
> Give me your arm, old toad;
> Help me down Cemetery Road.[16]

Yet, to end here would be to miss an important aspect of Larkin's verse. It would be to miss the pain and suffering caused for him by the limitations of human life. Having put the consolations of religion aside, Larkin finds no comfort in the rationalism which tells us that since death is not an experience, there is nothing to fear:

> This is a special way of being afraid
> No trick dispels. Religion used to try,
> That vast moth-eaten musical brocade
> Created to pretend we never die,
> And specious stuff that says *No rational being*
> *Can fear a thing it will not feel*, not seeing
> That this is what we fear — no sight, no sound,
> No touch or taste or smell, nothing to think with,
> Nothing to love or link with,
> The anaesthetic from which none come round.[17]

An 'armada of promises' threatens to hide this fear from us, convincing us that some form of compensation must turn up. Such expectations must be put aside:

> Only one ship is seeking us, a black–
> Sailed unfamiliar, towing at her back
> A huge and birdless silence. In her wake
> No waters breed or break.[18]

Larkin does not think that the permissiveness he describes as 'going down the long slide / To happiness', is any answer to this fear of the void. Neither is his own generation's rejection of religion:

> That'll be the life;
> No God any more, or sweating in the dark
> About hell and that, or having to hide
> What you think of the priest. He
> And his lot will go down the long slide
> Like free bloody birds. And immediately

Rather than words comes the thought of high windows:
The sun-comprehending glass,
And beyond it, the deep blue air, that shows
Nothing, and is nowhere, and is endless.[19]

There is an ache in the soul born of the contrast between the limits of human life in space and time, and the endless, indifferent, neutrality of the heavens. Like Hamm in Beckett's *Endgame*, Larkin is insisting: 'You're on earth; there's no cure for that'. But he does not advocate passive resignation. What Larkin says of Thomas Hardy can be said of his own verse:

> . . . the presence of pain . . . is a positive, not a negative qual-
> ity — not the mechanical working out of some predetermined
> allegiance to pessimism or any other concept, but the continual
> celebration of what is both the truest and the most important
> element in life, most important in the sense of most necessary
> to spiritual development.[20]

What of this development in Larkin? We have seen its negative side, the rejection of false answers — 'nothing to be said'. But it also has a positive side. The tension between a recognition of the limitations of human life and the yearning for freedom from these limitations, which can never be resolved by substantive answers, gives rise to a readiness to settle for what might be called 'charitable untruths' in our dealings with each other. Even in the most intimate relationships, a couple talking in bed, where one would expect talk to be open and free, it is not so.

It becomes still more difficult to find
Words at once true and kind,
Or not untrue and not unkind.[21]

And what of the inevitable end of all such relationships? Contemplating the *Arundel Tomb*, where the earl and countess lie in stone, hands unexpectedly clasped, he wants to say that 'Time has transfigured them into / Untruth'. The eternal love they swore was not a fidelity in stone which has outlasted them. On the other hand, the very different people who now visit the tomb are, in some sense or other, a testimony to the fact that what the earl and countess wanted to say of their love persists as a desire in them too.

The stone fidelity
They hardly meant has come to be
Their final blazon, and to prove
Our almost-instinct almost true:
What will survive of us is love.[22]

David Timms points out that Larkin's careful choice of words like 'almost true', 'not untrue' and 'not unkind' lack the harshness of their synonyms, 'lie' and 'falsehood'. For Timms, this is Larkin insisting on the truth gently: '. . . he is charitable towards our false beliefs. This unsentimental charity is his most valuable quality.'[23]

We are told that Larkin does not criticise our weaknesses from the outside, since he recognises their presence in himself. This answer will not do. Larkin's criticism of false hopes and expectations are explicit enough, as we have seen, so where is the difficulty?

I believe the tensions in Larkin's verse have a deeper source: he runs up against the limits of the language available to him. He both wants to go beyond them and yet cannot, and so gives us words which sound like something almost being said. The tension to which I refer is captured in the last stanza of *Church Going*. Stopping at a church on a bicycle ride, the poet wonders how long church-going will last, what churches will be used for in the future, whether superstitions will surround them, and so on. But, then, he has to answer the question, what made him stop and enter the church:

A serious house on serious earth it is,
In whose blent air all our compulsions meet,
Are recognised, and robed as destinies.
And that much never can be obsolete,
Since someone will forever be surprising
A hunger in himself to be more serious,
And gravitating with it to this ground,
Which, he once heard, was proper to grow wise in,
If only that so many dead lie round.[24]

Perhaps the conviction that this can never become obsolete is too optimistic. Whatever of that, as Timms says, the poem shows how 'the most intelligent and eloquent of men can be made uncomfortable by emotions they do not fully understand'.

Further reflections should take as their starting point the source of this discomfort and the character of these emotions. Attention would have to be given to the kind of religious perspectives Larkin seems unaware of; those which ask the believer, as forcefully as Larkin does, to die to the desire for compensation. Speaking of the poet today, Larkin says: 'The days when one could claim to be the priest of a mystery are gone: today mystery means either ignorance or hokum, neither fashionable qualities'.[25]

The possibility, however rare, of celebrating religious mysteries, a *Deus absconditus*, in verse, would have to be reopened. It would be to raise the possibility of there being, even now, a poet of the Hidden God.

Notes

1. Philip Larkin, *Myxomatosis*, in *The Less Deceived* (Marvell Press, 1977).
2. Larkin, *Sunny Prestatyn*, in *The Witsun Weddings* (Faber & Faber, 1983).
3. Larkin, 'The Booker Prize 1977' in *Required Writing* (Faber & Faber, 1983), p. 84.
4. Noel Hughes, 'The Young Mr Larkin' in Anthony Thwaite (ed.) *Larkin at Sixty* (Faber & Faber, 1982), p. 22.
5. Ibid.
6. Larkin, 'This Be the Verse' in *High Windows* (Faber & Faber, 1974).
7. Larkin, 'An Interview with *Paris Review*' in *Required Writing*, p. 67.
8. Larkin, 'Reasons for Attendance', in *The Less Deceived*.
9. Larkin, 'Love Songs in Age' in *The Witsun Weddings*.
10. Larkin, *Places, Loved Ones*, in *The Less Deceived*.

11. George Hartley, 'Nothing to Be Said' in *Larkin at Sixty*, p. 91.
12. Anthony Thwaite, 'Introduction' in *Larkin at Sixty*, p. 14.
13. Larkin, *Self's the Man*, in *The Whitsun Weddings*.
14. E. E. Cummings, Five: v 'if I have made, my lady, intricate' in *Collected Poems 1913–1962* (Harvest/HBJ Book, 1980), p. 306.
15. Larkin, 'Annus Mirabilis' in *High Windows*.
16. Larkin, 'Toads Revisited' in *The Whitsun Weddings*.
17. Larkin, Aubade.
18. Larkin, 'Next, Please' in *The Less Deceived*.
19. Larkin, 'High Windows' in *High Windows*.
20. Larkin, 'Wanted: Good Hardy Critic' in *Required Writing*, pp. 172 – 173.
21. Larkin, 'Talking in Bed' in *The Whitsun Weddings*.
22. Larkin, 'An Arundel Tomb' in Ibid.
23. David Timms, *Philip Larkin* (Oliver & Boyd, 1973), p. 109.
24. Larkin, 'Church Going' in *The Less Deceived*.
25. Larkin, 'Writing Poems' in *Required Writing*, p. 83.

Part II
Under a Godless Sky

. . . maybe we had neglected to tell these children
the rules of the game we happened to be playing. Maybe
we had stopped believing in the rules ourselves, maybe
we were having a failure of nerve about the game. Maybe
there were just too few people around to do the
telling.

7

Following Rules

If there is no God, from where does our guidance come to live in one way rather than another? It seems that, left to ourselves, we have to devise our own rules for human conduct. But how are we going to do that? What status can these rules have? What happens if not everyone agrees with them? What can we say if someone challenges their authority?

Suppose someone is confronted by a rule, 'Thou shalt . . .' or 'Thou shalt not . . .', but, instead of obeying it, says, 'What if I don't?' or 'What of it?' What can be done in face of this challenge? Sometimes, the answer is obvious. If someone wants to get to Swansea, and I give him a rule, 'Take the next turning on the right', it is clear what I would say if he then asked, 'What if I don't?' I'd tell him that he wouldn't get to Swansea; that he'd get lost. Similarly, when it says on the medicine bottle, 'Don't exceed the prescribed dosage', I know roughly what trouble to expect if I don't follow the rule. Since people, normally, do not want to get lost or to be ill, the rules regarding these matters, the 'Thou shalts' and the 'Thou shalt nots' have ready justifications at hand by which to answer challenges to the rule.

But it isn't always like this. There are other rules, moral and religious rules, which seem to lack such justifications. 'Thou shalt not lie', 'Thou shalt love the Lord thy God with all thy heart' — but, then, what if someone says 'What if I don't?' This question has haunted philosophers throughout the history of their subject. Faced by the challenge to the rule, 'What if I don't?' they have tried to answer it in various ways. For example, they have tried to point to the consequences for others if the rule is not followed, but this has not worked for a very simple reason: the person who challenged the rule is just as prepared to challenge the consequences for others. If he has said 'What of it?' in face of the rule, he can say 'What of it?' in face of the consequences for others too. Sometimes, when someone has not been alive to the consequences of his actions, when they are pointed out to him, he changes his ways.

But simply because this happens, sometimes, it would be foolish to think that all rule-breaking is a result of such lack of realisation, and that pointing out the consequences for others would be sufficient to ensure that the rules are kept. This can be illustrated by a simple cautionary tale: A teacher, observing a little boy bullying a little girl in the school playground, went up to him and remonstrated with him, saying, 'Don't you know you're hurting her?' to which the little boy replied, 'Yes, miss'. The little boy broke the school rule against bullying, not because he was unaware of the fact that he was hurting the little girl, but because he wanted to hurt her. The consequences have not, of themselves, guaranteed his keeping the rule. He is not interested in not hurting her, and so does not keep the rule. Well, why can't we settle for that? Why can't we say, 'Well, if he's not interested, that's that'? After all, we often do this with other rules. I give the rule, 'Take this train', 'Take this road', but then I find out that you are not interested in going where this train or road leads. I have to withdraw the rule in your case. The train and the road cease to be the right train and road for you. Their rightness was conditional on your interests. If you are not interested, the rule lacks the necessary support to have a hold on you. Why not say the same of moral and religious rules? But can we, do we? Well, some do and can, while others don't and can't. Or, better: sometimes we can and do, but sometimes we can't and don't. Either way, we have a problem. Moral rules do not depart, do not cease to make a demand on us, simply because we express no interest in them. Wittgenstein has illustrated this fact well:

Supposing that I could play tennis and one of you saw me playing and said 'Well, you play pretty badly' and suppose I answered 'I know, I'm playing badly but I don't want to play any better', all the other man could say would be 'Ah then that's all right'. But suppose I had told you a preposterous lie and he came up to me and said 'You're behaving like a beast' and then I were to say 'I know I behave badly, but then I don't want to behave any better', could he then say 'Ah, then that's all right'? Certainly not; he would say 'Well, you *ought* to want to behave better'.[1]

'You ought to.' 'You *must*.' But what do these 'oughts' and 'musts' come to? In what does the moral or religious necessity reside? How can we speak of the necessity of 'Thou shalt' and 'Thou shalt not' when, in face of them, despite knowing the consequences for others, someone can say with impunity, 'What if I don't?'

And so philosophers have tried again, tried to find a way to discover a necessary hold which moral and religious rules will have on the agent's will. Since appeal to the consequences for the interests of others need not move him, since he may not care about other people, philosophers have tried to show that moral and religious rules are necessarily linked with the agent's self-interest. The philosopher's dream is of a happy marriage between morality and religion on the one hand, and self-interest on the other. In attempts to realise this dream many desperate efforts have been made to show that man needs morality to get on in this world; attempts to show that it pays to be good. These attempts have not got very far for two very obvious reasons.

First, it is simply factually false that there is a neat fit between morality and religion and worldly success. There is no reason to suppose that, in worldly terms, goodness is rewarded more than wickedness. It is not for nothing that, throughout the centuries, the cry has been heard, 'Why do the wicked prosper?' Are we seriously going to argue that there has been a mistake, and that on recalculating we shall find that the wicked have not prospered after all? If it's the wicked you want to convince, on their own terms, there will be little point telling them that what you mean by 'prospering' is not what they mean. The wicked would be tolerant enough. 'By all means have your eccentric linguistic rule', they'd say, 'but we'll still laugh all the way to the bank'.

Second, let us suppose that you could give a thousand tough characters a reason to be just — a reason on their own terms. Suppose you convince them that the meting out of advantages and disadvantages is the sole discretion of God, so that, given eternity, self-interest is always on the side of the good. Would *this* be what we wanted in speaking of a respect for moral and religious rules? Hardly. All we have is self-interest, and a cringing servility to a vindictive God. On this external, worldly, view of divine reward and punishment, if we found out that goodness was to be punished and evil rewarded by a malignant deity, we would promptly give up our allegiance to the good. Surely, we contrast moral and religious rules with worldly self-interest. It is grotesque, therefore, to try to justify the rules in terms of this self-interest. The Danish philosopher, Søren Kierkegaard saw this clearly:

> But, my listener, . . . would you dare, as a father, to say to your child as you sent him out into the world, 'Go, with your mind at ease, my child, pay attention to what the many approve and what the world rewards, for that is the Good, but what the world punishes, that is evil . . . would you dare, if you should speak as a father to your own child, would you dare say any such thing?[2]

But now, where does all this leave us? If neither appeal to the interests of others, nor appeal to one's self-interest, can guarantee obedience to moral or religious rules, where does that leave the force, the necessity, the seemingly absolute claim, of the 'Thou shalts' and 'Thou shalt nots'? If appeal to consequences cannot account for these characteristics of the rules what can? Nothing external to the rules themselves it seems. And so we are left peering anxiously at the rules themselves, trying to discover that 'something' in them which creates their necessity, which 'makes' us follow them. But that 'something' has proved to be as elusive in this respect as the appeal to consequences turned out to be. So elusive, in fact, that it has led philosophers to denigrate the attempt to find it. It is as if we are searching, they say, for some magical property in the moral or religious 'must', which will force us, psychologically, to obey its dictates. They can make no sense of this 'magical must', and neither, I must confess, can I.

And so we come back once again to our initial question: Suppose someone is confronted by a rule, 'Thou shalt' or 'Thou shalt not', but, instead of obeying it, says 'What if I don't?' or 'What of it?' What can be done in face of this challenge?

It is to further the attempt to answer this question that I turn to examine the play, *The Rules of the Game* by the Italian dramatist Luigi Pirandello.[3] That I do so may seem surprising, since the opinion of many critics in this country is that Pirandello is rather a cynic and that *The Rules of the Game*, written in 1918–19 simply reveals his ruthless use of sardonic humour. I think that such an estimate of Pirandello misses a deeper dimension in his work, a dimension which has much to say to the question concerning rules we have been discussing.

When we look at *The Rules of the Game*, there seems to be a great deal, at first, to support the view of the dramatist as a cynic. The central character Leone Gala often refers to what he takes to be the rules of the game: 'But you must play your part, just as I am playing mine. It's all in the game . . . Each of us must play his part through to the end — In this game one wears a mask according to the role and one obeys the rules which are themselves created by the roles assumed.'

Not a very promising view of rules one might think. Rules are the function of roles which are themselves masks which hide the real self. But what substance has the real self? What game is *it* playing? It is tempting to reply: the game of not getting egg on your face. As John Linstrum says in his Introduction to *Pirandello: Three Plays*, the image of the egg is important in Pirandello's play: 'The "mask" of the egg is plain, smooth, logical, devoid of feeling: the "face" inside the mask is composed of different and contrasting elements, with an embryo of life that would be capable of feeling'.[4]

Leone Gala is a master at coping with eggs, because he has mastered what he calls 'the game of life'. He explains the rules of this game to Guido Venanzi, whom he knows is having an affair with his wife, Silia, from whom he is estranged. The rules of the game, he claims, are to establish a 'nothingness' inside you, so that whatever incident occurs, it cannot hurt you. You will always stay upright, retain your equilibrium, and turn the incident which threatens to engage your feelings into a fanciful conceit. Leone explains to Guido how this is to be done:

Leone. You must grapple with the incident without hesitation, before it gets a chance to engage your feelings, and get out of it anything that may be of advantage to you. The residue will be powerless to injure you, you can laugh at it, play with it, make it the fanciful conceit I mentioned just now.

Guido (*more and more bewildered*): I'm afraid I still don't quite . . .

Leone: Look, Venanzi. Imagine for a moment that you notice an egg suddenly hurtling through the air straight towards you . . .

Guido: . . . an egg?

Leone: Yes, an egg. A fresh one. It doesn't matter who has thrown it, or where it comes from; that's beside the point.

Guido: But suppose it turns out to be a bullet and not an egg?

Leone (*smiling*): Then it's too late to think about emptying your-

self. The bullet will do the job for you, and that's the end of
the matter.

Guido: All right — let's stick to your egg; although what a fresh
egg has to do with the matter, I'm blessed if I can see.

Leone: To give you a fresh image on events and ideas. Well,
now, if you're not prepared to catch the egg, what happens?
Either you stand still and the egg hits you and smashes, or
you duck and it misses you and smashes on the ground. In
either case the result is a wasted egg. But if you are prepared,
you catch it, and then — why there's no end to what you
can do with it, if you're a good cook. You can boil it, or poach
it, or fry it, or make an omelette of it. Or you can simply
pierce it at each end and suck out the yoke. What's left in
your hand then?

Guido: The empty shell.

Leone: Exactly. The empty shell is your fanciful conceit. You can
amuse yourself with it by sticking it on a pin and making it
spin, or you can toss it from one hand to the other like a
ping-pong ball. When you're tired of playing with it, what
do you do? You crush it in your hand and throw it away.

The common response to Pirandello's *The Rules of the Game* is to
see Leone as playing this tormenting game with his wife and her
lover, a game he plays until he is ready to crush them. It is easy
to gain this impression of the play. Despite their separation, her
husband's detached aloofness continues to be a burden for Silia.
So great is this burden that she feels she will never be free until
her husband is dead. She tells her lover: 'He's like a ghost, quite
detached from life, existing only to haunt other people's lives . . .
That man has paralysed me! I've only one idea continually gnaw-
ing at my brain: how to get rid of him, how to free myself from
him.'

Silia is determined not to be an empty egg-shell in her husband's
hand. So angry does she become at the way he has talked to
Guido about the rules of the game of life, that she throws an egg
at her husband's departing figure in the street. Unfortunately, it
hits Marquese Miglioriti one of four out on a drunken spree, and
they come to her room, mistaking her for a woman of easy virtue
who lives next door. Silia humours them, offering to dance naked
in the square for them. But when other tenants arrive, disturbed
at the noise, her tone changes. She charges the drunks with insult-

ing and assaulting her. When Miglioriti, realising their mistake, offers her his abject apologies, she refuses them, demanding that he must pay for this insult to her honour. He presents her with his card, agreeing that the question of honour must be satisfied. But what of Silia's attitude once Miglioriti and the tenants have gone? 'As soon as the Tenants have gone, Silia looks radiantly at Miglioriti's card, and laughs with gleeful, excited and malicious triumph.'

Silia hasn't been offended at all in reality. She has seen an opportunity to get rid of her husband by getting him to fight a dual to defend her honour. Guido is unhappy about the whole affair. He tries to warn Leone, but, in the end, weakly goes along with Silia's plan. Miglioriti is a fine swordsman and a good shot. The duel is arranged. Two shots are to be fired. If they are inconclusive, the duel is to continue with swords. Guido is to be Leone's second and his medical friend, Dr Spiga, is to be in attendance.

Leone has no experience with weapons, but shows no interest in acquainting himself with them prior to the duel. He remains perfectly calm. The duel is likely to be to the death, since not only is Miglioriti annoyed because his apologies have not been accepted, he has also discovered that Guido was in hiding in another room throughout the whole episode, a fact which casts doubt on Silia's protests about her honour.

On the morning of the duel, Dr Spiga arrives with his medical equipment to be told by Philip, Leone's servant, that his master is still asleep. When Guido arrives and learns of this fact, he marvels, as do they all, at Leone's equanimity. In a little time he would probably be dead, and yet he sleeps soundly. Guido goes to wake him, to tell him that the duel is only ten minutes away.

When Leone finally confronts them, he tells them that he sees no necessity to fight the duel. He does not care about its being his duty. But, he says, Guido will care. *He* won't let his beloved Silia be dishonoured. The rules of honour and dishonour mean nothing to him, but they do to Guido. Leone accuses him of conspiring with his wife to kill him: 'You thought you'd have a little game with me, didn't you? You thought between you, you could win my life from me? Well, you've lost the game my friends. I have outplayed you.'

Leone tells Guido that instead of fighting the duel, he intends having his breakfast. Guido and Barelli, a swordsman who had

hoped to prepare Leone for the duel, try to appeal to the rules of
the code of honour. It has no effect:

> *Guido*: . . . don't you realise that you will be dishonoured!
> *Barelli*: Disgraced! We shall be forced to expose your dishonour!
> (Leone *laughs loudly*)
> *Barelli*: How can you laugh? You'll be dishonoured, dis-
>   honoured!
> *Leone*: I understand my friends, and I can still laugh. Don't you
>   see how and where I live? Why should I worry my head
>   about honour?

Of course, Silia's honour does matter to her lover Guido. He
feels he *must* fight the duel. He goes to his death.

Here, we seem to have a perfect example of the problem with
which we began. People say to Leone, 'There is a code of honour;
there are rules'. He replies, 'So what?' What are we to make of
this? As I have said, it is tempting to see Pirandello's play as an
exercise in sardonic humour. In typical *commedia dell'arte* style,
Leone turns the table on his adversaries. The egg was thrown at
him. He ducks, and it hits Guido instead. He has beaten his wife
and her lover at their own game, the only game which life is
about.

Is that all Pirandello's play shows us? To think so is to miss the
deeper dimensions in his art, dimensions which, as John Linstrum
points out, take us far beyond the conventions of *commedia dell'arte*,
beyond the artful turning of the tables on one's adversaries. He
locates these dimensions in remarks on 'Humour' which Pirandello wrote in 1908:

> I see an old woman with her hair dyed and greasy with oil: she
> is made up garishly and is dressed like a young girl. I begin to
> laugh. I perceive that she is the exact opposite of what a respect-
> able old lady should be . . . The sense of the comic consists of
> this *perception of the opposite*. But if, at this point, I reflect and
> consider that she may not enjoy dressing up like an exotic
> parrot, that she is distressed by it and does it only because she
> deceives herself, pitifully, into believing that she can retain the
> love of her younger husband by making herself up like this . . .
> then I can no longer laugh at her . . . from the initial *perception*

of the opposite, reflection has led me to a *feeling of the opposite*. This is the difference between the comic and humour.'[5]

At first we may laugh at the way the tables are turned in *The Rules of the Game*, but, then, when we turn to share with Leone his elation at his success, a shock awaits us. We do not find the jubilant turner of tables of the *commedia dell'arte* tradition. On the contrary, after the duel, when Dr Spiga rushes in to get his medical equipment, Leone does not move. When Silia runs out frantically after the doctor, asking whether Guido is dead, already knowing the answer, he still does not move:

> (*Leone remains motionless, absorbed in deep, serious thought. A long pause.* Philip *enters . . . with the breakfast tray and puts it down on the table*).
> Philip (*calling in a hollow voice*): Hey!
> (*Leone barely turns his head.* Philip *indicates the breakfast with a vague gesture*): Breakfast time!
> (Leone, *as though he has not heard, does not move*)

Is this the jubilant turner of tables, or an object of pity? True, in face of the code of honour and its rules he has said, 'What of it?' But even to turn the tables on his wife and lover he has had to recognise certain things. He has had to recognise that his wife used the code of honour in her own self-interest; that, in fact, she perverted the code in an attempt to secure his death. He has also to recognise that her lover is not in the same category. Weak though he is, he had tried to resist her plans initially. And, at the end, Leone can only turn the tables on Guido by recognising that Guido does have a sense of duty, does love his wife; indeed, that he is prepared to die for her honour. Of course, he himself is outside all this. But the result is the still, motionless, figure we see at the end of the play.

'Thou shalt', 'Thou shalt not' — 'What if I don't?' Earlier we saw how philosophers sought in vain to make moral and religious rules have an automatic effect on people's behaviour. They tried to make the 'must' of the rules a 'magical must'. In the light of Pirandello's play, we can see that the rules were being asked to play a role they can never fulfil. If self-interest rules in a person's life, as it did with Silia, the rules will have no hold on that person. On the other hand, if someone cares for honour and is capable of love, despite all his stumblings and weaknesses, then, like Guido, he may even be prepared to die for love and honour. But the man who has created a 'nothingness' within himself, will feel no obligation. He has indeed sucked all the contents from the egg. As a result, however, not only the egg, but he too, is an empty shell.

We stare at moral and religious rules expecting them to have some kind of magical, necessary effect on us, not realising that it is not the rules which give life to our lives, but our lives which give life to our rules. In sordid surroundings the rules become sordid. Without the surroundings of love, respect and decency, moral and religious rules degenerate and may become, as Pirandello shows so well, what Leone calls, the rules of the game. If, then, it is our lives which give life to our rules, we cannot take it upon ourselves to devise rules which will, of themselves, as it were, secure the quality of those lives. There is no rule for a life in which there will be worthwhile rules. And so, if there is no God, if we live under a godless sky, left to our devices, rules, of themselves won't save us. Our attention turns from the rules to the lives we lead. But when our attention turns in this direction, what do we find?

Notes

1. Ludwig Wittgenstein, 'Lecture on Ethics', *Philosophical Review*, Jan. 1965.
2. Søren Kierkegaard, *Purity of Heart*, trans. Douglas Steere (Harper & Row, 1956), pp. 93–4.
3. Luigi Pirandello, all quotations from *The Rules of the Game* in *Pirandello: Three Plays* (Methuen, 1985).
4. John Linstrum, 'Introduction' in *Pirandello; Three Plays*, p. xxi.
5. Quoted by Linstrum, ibid., p. xvii.

8

Only Words?

In the previous essay we saw the difficulties which arise when, given that there is no God, people ask for a justification of moral rules. What authority do the rules have? Why should we follow them? Attempts to provide external justifications for moral rules seem to come to nothing, and so we are left, staring at the rules, as if searching for the compulsion which will show why we *must* follow them. But this necessity, like the external justifications for which we sought, seems to slip through our fingers. We saw, however, that our difficulties are born of misunderstandings. Rules do not underlie our lives. Our lives show the worth, or otherwise, of our rules.

But what of God's rules, God's commands? Do not the same conclusions follow for them? Do God's commands underlie our lives, or is it our lives which show what God's commands mean to us? Could it even be that, given what God's commands have become for many, this fact, *in itself*, has contributed enormously to the creation of a godless sky? How can this have happened? We can answer this question with the help of one of the most famous plays in twentieth century literature.

On a country road, two tramps, Vladimir and Estragon, are waiting. They are waiting for a Mr Godot with whom they believe they have an appointment. This is the opening scene of Samuel Beckett's play, *Waiting for Godot*, but the scene never changes throughout the play. At the end of the first Act, the tramps are told that Mr Godot cannot come that day, but that he will surely come tomorrow. But at the end of the play, Mr Godot still has not come. Vladimir and Estragon still wait, still believe that they have an appointment to keep. Put baldly in this way, the play seems to present a daunting prospect for the theatregoer. Yet, we know that it has captured the imagination as much as any twentieth-century drama. Why should this be so?

Many glib answers have been given to this question; answers which roll off the tongue with an unearned ease; answers which create the illusion of understanding where none is present. One such answer sees *Waiting for Godot* as a typical example of what has been unhelpfully called, *The Theatre of the Absurd*. Works which fall under this heading are supposed to show that life is meaningless. Life has become meaningless as a result of the realisation that there is no God. In his book, *The Theatre of the Absurd*, Martin Esslin describes the attitude which, he thinks, characterises this kind of theatre: 'The hallmark of this attitude is its sense that the certitudes and unshakeable basic assumptions of former ages have been swept away, that they have been tested and found wanting, that they have been discredited as somewhat cheap and childish illusions.'[1]

But do these words capture the mood of Vladimir and Estragon as they wait for Mr Godot? The picture Esslin presents is that of the liberated and liberating man, with rational tests at hand, who has been rescued, and who now wants to rescue us, from our cheap and childish illusions; who has been brought, and wants to bring us, into the light from the darkness of superstition. But how do we find Vladimir and Estragon at the opening of the play?

> (Estragon, *sitting on a low mound, is trying to take off his boot. He pulls at it with both hands, panting. He gives up, exhausted, rests, tries as before. Enter* Vladimir)
> *Estragon* (*giving up again*): Nothing to be done.
> *Vladimir*: I'm beginning to come round to that opinion. All my life I've tried to put it from me, saying, Vladimir, be reasonable, you haven't yet tried everything. And I resumed the struggle.[2]

A picture of liberated men? Hardly. Still, if we put *that* aside, may not Esslin still have a point, since he also wants to say that the *Theatre of the Absurd* '. . . strives to express its sense of the senselessness of the human condition'. Applying this to Beckett's plays, Esslin says: '. . . language in Beckett's plays serves to express the breakdown, the disintegration of language'.[3]

Doesn't this sum it up? Doesn't this capture perfectly the opening of Beckett's play? 'Nothing to be done', says Estragon. 'I'm beginning to come round to that opinion', replies Vladimir. Certainly, in my experience, many rush to embrace Esslin's vulgar response to Beckett. Essays in departments of literature, theology and philosophy testify to the appeal of the general thesis. Yet, on the most cursory examination, Esslin's response begins to disintegrate. He says that the Theatre of the Absurd 'strives to express its sense of the senselessness of the human condition'. Is the dramatist outside whatever is meant by 'the human condition'? How could he be? If something called 'the human condition' is said to be senseless as such, how is the dramatist to find the resources by which to express the sense of this senselessness? Again, when Esslin says that the language in Beckett's plays shows the disintegration of language, similar difficulties arise. If you speak in a general way, as Esslin does, about the inadequacy of language, the difficulty is that you are using language, successfully, presumably, to express the inadequacy. How does Esslin get out of these difficulties or try to grapple with them? He doesn't. He simply accepts the paradox unthinkingly and asserts that Beckett's play is a *tour de force* in face of the inherent inadequacy of language. Here is Esslin getting into all sorts of trouble while trying to put on a brave face in his predicament:

> But, if Beckett's use of language is designed to devalue language as a vehicle for conceptual thought or as an instrument for the communication of ready-made answers to the problems of the human condition, his continued use of language, must paradoxically, be regarded as an attempt to communicate on his own part, to communicate the incommunicable . . . Beckett's entire work can be seen as a search for reality that lies behind mere reasoning in conceptual terms. He may have devaluated language as an instrument for the communication of ultimate truths, but he has also shown himself a great master of language as an artistic medium.[4]

The familiar difficulty, disguised and, seemingly, excused as paradox, re-emerges. We have already heard it said that Beckett wants to express the sense of what is inherently senseless, wants to give us a language which shows the disintegration of language. Now we are told that Beckett is trying to communicate that which cannot be communicated, and that although he wants to devalue language, he is also a master of it. As I have said, this way of taking refuge in the licence of paradox is a vulgar response to Beckett's play.

The playwrights themselves do not indulge in paradox in this way. When someone tried to impose such paradoxical conse-

quences on Eugene Ionesco by asking him how he could write his
plays and say at the same time that communication is impossible,
Ionesco denied that he had ever advanced such a general thesis.
'The very fact of writing and presenting plays is surely incompat-
ible with such a view. I simply hold that it is difficult to make
oneself understood, not absolutely impossible.'[5]

Gessner accused Beckett of harbouring the same contradiction
in his views. He asked him how he could say that language could
not convey meaning, while at the same time write plays and
novels, which he obviously hoped people would appreciate and
understand. Beckett replied: 'What do you want, dear man? There
are words; we have nothing else.'

Esslin misses the point of this reply. Beckett, in *Waiting for
Godot*, is not propounding any general thesis about the inadequacy
of language. What he shows us is quite specific, namely, words
at work in the lives of Vladimir and Estragon. The predicament
of the tramps is not that words have no meaning, but that their
words have the meaning that they do. The trouble is not that the
tramps cannot speak, but that they speak in the way they do.
They have their words — what else could they have?

But why should we be interested in the fate of these tramps?
Why should their words interest us? Might it not be because their
words may be or may become our words, that their linguistic fate
may be or become ours? Might not the limits of their language,
become the limits of our world? Has this come about? How could
it come about?

Words do not have meanings *in vacuo*, but in the context of
what we do with them. Our responses, our reactions, play an
essential role where the meanings of words are concerned. This
is easy to see in the case of colours, smells and tastes. The distinctions between colours, pleasant and unpleasant odours, bitterness
and sweetness, have their sense in our common reactions. If,
normally, we did not react as we do where colours are concerned,
what would it mean to speak of *the* colour of anything? We do
not agree to react in the way we do. We react and find we agree
in our reactions. If we were not normally attracted by certain
smells and repelled by others, or did not react as we do to what
we call bitter and sweet, what would it mean to distinguish
between the pleasant and the unpleasant smell, the bitter and
sweet taste? Our normal reactions determine the life and meaning
of these distinctions. But this is true, not only of colours, smells

and tastes, but of words like 'chair', 'table' or 'stair'. Here, too, our actions are central in determining the sense of these words. What a chair, table or stair is, is bound up with our sitting on a chair or at the table, climbing the stair and so on. Cut these words off from these surroundings and they lose their meaning. We would not know what to do with them. They have their life in these surroundings, surroundings, in which our actions, responses and reactions play a vital part.

If all this is true of words like colour, smell, taste, chair, table, stair, it is certainly true of words which have moral and religious import. It is these words, more than any other, which Beckett explores in *Waiting for Godot*. Take, for example, the word 'repentance'. What kind of life surrounds it? Vladimir, wondering what alternative to consider next to relieve their boredom and stagnation, suddenly considers the possibility of repentance.

> *Vladimir*: One of the thieves was saved. (*Pause*) It's a reasonable
> percentage. (*Pause*) Gogo.
> *Estragon*: What?
> *Vladimir*: Suppose we repented.
> *Estragon:* Repented what?
> *Vladimir*: Oh . . . (*He reflects*) We wouldn't have to go into the
> details.

Notice how Vladimir has severed repentance from its religious surroundings. In order to repent, it appears that one does not have to worry about the details of the deeds one is repenting of. But, in that case, how serious is the repentance? How can one make sense of the sorrow and remorse which are involved in repentance if the details of what one has done are of no concern to me? What is one actually repenting *of*?

That question does not arise for Vladimir and Estragon. Their question is, rather, What is one repenting *for*? What will one get out of it? What are the odds that one will benefit from repenting? That is why Vladimir is impressed by the story of the thief who repents on the cross. It is said that he was saved as a result. The odds are fifty-fifty; quite impressive. Perhaps they ought to repent, in that case. Repentance is robbed of its normal, religious, surroundings and made a matter of calculated prudence.

But before they take this calculated risk and repent, Vladimir is anxious to find out whether the story of the thief who was saved

on the Cross is true. After all, if he was not saved, there would
be little point in repenting. And Vladimir is distinctly worried
about the state of Biblical scholarship on the matter:

> *Vladimir*: And yet . . . (*pause*) . . . how is it . . . this is not boring
> you I hope — how is it that of the four Evangelists only one
> speaks of a thief being saved. The four of them were there —
> or thereabouts — and only one speaks of a thief being saved.
> (*Pause*) Come on, Gogo, return the ball, can't you, once in a
> way?
> *Estragon*: (*with exaggerated enthusiasm*) I find this really most extra-
> ordinarily interesting.
> *Vladimir*: One out of four. Of the other three two don't mention
> any thieves at all and the third says both of them abused
> him.
> *Estragon*: Who?
> *Vladimir*: What?
> *Estragon*: What's all this about? Abused who?
> *Vladimir*: The Saviour.
> *Estragon*: Why?
> *Vladimir*: Because he wouldn't save them.
> *Estragon*: From hell?
> *Vladimir*: Imbecile! From death.
> *Estragon*: I thought you said hell.
> *Vladimir*: From death, from death.
> *Estragon*: Well what of it?
> *Vladimir*: Then the two of them must have been damned.
> *Estragon*: And why not?
> *Vladimir*: But one of the four says that one of the two was saved.
> *Estragon*: Well? They don't agree, and that's all there is to it.
> *Vladimir*: But all four were there. And only one speaks of a thief
> being saved. Why believe him rather than the others?
> *Estragon*: Who believes him?
> *Vladimir*: Everybody. It's the only version they know.
> *Estragon*: People are bloody ignorant apes.

The odds on salvation have shortened. If the story is true, the
odds are fifty-fifty, but only one of the four Evangelists record it
in this way. What odds repentance now? Once again we see that
the pseudo interest in Biblical scholarship subserves a prudential
goal. But, of course, Biblical testimony, on this argument, must

itself be based on a matter of fact, namely, whether God can in fact save an individual. If he can't that's the end of the matter. Vladimir and Estragon are waiting to be saved from their predicament. They hope Mr Godot, when he comes, will save them. But just as scripture can be doubted, so there is reason to doubt whether Godot can, in fact, deliver the goods. If he can't deliver the goods, if God can't deliver the goods, there would be no point in repenting.

Vladimir: Let's wait and see what he says.
Estragon: Who?
Vladimir: Godot.
Estragon: Good idea.
Vladimir: Let's wait till we know exactly how we stand.
Estragon: On the other hand it might be better to strike the iron before it freezes.
Vladimir: I'm curious to hear what he has to offer. Then we'll take it or leave it.
Estragon: What exactly did we ask him for?
Vladimir: Were you not there?
Estragon: I can't have been listening.
Vladimir: Oh . . . nothing very definite.
Estragon: A kind of prayer.
Vladimir: Precisely.
Estragon: A vague supplication.
Vladimir: Exactly.
Estragon: And what did he reply?
Vladimir: That he'd see.
Estragon: That he couldn't promise anything.
Vladimir: That he'd have to think it over.
Estragon: In the quiet of his home.
Vladimir: Consult his family
Estragon: His friends.
Vladimir: His agents.
Estragon: His correspondents.
Vladimir: His books.
Estragon: His bank account.
Vladimir: Before taking a decision.
Estragon: It's the normal thing.
Vladimir: Is it not?
Estragon: I think it is.

> *Vladimir*: I think so too.
> (*Silence*)
> *Estragon*: (*anxious*) And we?
> *Vladimir*: I beg your pardon?
> *Estragon*: I said, And we?
> *Vladimir*: I don't understand.
> *Estragon*: Where do we come in?
> *Vladimir* Come in?
> *Estragon*: Take your time.
> *Vladimir*: Come in? On our hands and knees.
> *Estragon*: As bad as that?

Godot is just like they are, procrastinating and fudging when confronted by a request for help. Notice, the tramps say that this is quite normal. It is what they have come to expect of themselves and others. It is what they expect of Godot too. Repentance, for them, is something they will do if it pays to do it. The Biblical evidence makes the odds uncertain and whether Godot or God can help is uncertain. The price the tramps may have to pay for help may be high — they may have to go on their hands and knees to get it. But all this is the normal language of the tramps. This is, for them, the kind of life the word 'repentence' has.

Earlier, when I spoke of words like colour, taste, smell, chair, table, stair, I made much of our normal responses and reactions in connection with them. Of course, 'normal' does not include everyone. There are those who do not respond in the normal way. Our normal responses, however, determine their fate. For example, we speak of a person as colour-blind when he is cut off from some normal responses where colours are concerned. When I spoke of the way Vladimir and Estragon speak of 'repentance'. I said that they had severed the word from its normal religious surroundings. But did I have the right to say this? What if *their* response is becoming the normal response both *to* and *within* religion? If that is happening, then the man who protests against it in the name of religion will himself be regarded as the strange one, the outcast, the blind one.

But *has* this way of talking become normality for many? Within the philosophy of religion this question must be answered in the affirmative. Here is Richard Swinburne, now Professor of Christian Philosophy at Oxford, defining faith in God in his book on *Faith and Reason*. It involves acting on the assumption 'that God will do for us what we want or need' where 'there is some danger that he may not'.[6]

The God with whom there is no variableness or shadow of turning has become a good tip for punters. Since this God won't save you unless you obey his commandments, you have good reasons for obeying them. For Swinburne a man can save his soul by making his salvation an aim. He thinks the charge of selfishness and self-interest can be avoided because a person's salvation is not in competition with anyone else's salvation. He does not see that what is at issue is the immoral character of the concern Swinburne presents as the desire for salvation. Swinburne says, 'You seek your own salvation partly by forwarding that of others'.[7] Other religious believers would say that forwarding the salvation of others is, in part, your salvation. For Swinburne, fear of divine punishment is like saying, 'Don't do that to me'. For other religious believers it is saying 'Don't let me become that'. In return for the salvation he can provide, Swinburne's God requires to be worshipped. Here is Swinburne's prudential pilgrim, Mr All Things Considered, assessing the odds at the start of another Lord's Day:

Suppose S believes that, on balance, just probably, there is a God, and that, on balance, just probably, God wants to be worshipped in church on Sunday morning, and that, on balance, just probably, if you do not do what God wants, you will suffer quite a bit for it in the next life. S has the purpose of avoiding such suffering, but also the purpose of staying in bed on Sunday morning. In the end he stays in bed. We accuse him of not 'acting on' his beliefs. The beliefs have failed to influence conduct because they were not strong enough for purposes of given strength. If S had believed the religious propositions with much greater confidence he would have got up and gone to church, but, as it was, he stayed in bed — the religious propositions seemed somewhat speculative, and so it seemed worth taking a gamble on their falsity. But if S had had a stronger purpose to avoid suffering in the after-life, then given the beliefs of the strength which he had, he would still have gone to church.[8]

This balancing of prudential possibilities goes on elsewhere. Swinburne simply applied it to religion He says: 'What applies to

beliefs generally applies to the belief that there is a God'.[9] Wouldn't
Vladimir and Estragon have understood? Of course, they would.
They'd play the same game as Swinburne except that they'd
haggle over the odds, but they'd understand:

> *Estragon*: It's the normal thing.
> *Vladimir*: Is it not
> *Estragon*: I think it is.
> *Vladimir*: I think so too.

But, now, listen to a very different response from another philosopher, Rush Rhees:

> Is the reason for not worshipping the devil instead of God that
> God is stronger than the devil? God will get you in the end, the
> devil will not be able to save you from his fury, and then you
> will be *for* it. 'Think of your future, boy, and don't throw away
> your chances.' What a creeping and vile sort of thing religion
> must be.

But what if this vile and creeping sort of thing threatens to become
normal religious language for many people? What if it has already
become such a language for many, if not the majority, of philosophers of religion?

Earlier I asked why the language of Beckett's tramps should
interest us. I suggested that their words might be or become ours,
that their linguistic fate may be or become ours. But their fate may
be read differently by different members of the play's audiences
and readers. Some will see the tramps as partly trapped by the
language of childish illusions and as partly seeing through this
language, but these readers will have no conception of anything
else religious language could be. Others see the tramps as victims
of what their language has become, a language of vulgar prudence.
Among these readers, some may be able to contrast this with a
deeper conception of religious faith. Others, including perhaps
Beckett himself, will find in the vulgarised language echoes of
something else it once was without being able to make this 'something else' explicit. For others, and they are many, the tramps are
lost souls who do not see what is in their interests; who do not
see that it pays to worship God.

Beckett says, 'There are words; we have nothing else'. True

enough, but the words in our lives and the life in our words reveal where and who we are.

Notes

1. Martin Esslin, *The Theatre of the Absurd* (Penguin Books, 1977) p. 23.
2. Samuel Beckett, all quotations from *Waiting for Godot* (Faber & Faber, 1977).
3. Esslin, op. cit., p. 85.
4. Ibid., p. 87.
5. Ionesco, Eugene, 'The Playwright's Role', *Observer*, 29 June 1958.
6. Richard Swinburne, *Faith and Reason* (Clarendon Press, 1981), p. 118.
7. Swinburne, ibid., p. 139.
8. Swinburne, ibid., p. 29.
9. Swinburne, ibid., p. 17.

9
Distorting Truth

We concluded the last essay by saying that the words in our lives reveal who we are. Of course, those lives do not conform to a neat pattern, but are, rather, a mixed bag. People's perspectives vary, so that the aspects under which they see the world cannot be taken for granted. One of the most difficult things is to see ourselves. We may not appreciate the distortions in our midst. We may not be ready to have them pointed out, least of all by one of our own kind.

In 1932, the painter, Evan Walters, offered to lend his fine portrait of the writer, Caradoc Evans, to the National Museum of Wales. The offer was declined on the grounds that the Museum already possessed a recent example of his portraiture. Everyone knew how to read this coded reply. The vast majority of letters sent to the newspaper the *Western Mail* supported the decision. One lady concluded her letter with the words: '*Câs gŵr na charo y wlad a'i magodd*' — 'Hateful is the man who does not love the land of his birth'. Evans was accused of distorting Welsh life: its people, its language and its religion. Here is the *Western Mail*'s critical reaction to his second volume of short stories *Capel Sion*, which it saw as carrying on the pattern established in his first collection, *My People*.

It may be that Mr Evans spent his early days among some people of the kind he depicts; if so, he seems to have lived in a sort of moral sewer. For all his characters are repulsive, and designedly so. They are certainly not Welsh; they are certainly not Welsh peasants; and the language they speak is not to be found anywhere in the world outside Mr Evans's books. It is charitable to believe that his knowledge of the language is of the slightest; if his idiotic representation of the talk of the peasantry is not due to ignorance, then may the Lord forgive him. For his offence is rank — as rank as the book itself. The stories are gross in tone, in intent, and in effect, and the reviewer's final feeling on finishing the work is to go and have a bath.

My People was published in 1915 and *Capel Sion* in 1916. Since then, Welsh Nonconformity and its political connections have ceased to be the power they once were. Nevertheless, even now, we have only to scratch the surface to find this attitude to Evans re-emerging. On attempting, without much hope of success, to get hold of T. L. Williams' useful study, *Caradoc Evans* in the University of Wales Press *Writers of Wales* series, in a Welsh book-shop, I was told, 'I'll have a look for it, but we didn't think much of him, mind'. Notice the confident use of 'we'. For her, Evans was the outsider, the betrayer, a man alienated from his people and from his roots in Wales.

It is often said that Wales, a small country, struggling to retain its language and its cultural distinctiveness, cannot afford to be critical of itself. There are plenty all too ready to deride it. Yet, understandable though that reaction may be, it will not do. Protec-tiveness kills the very culture it seeks to preserve. Furthermore, criticism of others and of oneself can manifest the distinctiveness of a culture just as much as praise of it.

In order to understand the reaction which faced Caradoc Evans, we have to understand that it is not one which is confined to Nonconformist Wales and its parochialism. Not at all. It is a reac-tion to be found, for example, in the most powerful country in the world. Flannery O'Connor refers to a challenge thrown out by an editorial in *Life* magazine. It asked, 'Who speaks for America today?' Commenting on this challenge in 1957, Flannery O'Connor said:

> The gist of the editorial was that in the last ten years this country had enjoyed an unparalleled prosperity, that it had come nearer to producing a classless society than any other nation, and that it was the most powerful country in the world, but that our novelists were writing as if they lived in packing boxes on the edge of the dump while they awaited admission to the poorhouse.[1]

The editorial went on to say that what was needed in literature was a 'redeeming quality of spiritual purpose' which would express 'the joy of life itself'. Literature was to be uplifting; it should feed *Life*'s image of America. It is a far cry from America to Nonconformist Wales, but in its essence, the demand is the same. What differs, of necessity, is the social and cultural milieu through which it is expressed. In Wales, that milieu prided itself on being religious. Literature, then, should give a spiritual uplift. Its humour should be 'healthy' humour and its criticisms reserved for the enemies of religion. Evans was held to have sinned against all these requirements. So far from giving spiritual uplift, his work indulged in savage satire. Its humour, if it can be called that, was black humour and the object of his criticisms was the very religion which literature should aim to sustain.

Flannery O'Connor often alluded to the challenge of *Life* magazine. Once, she said:

> What these editorial writers fail to realise is that the writer who emphasises spiritual values is very likely to take the darkest view of all of what he sees in this country today. For him, the fact that we are the most powerful and the wealthiest nation in the world doesn't mean a thing in any positive sense. The sharper the light of faith, the more glaring are apt to be the distortions the writer sees in the life around him.[2]

Here, the contrast is between secular materialism and religion. What made Evans so hard to take for many Welsh people was that the distortions he attacked were within religion itself. Little can be found in his work, if anything, about the spirituality of Welsh Nonconformity. His emphasis is almost entirely on the narrow code of do's and don'ts that Nonconformity can become. As T. L. Williams says:

> The code was nowhere more powerful than in its draconian enforcement of that sabbatarianism which came to be synonymous with the 'Welsh Sunday', but at the same time this strict Sunday observance was probably the most vulnerable point in the whole puritan ethic, for it encouraged secrecy, furtiveness and, above all, hypocrisy. In short, it tended to produce a situation in which one's 'sin' was less important than the *discovery* of one's sin, and in which there could be a great discrepancy between the ideals of Nonconformist behaviour and the actual behaviour of those who professed to subscribe to the code. There is of course nothing shocking in this very ordinary human

failure to live up to ideals; it is just that in rural Welsh society the clamour of public (chapel) censure against the wrongdoer (for example, the formal ceremony of 'breaking out' from the chapel the girl who was expecting an illegitimate baby) was such as to reinforce and perpetuate the tendency to cover things up hypocritically. A natural corollary to this situation was the paradox by which the worst offence against this Nonconformist (and politically radical) society was to be nonconformist, to be the outsider, who preferred his own moral, or immoral, code.[3]

Yet, it must be remembered, if Welsh Nonconformity can be the subject of strong satire, so can Roman Catholicism. The fitting comparison is not with the criticisms of James Joyce and others from a liberal, humanistic perspective, but with criticisms from within the fold by writers such as J. F. Powers. Speaking of him Flannery O'Connor says:

Catholic life as seen by a Catholic doesn't always make comfortable reading for Catholics . . . In this country we have J. F. Powers, for example, a very fine writer and a born Catholic who writes about Catholics. The Catholics that Mr Powers writes about are seen by him with a terrible accuracy. They are vulgar, ignorant, greedy, and fearfully drab, and all these qualities have an unmistakeable Catholic social flavour. Mr Powers doesn't write about such Catholics because he wants to embarrass the Church; he writes about them because, by the grace of God, he can't write about any other kind. A writer writes about what he is able to make believable.[4]

When Evans, a Welshman, wrote about Welsh Nonconformists, it did not make comfortable reading for them either. But what he saw, he too saw with a terrible accuracy: hypocrisy, greed, lust. He too gave these vices an umistakeable Welsh Nonconformist flavour. It will be objected that all Nonconformists were not of this kind. True enough, but, like Powers, Evans wrote about this kind of Nonconformist because he couldn't write about any other kind. It cannot be said that he did not want to embarrass the Chapel. He did. But what he wanted to embarrass was its respectability rather than its religion. It must be remembered that all his life he had a love-hate relationship with the Nonconformity he vilified. Drawing back from it in revulsion and disgust, nevertheless, he could not leave it alone, but was drawn to it again, aware of other things it had to offer, but which he could not write about. There were times when he regretted that he had not trained for its ministry, and to the end he was a great sermon-taster. When he died in 1945, the letters of condolence showed how much he was liked by ordinary people all over Wales. He was a kind-hearted man whom the community of New Cross, near Aberystwyth, came to know as such. George H. Green says:

> This was the Caradoc the neighbours came to know — the man whose body six of them carried on their shoulders up the steep hill behind his New Cross home, behind the little chapel where his friend, Tom Beynon, preached the simple sincere sermons that Caradoc admired and liked. He liked and admired them, not because they dealt with points of theology, but because they were free of the humbug and hypocrisy he saw about him, and hated and attacked consistently. If through hating hypocrisy he became hated by some, so much the worse for them. It is by themselves — not Caradoc — that they are condemned.[5]

But, it may be said, the issue of distortion has been ducked. Did not Evans distort what he saw about him, a distortion highlighted in the curious language in which he chose to express himself? Without a doubt, Evans used a distorted language in which to write, but the character of the distortion involved has been badly misunderstood by Welsh and English readers alike. Both shared a common assumption, namely, that Evans was translating straighforwardly from Welsh into English. For their part, the English concluded that his was how Welsh people spoke and were duly amused. The Welsh, on the other hand, saw nothing but grotesque failure on Evans' part and were duly infuriated. But since Evans was not attempting to translate in the first place, both reactions are ridiculously wide of the mark. Evans' language is a special creation on his part to bring about a desired artistic effect. The sources of the language are numerous: some literal translations from Welsh, some outlandish translations, use of stumbling efforts to speak English by predominantly Welsh speakers, use of Welsh slang, the coining of English words based on Welsh slang, and so on. But all these sources are blended together as befits the occasion, answering to no preordained pattern. One other essential element in Evans' use of language must be mentioned, namely,

the enormous influence on it of the Authorised Version of the
English Bible. According to Evans' own testimony, before writing
one of his stories he would read from the Old Testament. From
this he took the rhythm, economy and grandeur of its language.
Combining this with the Welsh sources we have mentioned, the
result was a brilliant parody, through distortion, of the Welsh
religious discourse of a people who lived by the Book.

The distortion, then, has to be admitted, but it is a distortion
intimately connected with truth. The Welsh were perfectly correct
to say that they did not speak and behave in the extreme ways
Evans depicted. But why should they assume that he was involved
in straightforward description? Flannery O'Connor was amused
at critics who said that she had convinced them that people in
Georgia actually behaved in the ways she depicted and were duly
horrified. They failed to understand her use of distortion as we
may fail to understand Evans'. Speaking of Kafka's *Metamorphosis*
which begins with a man waking up to find that he has turned
into a cockroach, Flannery O'Connor says: 'The truth is not distorted here, but rather, a certain distortion is used to get at the
truth'.[6]

The same is true with O'Connor and Evans. She said that in a
world in which religion was not understood, the writer is forced
to employ shock tactics. She said that for the deaf we have to
shout, and that for the almost blind we have to draw large and
startling figures. Evans found the deaf and the almost blind, not
outside religious circles, but within them. He wanted to forge a
language which would shock them into realising something about
themselves they would not see otherwise. The measure of his
success can be seen from the fact that many who expressed public
outrage, admitted in private that much of what he said was true.
To those who matched public outrage with private outrage,
respectability had penetrated the soul to recesses which even
Evans' brilliance could not reach.

One of the most savage short stories in *My People* is *Be This her
Memorial*.[7] It is the story of Nanni, by far the oldest member of
Capel Sion. Her income is three shillings and ninepence a week
which she receives from the Poor Relief Officer. It keeps her out
of the poorhouse and thus grants her the freedom to listen to
Respected Josiah Bryn-Bevan the minister of Capel Sion whom
she idolises. She helped to bring him into the world, knitted socks
for him when he was a farm servant, and, when he entered the

ministry, gave a tenth of her income to support him in Capel Sion.
'Unconsciously she came to regard Josiah as greater than God:
God was abstract; Josiah was real'.

A rumour comes to her that the Respected Josiah Bryn-Bevan
had received a call from a wealthy sister church in Aberystwyth.
Notice, 'Respected' not 'Reverend' which would be the normal
translation of the Welsh 'Parchedig'. The use of 'Respected' helps
him to play against it the fact that respect is the last thing this
minister deserves. Notice too that the minister gets a *call* (pre-
sumed to be from God), rather than an invitation from another
church. Evans slyly implies that God always calls his ministers to
chapels which will increase their salaries. 'Is it a good call?' one
minister will ask another, the salary featuring prominently in the
reply. With present salary structures, this has ceased to be a telling
point. Nanni prays to God:' "Dear little Big Man", she prayed,
"let not your son bach religious depart" '. Then she recalled how
good God had been to her, how He had permitted her to listen
to His son's voice; and another fear struck her heart. ' "Dear little
Big Man", she muttered between her blackened gums, "do you
now let me live to hear the boy's farewell words".'

She is visited by a Bible salesman from whom she buys a large
brass-clasped gaudy illustrated Bible as a farewell gift for the minister who has announced his departure. She is absent from Capel
Sion for many Sundays, following Josiah Bryn-Bevan wherever he
happened to be preaching. She was absent from the hay-making
too, but when Sadrach Danyrefail goes to remonstrate with her,
he is frightened by the gleaming-eyed creature who confronts him
and repulsed by the abominable smell from inside her cottage.
She begins to appear in chapel with oozing sores at the side of
her mouth. ' "Old Nanni," folk remarked while discussing her
over their dinner-tables, "is getting as dirty as an old sow".'

She makes the final payment on the Bible and asks Sadrach
Danyrefail to present it to the minister on her behalf when he
delivers his last sermon. But she is absent from the service. After
his sermon, the Respected Josiah Bryn-Bevan referred to her Bible
and dwelt on her sacrifice. But he then thoughtlessly presents the
Bible to Sadrach Danyrefail in recognition of his work with the
Sunday School. The next morning, making a tour of his flock, the
minister calls on Nanni. He finds her on the floor:

There was no movement from Nanni. Mishtir Bryn-Bevan went

on his knees and peered at her. Her hands were clasped tightly together, as though guarding some great treasure. The minister raised himself and prised them apart with the ferrule of his walking-stick. A roasted rat revealed itself. Mishtir Bryn-Bevan stood for several moments spellbound and silent; and in the stillness the rats crept boldly out of their hiding places and resumed their attack on Nanni's face. The minister, startled and horrified, fled from the house of sacrifice.

What was he horrified by? Well, the rats presumably, the half-eaten face and the stench. That is why many readers called the story a horror-story. That is what the protests were about — associating Nonconformity with such horrors. Is that what we are horrified at and protest against? Flannery O'Connor has said: 'I believe that there are many rough beasts now slouching towards Bethlehem to be born and that I have reported the progress of a few of them, and when I see these stories described as horror stories I am always amused because the reviewer always has hold of the wrong horror.'[8]

The real horror in Evans' story is the horror latent in Nonconformity which could allow Nanni's fate to befall her. Further, there is the horror of the way in which her incredible capacity for sacrifice is corrupted and distorted in the chapel and in herself. True religion and sacrifice are being eaten away. The story is based on a true incident of a woman who roasted rats to save a pound for the chapel collection. Speaking of the ruins of Nanni's cottage, Evans says: 'If you happen to be travelling that way you may still see the roofless walls which were silent witnesses to Nanni's great sacrifice — a sacrifice surely counted unto her for righteousness, though in her search for God she fell down and worshipped at the feet of a god'.

Evans has compassion and pity for those who suffer, but he is ruthless in his exposure of hypocrisy and respectability. Such exposure characterises what many regard as a second horror story in *My People*, namely, *A Father in Sion*.[9] The main character, Sadrach is described as follows:

He was a man whose thoughts were continually employed upon sacred subjects. He began the day and ended the day with the words of a chapter from the Book and a prayer on his lips. The

Sabbath he observed from first to last; he neither laboured himself nor allowed any in his household to labour.

In other words, Sadrach conforms to the Nonconformist sabbatarian code. But what of his conduct in other respects? He has eight children, a man of rampant sexuality. He tells the children that their mother Achsah, who brought the farm as a gift to the bridegroom, has gone mad, though this is not the case. She is 10 years older than him. To get rest from him she accepts the situation. Sadrach keeps her locked up. Her condition is said to be a disgrace and no one is allowed to see her. Occasionally, he gives her an airing in the fields with a cow's halter over her shoulders. He brings another woman, Martha, to the farm, in marrying whom he has committed bigamy. Because he is prosperous and eloquent all this is tolerated in Sion:

> Sadrach declared in the Seiat that the Lord was heaping blessings on the head of His servant. Of all who worshipped in Sion none was stronger than the male of Danyrefail; none more respected. The congregation elected him to the Big Seat. Sadrach was a tower of strength unto Sion.

But affliction follows in the wake of prosperity. Six of the eight children die. His one remaining son Sadrach the Small is to marry Sara Ann with whose family a prosperous arrangement has been made. He tells Achsah of the wedding and, somehow or other, she frees herself in order to see it. In an extremely moving part of the story, Evans describes her looking furtively at the wedding procession, searching for the faces of her children. When she cannot find them, she begins to think that she really is going mad. She then realises that they must be grown-up by now and thinks that is the reason she cannot find them. She looks again, but has to accept that only Miriam and Sadrach the Small remain. She remembers the circumstances of the birth of all her children; how she had never refused her husband his rights; been a woman to him as long as she lasted. She goes to the graveyard and finds the graves of her six children, tracing with her fingers the letters of their names. This is how the story ends: 'As Sara Ann crossed the threshold of Danyrefail, and as she set her feet on the flagstone on which Sadrach the Small is said to have been born, the door of the parlour was opened and a lunatic embraced her.'

Arranged madness ends in real madness. This is horror enough, along with the deaths of the children. But presiding over it all is the unspoken horror of the order and life imposed on his family by Sadrach the most respected of chapel deacons. Evans is not simply emphasising the gap between religion and respectability, but pointing out how, for many, respectability was the essence of their religion.

A final example from *My People*, is the story *The Way of the Earth*.[10] Simon and Beca, he paralysed and she blind are simply waiting for death. Their daughter Sara Jane had been born out of wedlock and so they were outcasts from Capel Sion. But they had not always been in this state of destitution. Their farm had flourished and Simon and Beca had saved their money confident in the knowledge that when they had enough the doors of Sion would open to them. Their avarice is in unison with the chapel's avarice. They are anxious to get their 24-year-old daughter respectably married and are ready to drive a hard bargain when William Jenkins of the General Shop courts her. The people of Capel Sion look on with interest. But William Jenkins has made her pregnant. Simon's and Beca's bargaining power is utterly destroyed. William Jenkins takes everything they have. They will never enter Capel Sion now. He pays off his creditors. He lives with Sara Jane for a year, but when the creditors return, he flees from the land. Notice the key line in the bargaining between Simon and William Jenkins:

Simon shivered. He was parting with his life. It was his life and Beca's life. She had made it, turning over the heather, and wringing it penny by penny from the stubborn earth. He, too, had helped her. He had served his neighbours, and thieved from them. He wept.

'He asks too much,' he cried. 'Too much.'

'Come, now, indeed,' said William Jenkins. 'Do you act religious by the wench fach.'

As T. L. Williams says, 'Even in the thoroughgoing examination of hypocrisy which *My People* is, that last remark still manages to stand out'.[11] *Act religious* — that equation of scheming avarice and respectability with religion says it all. A limited picture? Certainly. A complete picture? Certainly not. But a true picture nevertheless, even when what is shown employs distortion to reveal a truth.

In the 1985 miscellany of Caradoc Evans' work, *Fury Never Leaves*

Us, a miscellany made up, in the main, of hitherto unpublished
material, the editor John Harris, who is engaged on a Life of
Caradoc Evans, writes: 'You simply cannot get a Caradoc Evans
book these days', complained Rhys Davies in 1962, "you don't see
them in libraries and certainly never in bookshops".'[12] That position remained unchanged until very recently.[13] His literary reputation still depends on one or two contributions in anthologies of
Welsh short stories or horror stories. In the latter, as usual, he is
included for the wrong horror.

In a world of grants and subsidised publishing, respectable
Wales had a subtler way of responding to attack than with counter-
attack — the way of silence. But that silence is testimony to something we have every reason to be ashamed of: the ways we have,
not only in Wales, of creating, in the very name or religion, life
under a godless heaven.

Notes

1. Flannery O'Connor, 'The Fiction Writer and His Country' in *Mystery
    and Manners* (Farrar, Straus & Giroux, 1969), pp. 25–6.
2. Ibid., p. 26.
3. T. L. Williams, *Caradoc Evans* (University of Wales Press, 1970), pp.
    5–6.
4. Flannery O'Connor, 'Catholic Novelists and their Readers' in *Mystery
    and Manners*, p. 173.
5. George H. Green in *Caradoc Evans* by Oliver Sandys, (Hurst & Black-
    ett, 1946), p. 157.
6. Flannery O'Connor, 'Writing Short Stories' in *Mystery and Manners*,
    pp.97–8.
7. Caradoc Evans, all quotations from *Be This her Memorial* in *My People*
    (Andrew Melrose, 1919).
8. Flannery O'Connor, 'Writing Short Storeis' in *Mystery and Manners*,
    pp. 97–8.
9. Caradoc Evans, all quotations from *A Father in Sion* in *My People*,
10. Caradoc Evans, *The Way of the Earth* in *My People*.
11. T. L. Williams, op. cit., p. 67.
12. John Harris, 'Preface' in John Harris (ed.), *Fury Never Leaves Us*: *A
    Miscellany of Caradoc Evans* (Poetry Wales Press, 1985), p.7.
13. *My People* was finally reprinted by Poetry Wales Press in 1988.

10

The Shortest Way Home

Given the intellectual criticisms of religion we have considered, the often facile and vulgar defences offered in face of such criticisms, and what religion, in practice, can descend to, it is hardly surprising that there should be rebellions, not simply against religious authority, but against all forms of authority. Such a rebellion characterised the 1960s, that decade in which all rules were questioned in the name of a radical individualism.

But how does that decade look now? It may be felt that the cultural heritage it bequeathed to us is not a distinguished one. The contemporary American essayist, Joan Didion has described it as 'the morning after the sixties'; the 1960s, a decade in which old certainties, old stories, old authorities, seemed to lose their hold more than ever. What exactly were we witnessing? Joan Didion replies:

> This was not a traditional generational rebellion. At some point between 1945 and 1967 we had somehow neglected to tell these children the rules of the game we happened to be playing. Maybe we had stopped believing in the rules ourselves, maybe we were having a failure of nerve about the game. Maybe there were just too few people around to do the telling.[1]

What about religious rules? Had many stopped believing them, too; too many had a failure of nerve about them; with too few able to speak with spiritual authority about them? If religious rules are to speak, they must inform our daily lives. The nineteenth-century Danish thinker, Søren Kierkegaard, said that we often look on religion like a delightful coloured map, one which we can hold easily in the palm of our hands, and enjoy looking at. But we do not realise that the map is to be used. And so when we find ourselves in the real countryside, with its long miles and winding muddy lanes, we do not know our way about. We can't use the maps.

That's how Joan Didion came to feel about religious maps. We
know these maps well. They claim to show the territory to us, but
do we know how to use them any more? Do they tell us how to
find our way about? What use is God's map if it's man's world?
One of these religious maps, a house-blessing hung on the wall,
framed, in Joan Didion's mother-in-law's house in West Hartford,
Connecticut:

> God bless the corners of this house,
> And be the lintel blest —
> And bless the hearth and bless the board
> And bless each place of rest —
> And bless the crystal windowpane that lets the
> > starlight in
> And bless each door that opens wide, to
> > stranger as to kin.[2]

What did Joan Didion think of this religious story, this religious
map which claimed to show you how to behave towards your
neighbour?

This verse had on me the effect of a physical chill, so insistently
did it seem the kind of 'ironic' detail the reporters would seize
upon, the morning the bodies were found. In my neighbourhood in California we did not bless the door that opened wide
to stranger as to kin. Paul and Tommy Scott Ferguson were
the strangers at Ramon Novarro's door, up on Laurel Canyon.
Charles Manson was the stranger at Rosemary and Leno La
Bianca's door, over in Los Feliz. Some strangers at the door
knocked, and invented a reason to come inside; a call, say, to
the Triple A, about a car not in evidence. Others just opened
the door and walked in, and I would come across them in the
entrance hall. I recall asking one such stranger what he wanted.
We looked at each other for what seemed a long time, and then
he saw my husband on the stair landing. 'Chicken Delight', he
said finally, but we had ordered no Chicken Delight, nor was
he carrying any. I took the licence number of his panel truck.
It seems to me now that during those years I was always writing
down the licence numbers of panel trucks, panel trucks circling
the block, panel trucks parked across the street, panel trucks
idling at the intersection. I put these licence numbers in a dres-

sing-table drawer where they could be found by the police when the time came.[3]

During this period, from about 1965 to 1971, Joan Didion, like many others, began to doubt the promises various stories offered her. As each story disintegrated, unable to exercise a hold on the facts of human experience, a more primitive code emerged for her, one scarcely deserving the name 'morality': 'a code that has as its point only survival, not the attainment of the ideal good'.[4]

On 9 August 1969, Joan Didion was at her sister-in-law's house in Beverly Hills, when she received a telephone call from a friend who had just heard about the murders at Sharon Tate Polanski's house:

> The phone rang many times during the next hour. These early reports were garbled and contradictory. One caller would say hoods, the next would say chains. There were twenty dead, no, twelve, ten, eighteen. Black masses were imagined, and bad trips blamed. I remember all of the day's misinformation very clearly, and I also remember this, and wish I did not: I remember that no one was surprised.[5]

No one was surprised. To be surprised, there must be some sense of a limit, a sense of that which cannot be transgressed. But the stories that came Joan Didion's way carried no such sense; could find no place for it.

> There were rumours. There were stories. Everything was unmentionable but nothing was unimaginable. This mystical flirtation with the idea of 'sin' — this sense that it was possible to go 'too far', and that many people were doing it — was very much with us in Los Angeles in 1968 and 1969. A demented and vortical tension was building in the community. The jitters were setting in.[6]

Where do you turn to when the jitters have set in, if no notion of an ideal good beckons you? To the convictions of private conscience, I suppose. But when Joan Didion looked at what private consciences had recommended, her fears were not allayed.

'I followed my own conscience.' 'I did what I thought was right.'

How many madmen have said it and meant it? How many murderers? Klaus Fuchs said it, and the men who committed the Mountain Meadows Massacre said it, and Alfred Rosenberg said it. And, as we are rotely and rather presumptuously reminded by those who would say it now, Jesus said it. Maybe we have all said it, and maybe we have been wrong.[7]

Jesus said it! You must have thought I had forgotten him. Has he anything to say to Joan Didion, and the rest of us, barricaded behind our own doors, suspicious of those who knock on them demanding entry?

> Then said Jesus unto them again, Verily, verily, I say unto you, I am the door of the sheep . . .
> I am the door: by me if any man enter in, he shall be saved, and shall go in and out, and find pasture.

Is there any evidence that Joan Didion heard that voice? Well, she once heard some old people holding a prayer-sing at the Faith Community Church in Death Valley. She tells us they had come there to live in trailers, so that they could die in the sun. What she heard terrified her.

> Rock of ages, cleft for me
> Let me hide myself in thee.

I cannot hear them and do not want to. What I can hear are occasional coyotes and a constant chorus of 'Baby the Rain Must Fall' from the jukebox in the Smoke Room next door, and if I were also to hear those dying voices, those Midwestern voices drawn to this lunar country for some unimaginable atavistic rites, *rock of ages cleft for me*, I think I would lose my own reason.[8]

Joan Didion has told us that among the people she knew in Los Angeles in 1968 and 1969, nothing was unimaginable — nothing, that is, except this — a rock of ages, cleft for me! Yet, at this very same time, in 1968, an American philosopher, O. K. Bouwsma, was writing these words:

It's as though man lived in an enclosure with thick walls and dummy doors — which might also be described as doors for dummies — trying to push open or to pull open, but apart from their illusions that the dummy door has given way just a chink, the dummy door does not open. Men cannot find their way to look out. All the same they cannot get rid of the idea that there is something outside the wall. So they talk about it and talk about it — some say that there is nothing but darkness there, nothing at all. It frightens them.[9]

Joan Didion writes of plenty that frightens her, but does she still long for something else, something outside it all, which will give sense to it? I think she does. Surprisingly, she too seeks a rock of ages. One of her essays has that title, but the rock she writes about is Alcatraz, deserted, in 1966, apart from the care-taker, his wife, their dog and one other retired sea-man. What appeals to her about this deserted rock? As she says, she knows how the prison must have been 'with the big lights playing over the windows all night long and the guards patrolling the gun galleries and the silverware clattering into a bag as it was checked in after meals'. Yet, she cannot feel distaste for it now.

> But the fact of it was that I liked it out there, a ruin devoid of human vanities, clean of human illusions, an empty place reclaimed by the weather where a woman plays an organ to stop the wind's whining and an old man plays ball with a dog named Duke. I could tell you that I came back because I had promises to keep, but maybe it was because nobody asked me to stay.[10]

She wants somewhere devoid of human vanities, clean, unspot-ted from the world. That is an attempt to speak religious language without religion. Joan Didion finds no place for religious absolutes, but the need for absolutes keeps its hold on her. When the Chris-tian God retreats, what other god breaks in, demanding to be worshipped?

Ironically, in Joan Didion's case, she wants an instant, all-inclus-ive answer — the very romanticism she rightly rejected in the Californian dream. She is a critic of the dream, but she is also its victim. That is why her desire to stay on Alcatraz does not ring true. She yearns for some instant, magical cleansing, which can by-pass the messy details of life. One minute dirty; the next minute clean. The shortest way home to salvation. But that magical, quasi-religious solution does not work. And those who have done more than play around with the notion of the solitary place, who have embraced solitude, know that it does not work. Listen to the wise words of the Trappist monk, Thomas Merton: 'do not go into the desert to get away from the world, or you will find yourselves living with a legion of devils. But take the world with you into the desert, and pray for it.'

There is no shortest way home to salvation, no short-cut which by-passes the mundane details of everyday life. But the 1960s was a decade of short-cuts, of instant answers, instant love which was supposed to provide instant solutions; instant love which in fact made instant millionaires:

> All you need is love
> Love, love, love
> Love is all you need.

One of Joan Didion's essays is called a love song, and it celebrates the legend of John Wayne. She knows the facts as well as anyone; knows of his struggle against cancer. And yet the legend attracts her — a legend which offers another shortest way home — an instant answer, one offering instant freedom:

> . . . he suggested another world, one which may or may not have existed ever but in any case existed no more: a place where a man could move free, could make his own code and live by it; a world, in which, if a man did what he had to do, he could one day take the girl and go riding through the draw and find himself home free, not in a hospital with something going wrong inside him, not in a high bed with the flowers and the drugs and the forced smiles, but there at the bend in the bright river, the cottonwoods shimmering in the early morning sun.
>
> 'Hello there.' Where did he come from, before the tall grass? Even his history seemed right, for it was no history at all, nothing to intrude upon the dream.[11]

But if nothing can intrude upon the dream, how can the dream inform reality? When longing for God departs, often a longing for false, unattainable absolutes takes its place. Sometimes, something worse takes place, a false absolute plays at actually being God —

the deepest evil ensues. As we have seen, distressed by human cruelties, vanities and illusions, Joan Didion seeks the shortest way home to salvation; she longs for instant solutions. So did the people she found at Joan Baez's Institute for the Study of Nonviolence in Carmel Valley. Joan Didion sees through them. She sees through a Joan Baez song which says, 'Sometimes I get lonesome for a storm. A full-blown storm where everything changes'. Once again, one big answer for everything. As I say, Joan Didion sees through it. But she is also attracted by it. She doesn't trust her own conscience, because she knows this fatal attraction lurks there. If she listened to her conscience she'd find a dangerous desire to imitate God's omnipotence; to imitate it, falsely, in wanting to clean the world from all its faults in a terrifying nuclear holocaust. Where would Joan Didion be if she listened to her conscience?

> . . . were I to follow my conscience then, it would lead me out onto the desert with Marian Faye, out to where he stood in *The Deer Park* looking east to Los Alamos and praying, as if for rain, that it would happen: '. . . let it come and clear the rot and the stench and the stink, let it come for all of everywhere, just so it comes and the world stands clear in the white dead dawn'.[12]

But this world, according to Christianity, with all its faults, is the very same world that God so loved that he gave his only begotten Son to die for it. The world is God's world. When that sense fades or loses its hold, a longing for absolutes remains. In this longing various gods break in offering the shortest way home to salvation. But what if there is no short-cut to salvation? What if the way home is always a long one, calling at a garden called Gethsemane and a hill called Calvary? What if the long way to God is inescapable for those who desire him; as inescapable as God's reality to which prophets and psalmists testified so very long ago?

Notes

1. Joan Didion, 'Slouching towards Bethlehem' in *Slouching towards Bethlehem* (Touchstone, Simon & Shuster, 1979), p. 123.
2. Joan Didion, 'The White Album' in *The White Album* (Penguin, 1981), p. 18.

3. Ibid., p. 19.
4. Joan Didion, 'On Morality' in *Slouching towards Bethlehem*, p. 159.
5. Joan Didion, 'The White Album' in *The White Album*, p. 42.
6. Ibid., p. 41.
7. Joan Didion, 'On Morality' in *Slouching towards Bethlehem*, p. 161.
8. Ibid., p. 160.
9. O. K. Bouwsma, 'Faith, Evidence and Proof' in *Without Proof or Evidence* (University of Nebraska Press, 1984).
10. Joan Didion, 'Rock of Ages' in *Slouching towards Bethlehem*, p. 208.
11. Joan Didion, 'John Wayne: A Love Story' in *Slouching towards Bethlehem*, pp. 30 – 1.
12. Joan Didion, 'On Morality' in *Slouching towards Bethlehem*, p. 161.

11

Mental Gymnastics

In the last four essays, we have seen what ways of living may become. Rules get their significance from the place they occupy in our lives. We saw how religion can degenerate into a kind of vulgar prudence or deadly respectability, and how instant solutions can lead us astray with the idle dreams they peddle. But what of the intellectual analyses of these situations? They are not free of the diverse influences in the life that surrounds them. That being so, there is no guarantee that there will be illumination within intellectual enquiry itself; it may contribute to an obscuring of moral and religious possibilities.

Most professions invite jibes. The jibes are, usually, unfair, but never wholly untrue. They indicate a truth which needs to be recognised, a caution which needs to be heeded. Jibes against philosophy are no exception. The philosopher seems to doubt things we would not doubt ordinarily, and the jibe is, that in doing so, he cannot be taken seriously; he is playing around with words; performing mental gymnastics.

There have been philosophers who have said that no empirical proposition can be certain; that we cannot be certain that material objects, including our own bodies, exist. They have said that we never perceive other people; never see their joy, anger or grief. They have said I can be certain of my own pain, but can never be sure that others are in pain. They have said that we cannot be certain that $2 + 2 = 4$, or that the sun will rise tomorrow. What are these philosophers up to? Have they gone mad? Asylums house people who doubt or deny such things. But the philosophers are not locked up. They are up and about professing their subject, and telling others that, if only they reflected on the world about them, they would have these doubts and fears too. They are not neurotic doubts and fears, but rational doubts and fears — or so the philosophers say.

But this claim has proved too much for many. They have not deigned to argue with the philosophers, but, with a gesture, indicated the lack of seriousness they attribute to them. J. L. Craft has described two famous occasions when such gestures were made. Here is the first:

> Parmenides and his disciple Zeno argued for the thesis that motion is impossible and, by implication, that there is no motion . . . But Diogenes the Cynic, in the midst of a lecture by Zeno on the impossibility of motion, rose, perhaps at the moment Zeno was mentioning the unshootable arrow, and walked about in front of the lectern.[1]

Here is the occasion of the second gesture:

> Consider Dr Johnson kicking the stone, on the occasion of Boswell's saying that no refutation of Berkeley's thesis of the 'non-existence of matter' is possible. Boswell in the Life of Johnson writes of that occasion:
> 'I never shall forget the alacrity with which Johnson answered, striking his foot with a mighty force against a large stone, till he rebounded from it, "I refute it *thus*".'[2]

As Craft points out, walking around in a lecture or kicking a stone hardly qualify as arguments, let alone as intellectual refutations, but, nevertheless, these irreverent gestures do have a point. They are aimed, Craft says, 'at breaking the trance produced by the illusion of intelligibility'. 'But if motion is impossible, if Zeno is taken seriously, then how can one go home to dinner? And if there is no matter, if Berkeley is taken seriously, how can one sit on a chair or eat an apple?'[3]

But since Zeno as well as Diogenes can walk about, and Berkeley can kick stones as well as Dr Johnson, the effect of breaking the trance, induced by philosophy, may well be to treat the philosopher as one who plays around with words, indulges in verbal acrobatics, mental gymnastics. As such, he cuts a somewhat eccentric, comic, but, essentially, harmless figure.

Many see such a figure in George Moore, Professor of Moral Philosophy, the main character in Tom Stoppard's play, *Jumpers*.[4] The joke about philosophy as mental gymnastics looms large throughout the play. The gymnasts who give their name to the title are said to be 'a mixture of the more philosophical members of the university's gymnastics team and the more gymnastic members of the Philosophy School'. George says: 'The close association between gymnastics and philosophy is I believe unique to this university and owes itself to the Vice-Chancellor, who is of course a first-rate gymnast, though an indifferent philosopher'.

There are times when George, in discussing Zeno's arguements, wants to react to them with, as Diogenes did, with an irreverent gesture. If Zeno is to be taken seriously, a tortoise with a head start in a race with a hare, can never be caught. George has a tortoise and, if only he can find it, a hare, at hand to show how wrong Zeno is. He also has a bow and arrow at the ready to refute Zeno with yet another gesture and a joke worthy of Diogenes and Dr Johnson:

> But it was precisely this notion of an infinite series which in the sixth century BC led the Greek philosopher Zeno to conclude that since an arrow shot towards a target first had to cover half the distance, and then half the remainder and then half the remainder after that, and so on *ad infinitum*, the result was, as I will now demonstrate, that though an arrow is always approaching its target, it never quite gets there, and Saint Sebastian died of fright.

Immediately after this so-called demonstration, George discovers that he is wearing odd socks. The audience is invited to link this eccentricity with the eccentric arguments George has been discussing. Inevitably, at this point, with some justification, the conclusion will be drawn that Stoppard is simply sending-up philosophy in a way a non-philosophical audience can readily appreciate and embrace. To be content with that conclusion, however, is to miss entirely the savage comic thrust of the play, to appreciate which an appreciation of what has been happening in recent philosophy is needed.

The superficial conclusion that Stoppard is simply sending-up philosophy is easy to reach because Stoppard provides no corrective to the lack of seriousness with which George treats Zeno's arguments. He gives no indication of the deep difficulties which led Zeno to fly in the face of facts he knew as well as anyone else. Zeno might have avoided his conclusions about the immovability of the arrow if he had seen how he had run together physical divisibility and mathematical divisibility in his thinking. As George says, Zeno claims to show: '. . . that *before* reaching the half-way point, the arrow had to reach the quarter-mark, and before that the eighth, and before that the sixteenth, and so on, with the result . . . *that the arrow could not move at all!'*

If we think of the distance the arrow has to fly between A and B, there are in it an infinite number of mathematical points. What saying this amounts to is that if we follow the rule of dividing the distance between A and B by 2, it makes no sense to say that no further division is possible. But it is not true to say that the distance between A and B can be divided *physically* to infinity. There will come a point when no further physical division is possible. By thinking that the arrow has to pass through an infinite number of physical points to get from A to B, we are tempted to the unhappy conclusion that the arrow cannot get from A to B. Indeed, further reflection on these lines seems to show that the arrow cannot even get from one point to another, and so cannot move at all!

Zeno's difficulties are not trivial. They are deep-going. In unravelling how he came to fly in the face of the facts, we not only reveal confusion, but at the same time re-emphasise the importance of the distinction between mathematical and physical divisibility. There is no indication in Stoppard's play of ways, such as this, in which philosophical confusion may be *deep* confusion. There is hardly any deep or serious philosophy in the play at all. This has led the philosopher Jonathan Bennett to conclude, mistakenly, that in *Jumpers*, in contrast to Stoppard's other play, *Rosencrantz and Guildenstern are Dead*, Stoppard is not serious about philosophy:

> In contrast with this, the philosophy which is flaunted throughout *Jumpers* is thin and uninteresting, and it serves the play only in a decorative and marginal way. Its main effect has been to induce timidity in reviewers who could not see the relevance to the play of the large stretches of academic philosophy which it contains. Since the relevance doesn't exist, the timidity was misplaced, and so the kid gloves need not have been used.[5]

This conclusion could not be further from the truth. The philosophy Stoppard comments on *is* thin and uninteresting because his concern is with what morality and religion have become in the hands of such philosophy. If someone cannot free himself from the grip of Zeno's perplexity, arrows are not prevented from reaching their targets, or hares obstructed in overtaking tortoises. But what if someone acquainted with talk of absolute good and evil, and with talk of God, gives a philosophical account of such talk which obscures its character? More likely, what if someone unacquainted with such talk, propounds philosophical banalities which, he claims, capture the essence of such talk? What if this philosophy becomes prestigious? Can we say, with confidence, that the original language is safe, unusurpable by the philosophical banalities? Unfortunately not. The banalities may become normal discourse. This is the topic of Stoppard's *Jumpers*. He shows the struggles of George Moore to hold on to some kind of sense in a context in which a marginal and decorative philosophy has become a *used* language all around him; a use to which he himself is not immune. So far from such philosophy not being relevant to the play, as Bennett thinks, it is the very essence of it.

George Moore struggles for sense as a professor of moral philosophy in a university where most of the philosophers are engaged in what he regards as mental gymnastics. He is not in favour with Archie, the Vice-Chancellor, because he refuses to take part in gymnastics; he refuses to jump. He tells Inspector Bones, who is investigating the murder of one of the gymnasts:

In fact I will have nothing to do with it. And in spite of the Vice-Chancellor's insistence that I can jump better than I think, I have always maintained the opposite to be the case . . . In the circumstances I was lucky to get the Chair of Moral Philosophy. (*His tone suggests, rightly, that this is not much of a prize*.) Only the Chair of Divinity lies further below the salt, and that's been vacant for six months since the last occupant accepted a position as curate in a West Midland diocese.

Bones: Then why don't you . . . jump along with the rest?

Bones' question is one of the most important in the play. A philosopher, in a survey of recent philosophy, said that the brightest and cleverest philosophers have not been concerned, in the main, with issues concerning morality and religion. George would say, more accurately, that is was not bright or clever of a philosopher to make these topics his main preoccupations. To be bright and clever is to show that talk of absolute good or evil, and talk of God, does not mean anything. George is convinced that these refutations are themselves the product of confusion, but he lacks

the philosophical resources to show this. In justifying why he
won't engage in gymnastics, all he can say is: 'I belong to a school
which regards all sudden movements as ill-bred.'

That is all a denial of God can mean for George — a sign of ill-
breeding. His positive arguments for the existence of God suffer
from a deadly gentility:

> There is in mathematics a concept known as a limiting curve,
> that is the curve defined as the limit of a polygon with an infinite
> number of sides. For example, if I had never seen a circle and
> didn't know how to draw one, I could nevertheless postulate
> the existence of circles by thinking of them as regular polygons
> with numberless edges, so that an old three-penny bit would
> be a bumpy imperfect circle which would approach perfection
> if I kept doubling the number of its sides: at infinity the result
> would be the circle which I have never seen and do not know
> how to draw, and which is logically implied by the existence of
> polygons. And now and again, not necessarily in the contem-
> plation of polygons or new-born babes, nor in the extremities
> of pain and joy, but more probably in some quite trivial moment,
> it seems to me that life itself is the mundane figure which argues
> perfection at its limiting curve. And if I doubt it, the ability to
> doubt, to question, to *think*, seems to be the curve itself. *Cogito
> ergo deus est*.

Such attempts at arguing for the existence of God from math-
ematics, attempts which Kierkegaard described, mockingly, as
attempts at infinite approximation, characterised Oxford philosophy of religion in the recent past. At present, the same infinite
approximation is attempted on the basis of probability theory.
Unlike the perpetrators of these attempts, George is at least clear-
headed about what his own arguments, and his attempts to
resuscitate the traditional proofs of the existence of God, amount
to: 'The fact that I cut a ludicrous figure in the academic world is
largely due to my aptitude for traducing a complex and logical
thesis to a mysticism of staggering banality'.

George cannot cope with the so-called logical refutations of the
intelligibility of religious belief. The Vice-Chancellor is right:
George can jump better than he can think. His own arguments, his
very attempts to defend religion, are fodder for the anti-religious
refutations. George's positive arguments have little to do with the

natural contexts of a living faith: 'If God exists, he certainly existed before religion. He is a philosopher's God, logically inferred from self-evident premises. That he should have been taken up by a glorified supporters' club is only a matter of psychological interest.'

The refuters of religion need arguments of this kind. The efficacy of these refutations depends on keeping religion within such artificial parameters. In this way, philosophical arguments concerning religion, pro and contra, bypass religion by detaching it from its natural context. The bewildering and confused situation in which George finds himself has been well described by Kierkegaard:

> . . . the concepts have gradually been emasculated, and the words have been made to mean anything and everything, so that the disputes are sometimes as ridiculous as the agreements. For it is always ludicrous to engage in controversy on the basis of loose words, and to come to agreement on the basis of loose words . . . so modern discourse about Christianity has lost the vigour that can come only from an energetically sustained terminology, and the whole is reduced to a toothless twaddle.'

But the emasculated concepts of philosophy are not confined to George's professional life. Stoppard's comic effects are achieved by making George, and those around him, behave in the ways people would behave if confused moral philosophies and philosophies of religion were acted on; if the language of those philosophies became their everyday language.

George's wife, Dotty, is having an affair with the Vice-Chancellor. Any idiot should be able to see it. But because George is infected with the prevailing philosophical doctrine that truth can be no more than an interim judgement, the language in which he speaks to Dotty of her affair makes it impossible for him to take the situation by the scruff of the neck, and easy for her to allay his suspicions: 'I can put two and two together, you know. Putting two and two together is my *subject*. I do not leap to hasty conclusions. I do not deal in suspicion and wild surmise. I examine the data; I look for logical inferences.' This philosophical game keeps truth at a distance. Games become the essence of his relationship with his wife. Her various semi-naked posturings are simply occasions on which he has to guess the song, book or film

she is alluding to. Their infrequent sexual contact has also become
a game, the character of which sometimes comes home to him:

Dotty: George! — I'll let you.
George: I don't want to be 'let'. Can't you see that's it an insult?

At the outset of the play, George is making an anonymous
telephone call to the police in an attempt to silence the noise of
the party Dotty is giving for the gymnasts. It is at the party that
one of the gymnasts is murdered, a fact George does not discover
until the play's second act. He talks at cross-purposes with Inspector Bones. George is owning up to making the telephone call
complaining of a party held in his own house, whereas Bones
thinks he is protecting Dotty from a murder charge.

> *Bones*: I don't think the burden of being a householder extends
>   to responsibility for any crime committed on the premises.
> *George*: Crime? You call that a crime?
> *Bones*: (*with some heat*) Well, what would you call it?
> *George*: It was just a bit of *fun*! Where's you sense of humour,
>   man?
> *Bones*: (*staggered*) I don't know, you bloody philosophers are all
>   the same, aren't you? A man is dead and you're as cool as
>   you like.

As we have seen, this comic effect comes from the misunderstanding between George and Bones. On the other hand, when
George does realise that his philosophical rival, Professor McFee,
is the gymnast who has been murdered, the moral philosophies
he sees through, but cannot escape from, prevent him from
expressing any real horror at the death. He is more horrified at
the death of his pets, a goldfish and a hare. Dotty has inadvertently killed the fish by letting water out of the bath, and he the
hare with his bow and arrow. It is for these deaths that he reserves
a horrified reaction, as if to murder. And why shouldn't he if the
language of the moral philosophies he is wrestling with becomes
his language?

> *George*: The study of moral philosophy is an attempt to deter-
>   mine what we mean when we say that something is good
>   and that something else is bad. Not all value judgements,

however are the proper study of the moral philosopher . . .
modern philosophy has made itself ridiculous by analysing
such statements as, 'This is a good bacon sandwich', or
'Bedser had a good wicket'.

The joke against Oxford moral philosophy is a telling one: the
joke against those who said that although its descriptive objects
may vary, humans, goldfishes, hares, the meaning of commen-
dation remains the same in all cases, there being no distinctive
moral use of 'ought'. There were those who recommended that
philosophers should consider the most trivial examples possible,
since, it was said, the logic of concepts is unaffected by the seriousness or complexity of the issues involved. There were others who
held out high hopes for arriving at what it means to be a good
man by beginning with a consideration of what it means to talk
of a good knife. Poor George! Although he struggled against them,
he found the language of such theories becoming his language,
with the comic results Stoppard depicts.

Soon, George finds himself, like the colleagues of Tolstoy's Ivan
Ilych, seeing an opportunity in McFee's death for his own professional advancement. And why shouldn't he if McFee's views
on morals are correct; if he can make McFee's philosophical language his own language? He expounds McFee's views to Bones:

George: He thinks good and bad aren't actually *good* and *bad* in
   any absolute or metaphysical sense, he believes them to be
   categories of our making, social and psychological conventions which we have evolved in order to make living in
   groups a practical possibility in much the same way as we
   have evolved the rules of tennis without which Wimbledon
   Fortnight would be a complete shambles, do you see? . . . It
   allows him to conclude that telling lies is not *sinful*, but simply
   anti-social.
Bones: And murder?
George: And murder, too, yes.
Bones: He thinks there's nothing *wrong* with killing people?
George: Well, put like that, of course . . . But *philosophically*, he
   doesn't think it's actually, inherently wrong in itself, no.
Bones: (amazed) What sort of philosophy is that?
George: Mainstream, I'd call it. Orthodox mainstream.

Again, the joke hits home. In the attempt to revive ethical naturalism, an attempt was made to show that it pays to be good. Morality, it was said, is enlightened self-interest; that interest is morality's ultimate rationale. That being so, whether murder is condonable depends, in the end, on whether it is in my interests to murder. If this philosophical language threatens to become our everyday language, then, along with Dotty, we may not know what to make of the television news from the moon:

And so in the crippled space capsule, Captain Scott is on his way back to earth, the first Englishman to reach the moon, but his triumph will be overshadowed by the memory of Astronaut Oates, a tiny receding figure waving forlornly from the feature-less wastes of the lunar landscape . . . Millions of viewers saw the two astronauts struggling at the foot of the ladder until Oates was knocked to the ground by his commanding officer . . . Captain Scott has maintained radio silence since pulling up the ladder and closing the hatch with the remark, 'I am going up now. I may be gone for some time.'

Jonathan Bennett sees nothing here but a cheap joke. On the contrary, the joke could not be more serious. It is a *reductio ad absurdum* of what the philosophical view of morality as enlightened self-interest would make of our moral regard for the altruism of people like Oates. If that philosophy's language became our language, it would reverse much of what we cherish now. To admit that would be to admit the waywardness of philosophical theories. There is enormous resistance to admitting this. Stoppard depicts this professional resistance in the scene in which Archie, the Vice-Chancellor admits to having a motive for killing McFee. He had found that the professor of logic had come to God, and was contemplating entering a monastery.

Bones: Doesn't seem much of a reason.
Archie: It depends. Moore himself is not important — he is our tame believer, pointed out to visitors in much the same spirit as we point out the magnificent stained glass in what is now the gymnasium. But McFee was the guardian and figurehead of philosophical orthodoxy, and if he threatened to start call-ing on his masters to return to the true path, then I'm afraid

it would certainly have been an ice-pick in the back of the skull.

As long as traditional arguments for the existence of God, pro and contra, continue, philosophical jumpers are unperturbed. Logic can be relied on to put religion in its place. But there was quite a panic when that conception of logic was attacked, powerfully, from within philosophical logic itself, by Wittgenstein. He dared to say that language was idling in philosophical theories and that sense had gone on holiday! Worse, he made the comic remark that attackers of primitive religion are cruder than the savages. How could intellectuals stand such a thought? This intrusive philosophical voice had to be silenced. After a hiccup, the old arguments, within the comfortable philosophical game, regained their dominance. The fate of intrusive theologians must be the same. In the play's coda, we find Clegthorpe, a former veterinary scientist who has failed to get a cabinet post, a safe agnostic, who has been appointed Archbishop of Canterbury, suddenly panicking at the clamouring of his flock for what he cannot give them.

> *Clegthorpe*: They were shouting 'Give us the blood of the lamb. Give us the bread of the body of Christ' —
> *Archie*: That's hardly a rational demand.
> *Clegthorpe*: They won't go away! . . . Surely belief in man could find room for man's beliefs . . .?

The Archbishop, like the philosopher, is shot, silenced. Stoppard's comedy shows the perennial temptation for philosophy not to find room for man's beliefs. Further, it shows what happens to those beliefs if people actually make the confused philosophers' language their own language. Jonathan Bennett says '*Jumpers*, in short, lacks structure, and lacks seriousness'. On the contrary its comedy has very serious aims, and the play's pursuit of them is highly structured. Bennett says, 'Flattering as it may be to find our discipline represented on a West End stage, there is nothing here that deserves the attention of philosophers'.[6] To find the representation of philosophy on the West End stage flattering is to miss entirely the savage thrust of the comedy. As for the play not deserving the attention of philosophers, nothing could be further from the truth. Of course, if Stoppard is right, it will not get the attention of many. The philosophers are too busy thinking, jumping, to look.

Notes

1. J. L. Craft, 'Remarks on Bouwsma's Method of Failure', *Philosophical Investigations*, vol. 8, no. 3, July 1985, p. 163.
2. Ibid.
3. Ibid., p. 165.
4. All quotations from Tom Stoppard's *Jumpers* (Faber & Faber, 1975).
5. Jonathan Bennett, 'Philosophy and Mr Stoppard', *Philosophy*, vol. 50, 1975, p. 5.
6. Ibid., p. 8.

12

A Place without Qualities

As we listen to most contemporary debates about religion, to what passes for a defence of religion and to what passes for an attack on it, we may experience a sense of utter hopelessness. We find ourselves saying that nothing can be done. Our surroundings appear more and more absurd to us. But, then, doubts occur. Are these pessimistic reactions self-indulgent? Are they personal disappointments masquerading as perspectives, or the result of a predisposition to look on the black side? Such doubts must be faced. They may come and go, part of the general uncertainty of things.

But there is another voice which challenges the pessimistic reaction, a cleverer one which seeks to argue it out of existence. Sometimes, the voice comes from within, nagging and questioning. When it comes from without, from those who believe pessimism is misplaced, the voice is altogether brisker and more confident. But the essence of its argument is the same. Pessimism, it is said, is contradicted by the very attempt to express it. In order to say things are hopeless, we need to have a standard by which we can make this judgement. Things are really hopeless when people do not even know it; when they are in hell thinking they are in heaven. As long as we can recognise what is hopeless, all is not hopeless.

The argument is a powerful one, and its main point must be granted. But it is also a dangerously seductive argument, especially when linked to complacency and facile optimism. Even if the argument's main point is granted, it is important to realise how little need follow from it; how little it need disturb the pessimism it was meant to overthrow. An early chapter in Robert Musil's *The Man without Qualities* has the title, 'Even a man without qualities has a father with qualities'. Quite so. We cannot describe the son without invoking qualities. But let us not forget that they are invoked to show what a generation has lost. The fact that we can remember the father's qualities leaves entirely open the question of their intelligibility now, the extent to which they could be expressed in action now. Memories may inspire. They may also reduce us to stammerings and stutterings when we contrast ourselves with them.

Optimists hate this latter possibility and try to avoid it like the plague. Whenever a work of literature expresses it, they appropriate the work for some optimistic cause or other. This has been the fate of Franz Kafka's famous novel, *The Castle*. Roy Pascal reminds us of the variety of interpretations to which it has been subjected.

> Kafka became a crown witness for the religious message, Christian or Jewish, for the theology of crisis, for Freud, for existentialism, a critic of a dehumanized bureaucratic society and an appalled prophet of totalitarian savagery, an impotent petty bourgeois adoring his chains, the anguished spokesman of the alienation of man in modern society, abandoned by God.[1]

Yet, despite the apparent variety, these interpretations all have one thing in common: the creation of a confident, authoritative moral voice. All but one of them attribute such a voice to Kafka. The remaining characterisation of him as an impotent petty bourgeois attributes such a voice to the reader as he judges Kafka. All the interpretations, then, draw with confidence, on moral resources they think they possess. Kafka's *The Castle* is then read in the light of these perspectives.

But the perspectives have something else in common: they all ignore Kafka's text. They ignore what is evident in the novel, no matter in what direction we look, namely, the prevalence of shabbiness. Whether we look to the Castle or to the Village, what we see is a place without qualities.

Kafka's main character, K., comes to the Village claiming to be a land-surveyor. The whole novel is a record of his futile attempts to gain admission to the Castle. The novel is full of religious associations. K. is a man boasting of his qualifications, wanting the Castle to recognise his rights, and claiming he can gain admission to the Castle by his own endeavours. Of course, K. never does gain admission. The Castle never recognises his status, and there is no work awaiting a land-surveyor anyway. Soon, he has to accept the inferior post of school janitor, but it is made clear to him by the schoolteacher that he has only been given this post, too, as a favour. It is not his by right.

'The post has only been given to you as a personal favour, and
one can't stretch a favour too far, if one has any consciousness
of one's obvious responsibilities.' Now K. intervened at last,
almost against his will. 'As for the favour, teacher,' he said, 'it
seems to me that you're mistaken. The favour is perhaps rather
on my side.' 'No,' replied the teacher, smiling now that he had
compelled K. to speak at last. 'I'm completely grounded on that
point. Our need for a janitor is just about as urgent as our need
for a Land Surveyor. Janitor, Land Surveyor, in both cases it's
a burden on our shoulders . . .' 'That's just what I meant,'
replied K., 'you must take me on against your will. Although it
causes you great perturbation, you must take me on. But when
one is compelled to take someone else on, and this someone
else allows himself to be taken on, then he is the one who grants
the favour.' 'Strange!' said the teacher. 'What is it that compels
us to take you on? The only thing that compels us is the Superintendent's kind heart, his too kind heart. I see Land Surveyor,
that you'll have to rid yourself of a great many illusions, before
you become a serviceable janitor. And remarks such as these
hardly produce the right atmosphere for the granting of an
eventual salary.'[2]

The religious associations are obvious. If proud, rebellious man
wants to serve in the House of the Lord, he must die to the self,
realise that he cannot save himself by his own endeavours, humbly
accept God's gift of grace. Although not accepting a religious
reading of the novel, Erich Heller does show how K.'s claim to
the title of land-surveyor is symbolic of rebellion against God:

The German is *Landvermesser*, and its verbal associations are
significant. The first, is, of course, the land-surveyor's professional activity, consisting precisely in what K. desperately
desires and never achieves: to produce a workable order within
clearly defined boundaries and limits of earthly life, and to
find an acceptable compromise between conflicting claims of
possession. But *Vermesser* also alludes to *Vermessenheit*, 'hubris';
to the adjective *vermessen*, 'audacious'; to the verb *sich vermessen*,
'commit an act of spiritual pride,' *and* also 'apply the wrong
measure,' 'make a mistake in measurement.'[3]

God abases the proud of heart. K.'s long and futile struggle to

gain admission to the Castle is seen as the long journey by which
the sinner comes to a recognition of his dependence on God. It is
said that Kafka intended finishing his novel with K., having failed
to gain admission to the Castle, being allowed to live in peace in
the Village. For religious interpreters, K. is obviously a soul in
search of God. Edwin Muir goes as far as to conclude: '*The Castle*
is a picture on a scale never attempted since the seventeenth
century of the relation to God of the soul seeking salvation'.[4]

That is a truly astounding conclusion. It turns distant echoes
into spiritual realities. The echoes, as we have seen, cannot be
denied. Even a Castle without qualities recalls a Castle with qualities. But how very distant the echoes are. At no time did Kafka
ever suggest that the Castle was meant to be God's abode. How
could he, for what is obvious for all to see is what a shabby place
the Castle is. The women in the Village are expected to submit to
the sexual advances of the Castle officials. When the women are
discarded, they have to marry villagers, their drab existences said
to be made bearable only by the memories of those days when
the Castle favoured them. Refusal to submit to the officials leads,
as in the case of Amalia, to persecution of the whole family,
deprivation of livelihood for the father, loss of friends and ostracis-
ation by the Village. The victims are said to be in disgrace. K.
seduces Frieda who is mistress to Klamm, the highest official in
the Castle. She loses her job and is reinstated only when she
becomes the mistress of Jeremiah, who has pretended to be K.'s
assistant, but who is, in fact, a minor agent of the Castle sent to
spy on him and destroy his relationship with Frieda. What a
despicable bunch these Castle officials are!

And what of the administration of the Castle? Again, it is as
plain as day that it is a complete shambles. There is no rhyme nor
reason in the way it deals with correspondence from the Village
or its own documents. Documents may or may not be considered,
letters may or may not be answered, by whim, caprice, mistake,
but never as a result of proper consideration. K. receives a letter
thanking him for surveying work he has never done, a letter
which, it transpires, was meant for someone else. K. is told, again
and again, that the ordinary troubles of the Village are of no
concern to the Castle.

Religious interpreters have tried, with incredible desperation, to
find in all this a symbol of the incommensurability of God's laws
with the laws of man. God's ways are not our ways. True enough,

but why find a symbol in the sordid or claim to find the spiritual in the shabby? Heller says that to find people like Max Brod, Kafka's lifelong friend and editor, and Edwin Muir, his distinguished translator into English, grasping at these religious straws, is indicative of more than the confusion of individuals: 'It is the very spiritual uprootedness of the age which has deprived us of all sureness of religious discrimination. To men suffering from spiritual starvation, even a rotten fruit of the spirit may taste like bread from Heaven, and the liquid from a poisoned well like the water of life.'[5]

If we consider debates for and against religion in our day, things are no better. The god of contemporary theodicies is a shabby character, who justifies his dealings with men by appealing to sordid and vulgar reasons. The lessons he wants to teach us, by visiting us with afflictions, must be the product of unbridled malice. Philosophers and theologians, like the most subservient villagers, tell us to soldier on, believing that behind every seduction of the innocent there is a silver lining, a greater good to which it leads. There is one difference between these intellectuals and Kafka: they actually think they are talking about God! They have the audacity to parade their views in the name of orthodoxy, confusing the Faith with the orthodoxy of their intellectual practices, a very different matter. Their god is none other than Klamm, of whom Heller says: 'The most powerful official of the Castle . . . is called *Klamm*, a sound producing a sense of anxiety amounting almost to claustrophobia, suggesting straits, pincers, chains, clamps, but also a person's oppressive silence'.

But if the god depicted by many contemporary intellectuals is shabby, so are the worshippers they present. They are the equivalent of the most servile of Kafka's villagers, their highest motive for worship being self-interest. If we listen to their analyses, Big Brother in the Castle is indeed watching over us, and, if we know what's good for us, we had better obey him. On this view, if it were discovered that vice was rewarded rather than virtue, the virtues would immediately become the paradigms of irrational conduct. A shabby god attracts shabby worshippers.

But these conceptions prevail at the moment. Must we therefore try, for better or for worse, to make sense of religion in terms of them? Kafka thought, rightly, that this would lead to a sense of hopelessness, the kind of hopelessness anyone felt when trying to communicate with the Castle:

The receiver gave out a buzz of a kind K. had never heard on a telephone. It was like the hum of countless children's voices — but yet not a hum, the echo of voices singing at an infinite distance — blended by sheer impossibility into one high reason-ant sound which vibrated on the ear as if it were trying to penetrate beyond mere hearing.

But, then, the Superintendent tells K.:

You haven't once up till now come into real contact with our authorities. All those contacts of yours have been illusory, but owing to your ignorance of the circumstances you take them to be real. And as for the telephone . . . In the Castle the telephone works beautifully of course, I've been told it's going there all the time, that naturally speeds up the work a great deal. We can hear this continual telephoning in our telephones down here as a humming and singing, you must have heard it too. Now this humming and singing transmitted by our telephones is the only real and reliable thing you'll hear, everything else is deceptive. There's no fixed connexion with the Castle, no central exchange which transmits our calls further. When anybody calls up the Castle from here the instruments in all the subordinate departments ring, or rather they would all ring if practically all the departments — I know it for a certainty — didn't leave their receivers off. Now and then, however, a fatigued official may feel the need of a little distraction, especially in the evenings and at night and may hang the receiver on. Then we get an answer, but an answer of course that's merely a practical joke.

For Kafka, the language of those who cry to God and the langu-age of the replies they claim to receive, has placed God out of reach. What has happened in innumerable contemporary books and articles is that these alleged answers, the practical jokes, have been written up in all seriousness as the justifications of God's ways to men. The sounds on the telephone are more confused than ever.

This conclusion, of course, is one happily embraced by those who read *The Castle* from an anti-religious perspective. After all, they claim, isn't that what the novel is about: the exposure of the shabbiness and vulgarity, not only of religion, but of all forms of tyrannical oppression: religious, bureaucratic, totalitarian. What is celebrated is the fight against these oppressions, the fight of the free, autonomous, independent man. That is how these interpreters see K. Is he not inspired by his childhood memory of the way in which he scaled the high wall of the church graveyard?

> He stuck the flag in, it flew in the wind, he looked down and round about him, and over his shoulder too, at the crosses mouldering in the ground, nobody was greater than he at that place and that moment. By chance the teacher had come past and with a stern face had made K. descend. In jumping down he had hurt his knee and had found some difficulty in getting home, but still he had been on top of the wall.

It had seemed to the young boy that here was a victory for life. Many readers and critics of *The Castle* agree with him. Even if K. is defeated in his fight against the Castle, even if he is hurt in the process, it is a glorious defeat, the continuing affirmation of a free spirit against tyranny; he has been on top of the wall.

But, as with the religious interpretations, this interpretation is another case of theory determining the reading of the text. If we wait on the text, we have to admit that K.'s conduct is no less shabby than the Castle's. If the Castle is a place without qualities, K. is a person without qualities. His conception of his heroic calling is as romantically self-indulgent as that of Dostoyevsky's Raskolnikov in *Crime and Punishment*. He arrives in the Village to challenge the Castle single-handed, but soon he is embroiled in his seduction of Frieda.

> Instead of feeling his way with the prudence befitting the greatness of his enemy and of his ambition, he had spent a whole night wallowing in puddles of beer, the smell of which was nearly overpowering. 'What have you done?' he said as if to himself. 'We are both ruined.' 'No,' said Frieda, 'It's only me that's ruined, but then I've won you.'

K.'s dealings with Frieda are as shabby as the Castle's. He simply uses her as a way of getting in touch with Klamm. When he deserts her for Amalia's family, his relationship with them has the same ulterior motive. He plays Frieda's and Amalia's families off against each other shamefully, changing his tune constantly behind their backs. And what of his attitude towards the afflictions

of Amalia's family? He applauds their attempts to ingratiate themselves with the Castle once again. But of Amalia's brave stand
against the sexual advances of the wretched Castle official Sortini,
K. says: 'Innocently or not, she was the person who brought ruin
on the family. And instead of begging your pardon for it anew
every day she carries her head higher than anybody else.' This
really is an outrageous remark. Is this the remark of a free spirit,
the defender of liberties, the scourge of tyrannies? Any such
suggestion would be ludicrous. Is it not obvious that Kafka is not
only portraying a shabbiness which has infected religion, but a
shabbiness which has also infected talk of rights, liberty and
freedom.

It is important to remember that throughout the novel K. desires
admission to the Castle. He may want to scale its walls, see his
flag flutter in the wind. But if he wants to change the management,
he does not want to change the spirit of the place. He wants what
the Castle wants. After all, he admires Klamm.

> Once the landlady had compared Klamm to an eagle, and that
> had seemed absurd in K.'s eyes, but it did not seem absurd
> now; he thought of Klamm's remoteness, of his impregnable
> dwelling, of his silence broken perhaps only by cries such as K.
> had never yet heard, of his downward-pressing gaze, which
> could never be proved or disproved, of his wheelings which
> could never be disturbed by anything that K. did down below,
> which far above he followed at the behest of incomprehensible
> laws and which only for instants were visible — all these things
> Klamm and the eagle had in common.

But everything we have actually seen and heard of Klamm is
shabby in the extreme. There is a gap between this idealised
picture and Klamm's actual conduct, just as there is a gap between
the idealisation of K.'s boyhood memory of his scaling the wall,
and his conduct as an adult. Kafka is satirising the shabby gaps
that exist between liberal and revolutionary ideals and the actual
conduct of those who proclaim them. Those who protest against
tyranny too often share the character of the tyrants they seek to
overthrow. A little violence will usher in a new dawn, but, in
reality, one form of darkness gives way to another. Protesters
claim a moral authority they often do not earn. Observing that
others do not share their moral convictions, they grow impatient

when fate does not win them over to their cause. So perhaps a little persuasion is justified, a little force perhaps, the curtailing of certain freedoms, temporarily, of course, and so on. And none of this is supposed to impair the morality of the original intentions. With others, of course, their souls have been contaminated, but, in their case, it is supposed to be different. And so self-righteousness becomes the road to slaughter. The revolutionary depends on the liberal, who cannot distinguish between freedom and licence, to open the door, in the name of freedom, to those who would close the door on freedom forever. Principle gives way to power, standards to strategy, criticism to cant, and morality to manipulation. When this happens, Kafka the artist, who also surveys the land, sees how pervasive the shabbiness has become. Talk of authority and talk of freedom become equally dubious. But Kafka has no authoritative moral voice of his own because he sees no alternative. His world is the one Eliot described as ending, not with a bang, but with a whimper. In the fourth of his Prometheus legends, Kafka says: 'Everyone grew weary of the meaningless affair. The gods grew weary, the eagles grew weary, the wound closed wearily.'

Amalia is the only one who sees through the shabbiness surrounding her. She sees through the Castle and she sees through K. She knows she is living in a place without qualities. But there is not much she can do beyond recognising the fact. She withdraws from those around her, refuses to play their games or indulge in the language they speak. But she can do little against the prevalence of these games or the prestige of the language. This pessimistic conclusion people find hard to accept. Albert Camus, despite all the evidence to the contrary, says that K. is someone who dares to hope. He says that Amalia, by contrast, has no hope, and seems critical of her because of it. Even Erich Heller, in his otherwise perceptive paper, has to say at the end of it that 'the melancholy of spiritual failure' carries 'with it a subtle promise', to which the reply must be that it may or may not. In the world Kafka depicts, the odds are against it.

This chapter began with the claim that as we listen to most contemporary debates about religion, we may experience a sense of utter hopelessness. But when I say 'we' listen, who does the 'we' refer to? What if the 'we' refers to very few people, and that the vast majority are prepared to accept the debate on its own shabby terms? What, then?

Among those who accept the terms of the debate are the time-servers, those with an eye for what it is profitable, professionally, to say. Kafka was acquainted with these followers of fashion:

And besides, there are several roads to the Castle. Now one of them is in fashion, and most carriages go by that, now it's another and everything drives pell-mell there. And what governs this change of fashion has never yet been found out. At eight o'clock one morning they'll all be on another road, ten minutes later on a third, and half an hour after that on the first road again, and then they may stick to that road all day, but every minute there's the possibility of a change.

Yet, these are not the worst of it. After all, they do not really believe what they say, and they know what they are up to. But having put these cases aside, it must be admitted that there are many who are genuinely at home in the shabby language they employ when discussing religion or when acting for or against it. When this situation is the norm, it gives rise to the sense of hopelessness referred to. Individual voices may break through, but the likelihood is that they will seem forced, extreme, distorted, or even absurd. For the moment, at least, might it not be true that little can be done, that things are pretty hopeless? We must be ready to admit that this view could be the product of self-indulgence. We must be equally ready to admit that it could be true.

Notes

1. Roy Pascal, 'Critical Approaches to Kafka' in Angel Flores, *The Kafka Debate* (Gordian Press, 1977), p. 4.
2. All quotations from Franz Kafka's *The Castle* (Penguin, 1957).
3. Erich Heller, 'The World of Franz Kafka' in Peter F. Neumeyer (ed.), *Twentieth Century Interpretations of The Castle* (Prentice-Hall, 1969), p. 70.
4. Edwin Muir, 'Franz Kafka' in Ronald Gray (ed.), *Kafka* (Prentice-Hall, 1963, p. 42.
5. Heller, op. cit., p. 61.

13

Meaning What We Say

Looking back at the essays in the second part of this collection, may have a discouraging effect on hopes to express what it means to believe in God. It we claim that we do believe, we have to be behind our words. But, as we have seen, what words come to may itself reveal a vulgarisation of religious perspectives. We concluded the last essay by admitting that we may have to recognise, at times, that little can be done other than to hang on, in some way, at least recognising the crisis.

Faced with such difficulties, it is tempting to reply, 'Well, show us how words mean, and we will see to it that religious belief uses its words accordingly'. Such an expectation, however, is misplaced. It ignores how complex a matter 'meaning what we say' can be. The point of the present essay is simply to give some indication of this complexity, since it is only by taking it into account, that religious belief can inform people's lives.

It is easy to be captivated by the wonder of words. After all, we use them every day of our lives. We say one thing, a face lights up; we say another, it frowns. We give an order and things happen. We make a joke and people laugh. It is easy to start speculating about the meanings involved in this discourse; about how we mean what we say. It is easy also to expect one answer to the question, an answer which will cover all cases. 'When we mean what we say we — ' and we fill in the blank with the theory of our choice. The theories are shortlived, because people keep finding exceptions to them. Undeterred, we attempt to formulate wider theories to accommodate them. We are not prepared to change direction, to stop looking for all-embracing theories, and wait on the myriad ways in which we can mean what we say. A consideration of some interesting examples will show how necessary this change of direction is.

No discussion of what we mean by our words proceeds very far without a consideration of the phenomenon of deceit. It has seemed to some that whether someone means what he says is

hard, if not impossible, to determine, since it is always possible
that he is deceiving us. How can we take the meaning of what is
said on trust? Consider, for example, a promise made by a pleasure
plane pilot to a girl of 15: 'I'm going to write you a letter. I'll tell
you where I am and maybe you can come and see me. Would you
like that? Okay then. You wait.'

How, it may be asked, do we know what these words mean?
Does not that depend on the intentions of the speaker, on whether
he is deceiving her or not? Is that right? Let's consider the facts
of the case. Chris, the pilot, is, in fact, deceiving the young girl,
Edie, who has been infatuated with him ever since he has come
to fly his pleasure trips in her small town. She is not deterred
even when his fiancée of long-standing comes looking for him.
The pilot makes a hasty departure to get away from his fiancée,
but not before taking Edie into his tent, caressing and petting her
and making her the promise we have referred to. Do we understand what he says? Of course we do. So did Edie. What she fails
to understand are not his words, but him. The pilot does not use
words in any special sense when he deceives her. Not at all, the
meanings of his words are ordinary enough: he'll write a letter;
he'll tell her where he is; she can come to him; she is to wait. This
deceit, a product of romantic thoughtlessness rather than malice,
depends on the meanings of ordinary words to achieve its ends.
It is only because Edie understands the words in their ordinary
sense that she waits for him. He made a promise. He simply had
no intention of keeping it.

If, then, we know what the words mean, a meaning which is
found in the purchase these words have in our normal discourse
with each other, are people's intentions secrets we can never
discover, hidden behind their words? No, what these intentions
are can emerge too in our dealings with each other. Chris' promise
to Edie creates certain normal expectations. When those expectations are not fulfilled, the meanings of the words in the promise
do not change. What changes is one's understanding of the
relation of the person who made the promise to his words. That
is what happened to Edie: 'No letter was ever going to come. It was
an impossible idea to get used to. No, not impossible. If I thought
about Chris's face when he said he was going to write to me, it
was impossible, but if I forgot that and thought about the actual
tin mailbox, empty, it was plain and true.'

We see a distinction emerging between what words mean and

what a man means by his words. But the distinction is a complex one, because what words mean is determined by what we mean normally when we use them. As we have seen, what a man means by his words, what he is up to in using them, trades on these normal meanings. So far, we might conclude that when the pilot deceived Edie he told her what was not the case; he had no intention of writing to her or of letting her come to him. But we must not generalise from this incident. We must not think, for example, that whenever someone does not say what is the case, or allows what is not the case to be said, he too is a deceiver or someone who does not mean what he says. The rest of the story shows how wrong that general conclusion would be.

Edie resolves not to be one of those women who wait for letters which never come. Carmichael, the mailman, gets in touch with her. Now that she no longer goes to the mailbox, he finds that he has missed their friendly chats. He asks her out, and two years later they marry: 'He always tells the children the story of how I went after him by sitting by the mailbox every day, and naturally I laugh and let him because I like for people to think what pleases them and makes them happy'.

The story is called, *How I Met my Husband*.[1] Chris deceived Edie by telling her that he would write and by asking her to wait for him. Does Edie deceive her husband in allowing him to think that she was waiting for him every day? If we define deceit as saying or going along with what is not the case, we have to answer 'Yes'. But, then, long ago, Plato warned us not to confuse a truthful man with a man who always says what is the case. For example, a man who says what is the case no matter what harm it causes, and even to bring about that harm, is no lover of the truth. People who, acting in such ways, think that at least they have kept possession of truthfulness, would discover, if only their grip and their hearts could be opened, that they had been possessed by something very different. Whether we mean what we say cannot be determined by a formula, by whether, for example, our words correspond to what is the case. We have to look at the place words have in the whole complex network of relations they enter into. When we do this we see why Edie, laughing along with her husband and children, is no deceiver.

The story we've been discussing was written by the Canadian writer, Alice Munro. It is in her third collection of short stories, *Something I've been Meaning to Tell You*, first published in 1974, but not available her in Penguin Books until 1985. Alice Munro is an extremely impressive short-story writer. Although her first collection was published in 1968, she is not as well known this side of the Atlantic as she deserves to be. The stories from her third collection, discussed here, all bear in interesting, but complex, ways on the question of how and whether we mean what we say.

So far, in discussing this question, we have emphasised the meanings we share with one another in our daily dealings and discourse. We have also discussed how someone may trade on the normal meanings of our words and the expectations they create, in order to deceive another. We have seen how this deceit itself may become known to others in familiar ways. In these discussions, the meanings discussed are realised meanings: we know how to take words in their normal context; the willful deceiver knows what he is up to when he makes promises he does not intend to keep. Yet, from cases such as these, it would be wrong to conclude that, when we speak, we always know what our words signify. If asked, we would be ready enough with an answer. But it may be that in that answer, while we are not deceiving another, we may be deceiving ourselves. We do not realise this at the time. It may take some later event to put our words into proper perspective; to make us realise what we meant by our words. Alice Munro shows what such a realisation may come to in her impressive short story, *Forgiveness in Families*.[2]

Val has every reason to be fed up with her brother Cam. He goes from disaster to disaster, but their mother will never give up her faith in him. Despite being an atheist, she says, '. . . the Lord loves a lunatic'. Their widowed mother says that Cam could have been brilliant in school had he wanted to be, but he always played truant. He had a violent bout of 'flu which made him sick all over the table at Val's wedding to Haro. He was as absent from jobs as he was from school. He said he wanted the out-door life, but left a farm saying that people were religious there and after his soul. And so it goes on. Requests for money for mad schemes are always met, though his mother can ill afford to give what she works so hard to earn. He becomes engaged, but breaks it off, lying about a fatal hereditary kidney disease in his family. Still his mother seeks to excuse him; will not have anything bad said about him. After his wanderings, Cam comes home and lives there, on and off, for a year-and-a-half. Val describes him:

His hair is thin in front, not surprising in a man of thirty-four years of age, but shoulder-length behind, straggly, greying. He wears a sort of rough brown robe that looks as if it might be made out of a sack . . . and hanging down on his chest he has all sorts of chains, medallions, crosses, elk's teeth or whatnot. Rope sandals on his feet . . . He collects welfare. Nobody asks him to work. Who could be so crude? If he has to write down his occupation he writes priest

It's true. There is a whole school of them, calling themselves priests . . . They're in competition with the Hare Krishna bunch, only these ones don't chant, they just walk around smiling. He has developed this voice I can't stand, a very thin, sweet voice, all on one level. It makes me want to stand in front of him and say 'There's an earthquake in Chile, two hundred thousand people just died, they've burned up another village in Vietnam, famine as usual in India.' Just to see if he'd keep saying, 'Ve-ery ni-ice, ve-ery ni-ice,' in that sweet way.

Their mother collapses and is taken to hospital. They hold out little hope for her. Haro persuades Val to let her brother know. She does so, reluctantly. To her horror, he brings a whole troupe with him who chant in Swahili, Sanskrit or something outside the sick woman's room. Cam gives crazy justifications for the chanting. 'You're very mistaken if you think the tones of our voices are hurting or disturbing any sick person. This whole ceremony is pitched at a level which will reach and comfort the unconscious mind and draw the demonic influences out of the body. It's a ceremony that goes back five thousand years.'

Val gets the orderlies to throw them out. She tells her husband that Cam had turned the whole thing into a circus for his own benefit, and that it was sure to get in the papers. Her husband persuades her to get some sleep. She sleeps longer than she intended and is awakened by the telephone. She expects the worst, but the message is from her doctor to tell her that amazingly, against all the odds, her mother was much better that morning. She can't believe it. Her husband tell her it's due to tension. She says:

'I know. You build yourself up ready for something bad to happen and then when it doesn't it's a queer feeling, you can't feel good right away, it's almost like a disappointment.'

Disappointment. That was the word that stayed with me. I
was so glad, really, grateful, but underneath I was thinking, so
Cam didn't kill her after all, with his carelessness and craziness
and going out and neglecting her he didn't kill her, and I was,
yes, I was, sorry in some part of me to find out that was true.
And I knew Haro knew this but wouldn't speak of it to me,
ever. That was the real shock to me, why I kept shaking. Not
whether Mother lived or died. It was what was so plain about
myself.

Her mother goes from strength to strength. In three weeks,
reducing her hours a little, she is back at work: 'She told everybody
about Cam and his friends coming to the hospital. She began to
say things like, "Well, that boy of mine may not be much of a
success at anything else but you have to admit that he has the
knack of saving lives." Or, "Maybe Cam should go into the miracle
business, he certainly pulled it off with me" '.

But by this time Cam has tired of religion. He looks on it as a
stage in his journey of self-discovery. He is trying on old suits
and thinking of a career in accountancy. But Val is reflecting on
her own conduct, on the outwardly moralistic judgements she had
indulged in. Was it Cam who had made her mother's illness into
something for himself? She contrasted her own severity towards
him with her mother's simple generosity of thought. Had she not
fed a self-righteous image of herself? 'What has Cam ever done
that actually hurt me, anyway, as Haro once said. And how am I
better than he is after the way I felt the night Mother lived instead
of died?'

Looking back at her words, seeing for the first time what she
meant by them, she comes to think that she is the one who needs
forgiveness: 'I had a strange feeling, like I was walking on coals
and trying a spell so I wouldn't get burned. Forgiveness in families
is a mystery to me, how it comes or how it lasts.'

Here, what Val meant by her words is brought home to her.
What her words amounted to had always been clear to her husband, although he would never have dreamt of telling her. But
need things always be like this? It is tempting to assume that since
our words normally mean something, it should be possible, in
any situation, to work out, given sufficient patience, what they
mean. But if, as we have said, words have their meanings in the
network of complex relations and situations into which they enter,

why should this be so? Why should there not be unresolved
ambiguities, a tangle of circumstances, such that what someone's
words amount to in them, momentous though those words may
have been, cannot be summed up once and for all or determined
in any straightforward way? Alice Monro depicts such a situation
in her most powerful short story which gives its name to the
collection, *Something I've been Meaning to Tell You*.

Et realised young in life that her sister Char was beautiful. It
was not surprising that Blaikie Noble, who ran the local bus, and
who had a way with women, should be attracted to her. Char
acted as though she was indifferent to him, but, one night, when
she cannot sleep, Et discovers the two of them making love in the
back garden. But, then, just before Christmas, the shock news
breaks that Blaikie Noble, at 19, has gone off and married a lady
ventriloquist who is 40 at least. Char swallows blueing, thinking
it was poison. Et discovers her and gets her to induce vomiting:
'I didn't do this on account of Blaikie Noble,' she said between
spasms. 'Don't you ever think that. I wouldn't be such a fool. A
pervert like him. I did it because I'm sick of living'.

No mention is ever made of the incident. In time, Char marries
Arthur, her history teacher. He is much older than Char, a bum-
bling, awkward sort of fellow whom Char had always mocked. In
marriage these characteristics prompt her scorn and fury, which
she does her best to hide. But Et observes it all. Char has a
miscarriage in the first year of her marriage and never becomes
pregnant again. Soon, she and her husband are sleeping apart.
Blaikie Noble is back in attendance and has become her lover. All
this Et knows. Arthur's health is not good. Et is suspicious when
she discovers rat poison in a cupboard. She contrives every day
to check that the level in the bottle has not gone down. Arthur
'knew about history but not about what went on, in front of his
eyes, in his house, anywhere. Et differed from Arthur in knowing
that something went on, even if she could not understand why;
she differed from him in knowing there were those you could not
trust.'

Et has set up her own dress-making business. Her excellence is
such that customers tolerate her sharp tongue when they are
found to have shopped elsewhere. She visits Arthur regularly, but
she is no more than a companion to him. For him, Char remains
adorable, a mystery to be neither justified nor explained. Blaikie
goes off for a day or two to Toronto. Arthur misses him and asks

Et what plans he has for the winter. Without planning it, she says
she has heard that he has taken up with a rich widow. She asks
Char if she has heard anything reminding her that this has happened once before. She tells Arthur about Blaikie and the lady
ventriloquist, omitting any mention of Char's attempt at suicide.
The morning after this incident Char is found dead in bed. Et can
find no trace of the rat poison. The old doctor said heart-attack,
and let it go at that.

Suppose we ask what Et's unplanned lying words amount to?
How is that question to be answered? Is it at all clear? There is
little point in seeking clarity by asking what she had in mind at
the time.

The question often crossed Et's mind in later years— what did
she mean to do about this story when Blaikie got back? For she
had no reason to believe he would not come back. The answer
was that she had not planned anything. She supposed she might
have wanted to make trouble between him and Char — make
Char pick a fight with him, her suspicions roused even if
rumours had not been borne out, make Char read what he
might do in the light of what he had done before. She did not
know what she wanted. Only to throw things into confusion,
for she believed that somebody had to, before it was too late.

But what does she think she meant by her words, what did her
lie become to her, when she looked back at the whole sorry trail
of events? Again, there is no clear answer. Sometimes, her reflections are trivial. Blaikie Noble had returned to Toronto after the
funeral. He sent Christmas cards for a year or two, but then was
heard of no more. 'Et would not be surprised if her story of
marrying had not come true in the end. Only her timing was
mistaken.'

At other times, she wonders what she is responsible for; how
much moral weight her lying words should bear. Without determining that, how can she have a clear view of what her words
amounted to?

Nor would Et ever know. Would what was in that bottle leave
a body undisfigured as Char's was? Perhaps what was in the
bottle was not what it said. She was not even sure that it had
been there that last evening, she had been too carried away

with what she was saying to go and look, as she usually did. Perhaps it had been thrown out earlier and Char had taken something else, pills maybe. Perhaps it really was her heart. All that purging would have weakened anybody's heart.

But if Et is not clear what moral weight to put on her own words, what about us as readers? Here, too, reactions will vary. Many will want a more definite answer than that which Et herself arrives at. After all, part of the point of the story is to show us a woman who is unaware of certain facts about herself: her barely suppressed envy of Char and Blaikie, her probably suppressed love of a kind for Arthur. If we emphasise these factors, we are unlikely to accept that Et lied simply from a genuine concern about the situation and a desire to bring matters to a head. Although that concern and desire are there, it would be hard to make them the whole story. Others may say that important though these factors are, the most important truth by far which is, at best, half-realised, but more probably, not realised, by Et, is that she is revealed to be the kind of person she prided herself on detecting: a person not to be trusted and capable of wounding others deeply. Those influenced by psychoanalysis will want to go further. We can imagine them wanting to make far more of Et's suppressions. In their hands she will soon become someone who hates Char, who wants her out of the way, dead. Too extravagant no doubt, but not without a grain of truth. Et in lying about Blaikie reminds Char of what Blaikie has done once before. But on that previous occasion Char had tried to kill herself. Isn't Et, without mentioning it, reminding her of that too?

So what meaning do we find in Et's lying words? She has no clear idea of how to answer that question. Any answer we care to give will be determined partly by our own moral perspectives, and partly by which factors in the story we choose to emphasise. But does there have to be a clear, unambiguous answer concerning what Et's words amount to? For my part, Alice Munro's impressiveness as a writer is due, in no small measure, to her ability to show in this story that an affirmative answer to that question is not necessary. She shows us a situation in which aspects are constantly shifting, eluding any final conclusion. That is a phenomenon which is important in considering the complexity of people's relationships with each other. In this story, in considering what words mean, and what people mean by their words, we have come a long way from those shared meanings we mentioned at the outset, meanings which are unambiguously clear to speaker and hearer alike. That long journey from the simple to the complex, from the clear to the indeterminate, should at least discourage us from looking for one all-embracing answer to the question of how we mean what we say.

Perhaps we feel that Et should at least straighten things out with Arthur as they grow old together. But, then, what would straightening things out amount to? Would she be straightening things out, or still pursuing Char by destroying Arthur's image of her? Is there a clear answer to that question? And so our discussion would start all over again:

> Sometimes Et had it on the tip of her tongue to say to Arthur, 'There's something I've been meaning to tell you.' She didn't believe she was going to let him die without knowing. He shouldn't be allowed. He kept a picture of Char on his bureau . . . But Et let it go, day to day. She and Arthur still played rummy and kept up a bit of a garden, along with raspberry canes. If they had been married, people would have said they were very happy.

Perhaps none of us should die without knowing. Without knowing what? Presumably, how things are with us in fundamental respects. Religion claims to have something to say about this. If if does, its words must speak in a world where words can deceive, be involved in charitable untruths, have their aspects changed, and be involved, perhaps permanently, in unresolvable ambiguities. It is amid words such as these that the Word has to speak.

Notes

1. *How I Met my Husband* in Alice Munro's *Something I've been Meaning to Tell You* (Penguin, 1985).
2. In *Something I've Been Meaning to Tell You*.

Part III
Heroes of the Horizon

. . . what counts is how you conduct
yourself while you are being destroyed

14

Of Fishers and Men

No one would deny that believers in God are called on to turn their backs on the ways of the world; to live life according to the will of God, rather than according to the opinions of men; to turn from the temporal to the eternal. That much is uncontentious. Many religious believers, however, think that these distinctions are their sole prerogative. For them, to be an unbeliever is to be worldly, a slave to the opinions of men. They are reluctant to recognise that there can be ways of life, other than their own, which call *their* adherents away from worldliness, and which *also* emphasise the difference between the temporal and the eternal. They are reluctant to grant the atheist his prayer. Instead, when they come across these ways of life, believers misrepresent their character, suggesting that these ways of life are *really* religious after all. Such misrepresentation is in no one's interest. By marking the contrast between service of God and service of other ideals, and by giving a faithful account of it, the believer avoids a condescending misunderstanding of other ways of life and comes to a better understanding of his own.

I want to illustrate this by reference to one of the most famous short novels in twentieth-century American literature, Ernest Hemingway's *The Old Man and the Sea*. The misunderstanding and mischaracterisation I have referred to can be seen in the determination of many critics to turn the story into a Christian fable. Philip Young reminds us of the bare details of Hemingway's story:

After eighty-four days without a fish Santiago ventures far out to sea alone, and hooks a giant marlin in the Gulf Stream. For two days and two nights the old man holds on while he is towed further out to sea; finally he brings the fish alongside, harpoons it, and lashes it to his skiff. Almost at once the sharks begin to take his prize away from him. He kills them until he has only his broken tiller to fight them. Then they eat all but the skeleton, and he tows that home, half-dead with exhaustion, and makes his way to bed to sleep and dream of other things.[1]

Critics have widely noted that Santiago is Spanish for St James, and many have seen in the Old Man's struggle with the fish a prototype of Christian discipleship, a voyage from hubris to humility. Reviewing the novel, William Faulkner said:

This time, he discovered God, a Creator. Until now, his men and women had made themselves, shaped themselves out of their own clay; their victories and defeats were at the hands of each other, just to prove to themselves or one another how tough they could be. But this time, he wrote about pity: about something somewhere that made them all: the old man who had to catch the fish and then lose it, the fish that had to be caught and then lost, the sharks which had to rob the old man of his fish; made them all and loved them all and pitied them all.[2]

The religious echoes Faulkner finds in the novel are clear enough: Santiago, the disciple, has to let go before he can find, lose before he can gain. He must see, and accept, the loss of the greatest prize he had desired in the whole world, the big fish, in order to achieve a new humility before God. He must see the object of his dearest ambition stripped clean by sharks. Only when faced by the skeleton of all his former endeavours can he come to bow before his God. Everything is taken from him. He has to cast aside all his weapons. Defenceless, at last, he is brought home to a safe haven, to the completion of a spiritual pilgrimage which echoes that which began for those other fishers, Simon and Andrew, on the sea of Galilee:

Now as he walked by the sea of Galilee, he saw Simon and Andrew his brother, casting a net into the sea; for they were fishers.
And Jesus said unto them, Come ye after me, and I will make you fishers of men.
And straightway they forsook their nets, and followed him.

How tempting that reading is! How comforting to be able to bring Santiago, who, after all, has coloured pictures of the Sacred

Heart of Jesus and the Virgin of Cobre on the wall of his shack, firmly within the orbit of the Faith. But have we any right to try to do this? Have we not misrepresented the Old Man and his world in the attempt? True, in his adventure with the big fish, Santiago loses something and gains something, but is what he loses and gains that which Christians are said to lose and gain? Hemingway did not think so, and he did not welcome Faulkner's suggestion to the contrary: 'The Old Man in the story was a born Catholic in the island of Langa Rota in the Canary Islands. But he certainly believed in something more than the church and I do not think Mr Faulkner understands it very well.'[3]

In the story, the Old Man says he is not religious, yet, Faulkner and other critics think he is. Why should this be so? Is it not because the Old Man's story, which reads like a fable, and his life, which is a kind of prayer, speak of turning away from commercial concerns of worldliness? He goes out into deep waters to realise his conception of the eternal, leaving far behind those fishermen in their motor-boats for whom the sea simply provided a means of earning a living. In a world dominated by utilitarian concerns, the Old Man's relation to the sea is as far removed from them as any religious attitude. Just as many mock the other-worldliness of Christianity, so the younger fishermen laugh at Santiago's dream of encountering the big fish. But his dream is not a religious dream, though it encompasses the whole of his life, providing a style in which to live and die.

For religious believers, the sea has always spoken of God. The psalmist knew this well:

They that go down to the sea in ships, that do business in great waters.
These see the works of the Lord, and his wonders in the deep.
(Psalm 107)

Santiago certainly sees wonders in the deep, but does he see the works of the Lord? His relation to the sea is very different:

He always thought of the sea as *la mar* which is what people call her in Spanish when they love her. Sometimes those who love her say bad things of her but they are always said as though she were a woman. Some of the younger fishermen, those who used buoys as floats for their lines and had brought much money, spoke of her as *el mar* which is masculine. They spoke of her as a contestant or a place or even as an enemy. But the old man always thought of her as feminine and as something that gave or witheld great favours, and if she did wild or wicked things it was because she could not help them. The moon affects her as it does a woman, he thought.[4]

He loves the sea because it is in it that he is to pursue his eternal vocation, that for which he believes he was born. His vocation, however, is not that of the Christian. It is the vocation of a warrior, a hunter, put to the test in deep waters. That test is to exhibit what Hemingway himself calls 'grace under pleasure'. As Philip Young says of Santiago:

The chief point about him is that he behaves perfectly — honourably, with great courage and endurance — while losing to the sharks the giant fish he has caught. This, to epitomise the message the code hero always brings, is life: you lose, of course; what counts is how you conduct yourself while you are being destroyed.[5]

It is in this context that Hemingway's novel is to be understood. As Philip Young says:

To take the broadest view, however, the novel is a representation of life as a struggle against unconquerable natural forces in which a kind of victory is possible. It is an epic metaphor for life, a contest in which even the problem of right and wrong seems paltry before the great thing that is the struggle.[6]

Despite these remarks, Philip Young also wants to see the story as a Christian tragedy, a view hardly consistent with the hunter's vision and perspective he has just talked about. Other critics go much further in this mistaken direction. Wirt Williams thinks Santiago is a victim of hubris for which he must be punished. The Old Man has over-reached himself, strayed from his proper place:

His choice had been to stay in the deep dark water far out beyond all snares and traps and treacheries. My choice was to go there to find him beyond all people. Beyond all people in the world. Now we are joined together and have been since noon. And no one to help either one of us.[7]

Hemingway is not depicting hubris in these words. He is depicting the context in which the Old Man has to show grace under pressure; a challenge he must face alone and meet for himself without the help of others. It is a challenge which awaits him in the deep, far out from the comparative shallows, in which, in their motor boats, the new breed of fishers lay their commercial traps and snares. He has gone beyond a shallow way of life and launched into the deep to meet the challenge a hunter has to face, a challenge which creates a bond between the hunter and the hunted. He holds the big fish in greater respect than those who simply have a commercial attitude to the sea. 'How many people will he feed, he thought. But are they worthy to eat him. No, of course not. There is no one worthy of eating him from the manner of his behaviour and his great dignity.'

For the religious believer in peril on the sea, to see the will of God in the storm is to see his own creatureliness at the same time. The will of God is in his own survival or destruction as it is in the waves of the sea. Man ceases to be the centre of his world. His own existence, its radical precariousness, is seen by him as a gift of grace, something which is not his by right. He humbles himself before God. He becomes his servant.

Hemingway's Old Man is in awe before the forces of nature, but that awe calls out to him, not to become a servant, but to become a hero. His struggle with the big fish is meant to show whether he is still worthy to be called what his baseball hero Di Maggio is called — a champion. True, he has a deep bond with the big fish: ' "Fish," he said softly, "I'll stay with you until I am dead." ' But this unity between him and the fish is not a unity between God's creatures. It is a unity which comes from a warrior's perspective. ' "Fish," he said, "I love you and respect you very much. But I will kill you dead before this day ends." '

A quick pull by the fish causes a line burn on his hand. This does not concern him. It is part of what the hunter must endure. But he must endure with style. When the fish leaps out of the water for the first time, it is the biggest he has ever seen. To his annoyance, he has cramp in one of his hands. There is nothing fine in cramp as there is in bleeding hands. He regards the cramp as a humiliation. 'It will uncramp though, he thought. Surely it will uncramp to help my right hand. There are three things that are brothers: the fish and my two hands. It must uncramp. It is unworthy of it to be cramped.'

This is the talk of a proud hunter. It is a far cry from Saint Paul thanking God for the thorn in his flesh, since it served to remind him that he was not sufficient unto himself. Santiago speaks of the fish with all the pride of a warrior:

'I'll kill him though,' he said. 'In all his pride and glory.'

Although it is unjust, he thought. But I will show him what a man can do and what a man endures.

'I told the boy I was a strange old man,' he said. 'Now is when I must prove it.'

The thousand times that he has proved it meant nothing. Now he was proving it again. Each time was a new time and he never thought about the past when he was doing it.

Some critics have made much of the fact that the Old Man prays to God in his struggle with the big fish. It is difficult to see why they do, since the prayers are of no religious significance, being little more than attempts to drive a cheap bargain. Before uttering them the Old Man says he is not religious. He is right, but neither are his prayers: ' "I am not religious," he said "But I will say ten Our Fathers and ten Hail Marys that I should catch this fish, and I promise to make a pilgrimage to the Virgin de Cobre if I catch him. That is a promise." ' He begins repeating Hail Marys because they are easier to say than Our Fathers, but he says them quite mechanically. His prayer only becomes alive when it ceases to be a Hail Mary and becomes a hunter's prayer: ' "Blessed Virgin, pray for the death of this fish. Wonderful though he is." '

This is not hunting seen religiously, but the religion, such as it is, subserving the vision of the hunter. The Old Man regards himself as a champion but champions must not rest on their laurels. He recalls defeating a powerful black man at the hand game and, whenever he dreams, he dreams of lions. But, now, once again, he must meet the challenge of the big fish in the deep; meet it in the style of a champion. When the fish jumps again, cutting his hands badly, he says: 'pain does not matter to a man'. This is a far cry from Christianity's notion of the suffering servant. Absorbed in the battle with the fish he accords it equal rights and an equality of respect. 'You are killing me, fish, the old man thought. But you have a right to. Never have I seen a greater, or more beautiful, or a calmer or more noble thing than you, brother. Come on kill me. I don't care who kills who.'

Some critics may argue, however, that although all I have said is true, it does not detract from the view of Hemingway's story as a Christian fable. Up to the point where the fish is killed, it is argued, the story is indeed a hunter's tale; the outward voyage of hubris. The specific Christian dimension is precisely the homeward voyage from hubris to humility; from the fight against God to the haven of reconciliation. This Christian perspective on the story cannot be maintained.

When the Old Man realises that sharks are on the trail of the dead fish, he says he is sorry he has killed it. But these are not the accents of remorse or regret for the way of life he has led, as Wirt Williams thinks. Quite the opposite, in fact. It is in terms of the values of that way of life that he apologises to the great fish. Noble in defeat and death, it must now suffer the indignity of being eaten by the scavenging sharks he detests. Just as he distinguishes between shabby commercial fishers and great fishers, so he distinguishes between noble creatures like the big fish and the *galanos*, the scavenging sharks which come to eat like pigs at the trough. It is in this context that the Old Man's apology is to be understood: ' "I shouldn't have gone out so far, fish," he said. "Neither for you nor for me. I'm sorry, fish." ' But the apology is not the last word. As we have seen, part of the hero's code is how you conduct yourself even when you are being destroyed. That is why the Old Man says: 'But man is not made for defeat . . . A man may be destroyed but not defeated.'

What is true of man is also true of the noble fish, even when it has been half-eaten by the sharks: ' "Half-fish," he said. ' "Fish that you were. I am sorry that I went too far out. I ruined us both. But we have killed many sharks, you and I, and ruined many others. How many did you kill, old fish? You do not have that spear on your head for nothing." '

It is true that when the Old Man comes home to the harbour lights of Havana, he has been beaten. He has lost his prize and his weapons and is too exhausted to fight any longer. Nevertheless, this is not the return of a Christian soul, raised up from the trespasses and sins of the hunter's way of life. No; a hunter voyaged out and it is a hunter who returns: almost destroyed, but not defeated.

How different is his return home from that of another famous mariner in literature, Coleridge's Ancient Mariner, and how different is the tale he has to tell. You will remember how the Mariner brings a curse on himself and his fellow seamen by killing the albatross out of sheer devilry. The curse carries them to a region of deadly calm under a withering sun:

> We were the first that ever burst
> Into that silent sea.
> The very deep did rot, O Christ
> That ever this should be;
> And slimy things did crawl with legs
> Upon the slimy sea. [8]

Another ghostly ship approaches, striking terror into the hearts of the seamen who drop dead, one by one, until the guilty Mariner is left alone with the great rotting albatross around his neck. It is in this terrible situation that the Mariner comes to a love of God, a love quite foreign to Hemingway's mariner. This is how the philosopher, J. R. Jones, describes this radical change; a change which enables the Mariner to pray for the first time since killing the albatross:

Then in the silence under the blazing sun he began to look at what had earlier simply been an added loathsomeness — the slimy things which infested the water round the ship, and he began to be *aware* of them. A fascination with their sheer existance gripped him. His perception took on a timeless quality. The swarming water-snakes suddenly seemed to lie there with the whole world — the whole of existence — as their background. And this meant seeing them as they might be seen from Eternity. Something then welled up within him to which he could only give the name of 'love' and he *suddenly felt grateful for them*. Not because they were of any use to him, because they were not; and not necessarily because he *liked* them: he found them strangely beautiful but possibly not attractive. The experience was something quite different from this — it was a gratitude for their existence. It is said in Genesis that 'God saw everything that he had made, and behold it was very good'. Sunk as he must have been in the depths of despair, it was something of this very fundamental experience that came to the

Mariner; he saw existence objectively, as God might see it, and
he saw it to be good. He gave thanks for it.[9]

> O happy living things! No tongue
> Their beauty might declare,
> A spring of love gushed from my heart
> And I blessed them unaware.
> Sure my kind saint took pity on me
> And I blessed them unaware.
>
> The selfsame moment I could pray;
> And from my neck so free
> The Albatross fell off, and sank
> Like lead into the sea.[10]

Could Hemingway's Old Man have blessed the slimy water-
snakes? Hardly. They lack style. They could not count as one of
the noble creatures of the sea, the hunted with which the hunter
feels deep bonds of identity. Hemingway's story is not a Christian
fable, and his old fisherman does not come to a love of God's
creatures. As we have seen, he returns home a hero and a warrior:
almost destroyed, but not defeated. When the young boy sees the
Old Man's bleeding hands he cries. But what of the Old Man
himself? 'Up the road, in his shack, the old man was sleeping
again. He was still sleeping on his face and the boy was sitting
by him watching him. The old man was dreaming about the lions.'

Notes

1. Philip Young, *Ernest Hemingway* (University of Minnesota Press, 1960), p. 22.
2. William Faulkner, Review of *The Old Man and the Sea* in Jeffrey Meyers *Hemingway: The Critical Heritage* (Routledge & Kegan Paul, 1982), pp. 414–15.
3. Hemingway's response to Faulkner quoted in Peter Hays, 'Exchange between Rivals', in James Nagel (ed.), *Ernest Hemingway, The Writer in Context* (University of Wisconsin Press, 1984), p. 163, f.n. 27.
4. All quotations from Ernest Hemingway's *The Old Man and the Sea*, (Triad/Panther, 1970).
5. Philip Young, ibid., p. 11.
6. Philip Young, ibid., p. 23.
7. See Wirt Williams, *The Tragic Art of Ernest Hemingway*, (Louisiana State University Press, 1981), p. 172 f.

8.   Coleridge, *The Ancient Mariner*.
9.   J. R. Jones, 'Love as Perception of Meaning' in D.Z. Phillips (ed.), *Religion and Understanding* (Basil Blackwell, 1967).
10. Coleridge, ibid.

15

Kill or Be Killed

However hard its sayings may be, Christians cannot escape the challenge of Christ's sermon on the mount:

And he opened his mouth, and taught them saying,
Blessed are the poor in spirit: for theirs is the kingdom of heaven.
Blessed are they that mourn: for they shall be comforted.
Blessed are the meek: for they shall inherit the earth.
Blessed are they which do hunger and thirst after righteousness: for they shall be filled.
  Blessed are the merciful: for they shall obtain mercy.
Blessed are the pure in heart: for they shall see God.
Blessed are the peacemakers: for they shall be called the children of God.
Blessed are ye when men shall revile you, and persecute you, and shall say all manner of evil against you falsely, for my sake.
Rejoice, and be exceeding glad; for great is your reward in heaven: for so persecuted they the prophets which were before you . . .
Ye have heard that it hath been said, An eye for an eye, and a tooth for a tooth:
But I say unto you: That ye resist not evil; but whosoever smite thee on thy right cheek, turn to him the other also . . .
Ye have heard that it hath been said, Thou shalt love thy neighbour, and hate thine enemy:
But I say unto you, Love your enemies, bless them that curse you, do good to them that hate you, and pray for them which despitefully use you, and persecute you;
That ye may be the children of your father which is in heaven.

Put alongside Christ's words, the following imploring of fate by a soldier who has been scorned and rebuked for going into battle without cartridges in his rifle:

'You didn't put no cartridges in,' Akinfiev whispered faintly
into my ear, and tried to tear my mouth with his big fingers.
'You worship God, you traitor!'

He tugged and tore at my mouth. I pushed the epileptic away
and struck him in the face. Akinfiev fell sideways to the ground
and began to bleed from his fall.

Then Sasha went over to him with her wobbling breasts . . .

'Cocks have only one thought in life — to go and tear at
one another,' said Sasha. 'And everything that's gone on today
makes me want to go and hide my face.'

She said this sorrowfully and led the injured Akinfiev off with
her. And I plodded on to the village of Chesniki, slipping in
the tireless rain of Galicia.

The village was swimming and swelling, and blood-red clay
was oozing from its dismal wounds. The first star glimmered
above me, and fell into the clouds. Rain lashed the willows and
spent itself. Evening flew up to the sky like a flock of birds, and
darkness crowned me with its watery wreath. I felt my strength
all ebbing away. Bent beneath the funereal garland, I continued
on my way, imploring fate to grant me the simplest of pro-
ficiencies — the ability to kill my fellow-men.[1]

What would the Christian reaction be to this request? Would it
not be one of revulsion? Would the Christian not see it as an
advocacy of the way of violence, which is fundamentally at odds
with the way of peace? Would not members of the Jewish Faith
react in the same way? Yet, the remarkable fact is that the words
I have just quoted were written by a Jew, albeit by one whose life
and work seem to be riddled with paradox, contradiction and
tension. Isaac Babel, born in Odessa in 1894, fought with the
Cossack cavalry during the Russian Revolution. The Cossacks
were the symbols of Tsarist oppression, but the Cossacks Babel
rode with were on the side of the Revolution. The incident referred
to comes from *After the Battle*, one of Babel's famous *Red Cavalry*
stories. But if the anomaly of Cossacks fighting for the Revolution
strikes one as bizzare, far more bizarre is the thought of a Jew
riding and fighting with these Cossacks. As Lionel Trilling points
out, the Cossacks and the Jews were fundamentally opposed to
each other:

Traditionally the Cossack was the feared and hated enemy of

the Jew. But he was more than that. The principle of his existence stood in total antithesis to the principle of the Jew's existence. The Jew conceived his own ideal character to consist in his
being intellectual, pacific, humane. The Cossack was physical,
violent, without mind or manners . . . an image of animal violence, of aimless destructiveness.[2]

For Christian and Jew, the struggle between the way of peace
and the way of violence, is a struggle between good and evil
respectively. For them, anyone extolling the way of violence
would, for one reason or another, be hiding from himself what
he knew to be good, the way of peace. Of course, if people are
deeply alienated from the good, the picture darkens. The victims
of such people are not the victims of merely immoral actions, but
of monstrous and demonic actions. The Jews were such victims
in the Nazi holocaust, a holocaust Babel would find as repugnant
as anyone else. And yet, in his writings, he strives to appreciate
what is involved in the Cossack ethos, suggesting that in doing
so one discovers disturbing challenges for the Jewish, and, no
doubt, Christian perspectives. In the story, worship of God is
called betrayal. But how can this be? If worshipping God is identified with goodness, how can it be talked of as betrayal?

In calling the worshipper a traitor, the Cossack is suggesting
that there is an ideal, a conception of the good, which religious
belief violates. This is what many believers would find difficult to
accept. For them, outside religion, there are only unrepentant
sinners and monsters. They find it hard to accept that there are
moralities outside religion; even harder to accept that some of
these moralities are positively anti-religious in character. Once
this is recognised, we can see that from the perspectives of such
moralities, religious belief and worship may actually be regarded
as immoral. Believers feel, mistakenly, that to call these viewpoints
moralities, is somehow to bestow approval on them. But this is
not so. There is no contradiction in speaking of a terrible morality.
On the contrary, in the case of conduct one strongly disapproves
of, one may feel it is all the worse for being embodied in a morality.
Further, by recognising that there are these moralities, though
one's opposition to them need not be lessened one jot, one is
rescued from a condescending misunderstanding of them. One
ceases to think of the Cossack as someone who really knows he
ought to love his enemies, as Christ commanded, but who, in

moments of unthinking abandon, chooses to ignore the commandment.

But Babel's situation is an extremely complicated one. He did not think the Cossack morality was a terrible morality. On the contrary, elements in it attract him strongly. And this is the difficulty for Jews and Christians who read his stories: the difficulty of seeing what that attraction is, since it is one closely associated with killing and the threat of death. Lionel Trilling has summed up the difficulty well:

> The author, who represented himself in the stories, was a Jew; and a Jew in a Cossack regiment was more than an anomaly, it was a Joke, for between Cossack and Jew there existed not merely hatred but a polar opposition. Yet here was a Jew riding as a Cossack and trying to come to terms with the Cossack ethos. At that first reading it seemed to me — although it does not now — that the stories were touched with cruelty. They were about violence of the most extreme kind, yet they were composed with a striking elegance and precision of objectivity, and also with a kind of lyric *joy*, so that one could not at once know just how the author was responding to the brutality he recorded, whether he thought it good or bad, justified or not justified. Nor was this the only thing to be in doubt about. It was not really clear how the author felt about, say, Jews; or about religion; or about the goodness of man.[3]

These questions are difficult for the reader because without doubt, there are stories which re-inforce Trilling's first impression of brutality. Consider, for example, the story, *The Life and Adventures of Matthew Pavilchenko*.[4] Matthew has become a Red general, but he returns to mete out a terrible revenge on his master for the indignities which he and his wife had suffered at his hands. He tramples his former master to death.

> Then I stamped on my master . . . trampled on him for an hour or maybe more. And in that time I got to know life through and through. With shooting — I'll put it this way — with shooting you only get rid of a chap. Shooting's letting him off, and too damn easy for yourself. With shooting you'll never get at the soul, to where it is in a fellow and how it shows itself. But I don't spare myself, and I've more than once trampled an enemy

for over an hour. You see, I want to get to know what life really is, what life's like down our way.

Part of what Babel is trying to express in what he says about shooting, the suddenness of it for the shooter and his victim, is that it gives no opportunity for character to be displayed by either, a character involved in killing and in being killed. The trouble with this story, however, is in the character that *is* displayed in the way revenge is taken. Brutality predominates. It is inflicted in the name of just revenge, but falls foul of the danger for all those who act in this way: they take on something of the character of the persecutor they punish. We hear people say that a tormenting persecutor should be repaid in kind: visited by the same torments he inflicted on others. But can those who speak in this way be confident that they will not end up as tormentors too? Cruelty and violence go deep with us. If we dabble in them, may they not enter our souls as things we delight in?

Isn't that our justifiable reaction to Babel's story? Matthew seems to delight in trampling his former master to death. He says he does it to find out what life really is. But all he does is to exhibit power in ways alarmingly similar to the power once exhibited by the master he kills. The story seems to show little more than someone saying: my turn now. Lionel Trilling finds this story disturbing too, but he offers a suggestion as to what Babel may be doing here: 'Let us suppose, however, that he is setting down the truth as he heard it; let us suppose too that he has it in mind not to spare himself — this is part, and a terrible part, of the actuality of the Cossack directness and immediacy, this is what goes along with the grace and charm.'[5]

But what is the grace and charm about? They concern action, action in which a man faces danger and death. The virtues he exhibits on occasions such as these are all important: courage, bravery, endurance, panache. The opposite of these virtues, the vices Babel despised were cowardice, servility, weakness, small-mindedness, pettiness. Babel's distinction between virtues and vices does not correspond neatly to the distinction between Cossacks and Jews. Among the prosperous Jews of Odessa, Jews who contrasted violently with the poor Polish Jews Babel met later, there was a flourishing Jewish gangster racket. Babel expresses his admiration for the panache of Benya Krik, king of the gangsters, 'for he was passionate, and passion rules the universe'. He contrasts himself and his father unfavourably with him:

> Then see here, forget for a while that you have spectacles on your nose and autumn in your heart. Cease playing the rowdy at your desk and stammering while others are about. Imagine for a moment that you play the rowdy in public places and stammer on paper. You are a tiger, you are a lion, you are a cat. You can spend the night with a Russian woman, and satisfy her. You are twenty-five. If rings were fastened to heaven and earth, you would grasp them and draw heaven and earth together. And your father is Mendel Krik the drayman. What does such a father think about? He thinks about drinking a good glass of vodka, of smashing somebody in the face, of his horses — and nothing more. You want to live, and he makes you die twenty times a day. What would you have done in Benya Krik's place? You would have done nothing. But *he* did something. That's why he's the King, while you thumb your nose in the privy.

And what would happen when the time for action came? What did happen when the Jews of Odessa became victims of the pogrom that broke out in 1905? Babel saw his father kneel before a Cossack officer:

> 'Captain,' my father mumbled when the Cossacks came abreast of him; 'captain,' my father said, grasping his head in his hands and kneeling in the mud.
> 'Do what I can,' the officer answered, still looking straight ahead, and raising his hand in its lemon-coloured chamois glove to the peak of his cap.
> Right in front of them, at the corner of Fish Street, the mob was looting and smashing up our shop, throwing out into the street boxes filled with nails, machines, and my new photo in school uniform.
> 'Look,' my father said, still on his knees, 'they are destroying everything dear to me, Captain, why is it?'
> The officer murmured something, and again put the lemon glove to his cap. He touched the reins, but his horse did not move. My father crawled in front of the horse on his knees, rubbing up against its short, kindly, tousled legs.

'At your service,' the officer said, tugged at the reins, and rode off, the Cossacks following. They sat passionless on their high saddles, riding through their imaginary mountain pass and disappearing into Cathedral Street.

The striking distinction between the fine figure of the Cossack captain and his father's servility went deep with the young boy. When he is placed in the first class in his school, his family rejoices. Babel gives an ironic description of how his achievement was regarded:

In this toast the old man congratulated my parents and said I had vanquished all my foes in single combat: I had vanquished the Russian boys with their fat cheeks, and I had vanquished the sons of our own vulgar parvenus. So too in ancient times David King of Judah had overcome Goliath, and just as I had triumphed over Goliath, so too would our people by the strength of their intellect conquer the foes who had encircled us and were thirsting for our blood.

But Babel did not believe that strength of intellect did conquer. He had seen his father crawl, and was determined not to crawl himself. But he found his induction into Cossack life difficult. His whole background resisted such an induction. Further, he was an intellectual, a thinker not a doer, despised by Cossacks. He soon finds out how he is thought of when the Cossack commander asks if he can read and write:

'Yes I can read and write,' I replied, enjoying the flower and iron of that youthfulness. 'I graduated in law from St Petersburg University.'
'Oh are you one of those grinds?' he laughed. 'Specs on your nose, too! What a nasty little object! They've sent you along without making any inquiries; and this is a hot place for specs. Think you'll get on with us?'

Babel is accepted by them, but not through any display of his intellect. He loses his temper with an old woman who is reluctant to cook a goose for him:

And turning around I saw somebody's sword lying within

reach. A severe-looking goose was waddling about the yard,
inoffensively preening its feathers. I overtook it and pressed it
to the ground. Its head cracked beneath my boot, cracked and
emptied itself. The white neck lay stretched out in the dung,
the wings twitched.

'Christ!' I said, digging into the goose with my sword. 'Go
and cook it for me, landlady.' . . .

The Cossacks in the yard were already sitting around their
cauldron. They sat motionless, stiff as heathen priests at a sacrifice, and had not looked at the goose.

'The lad's all right,' one of them said, winking and scooping
up the cabbage soup with his spoon.

As we have already noted, this was not the last time that Babel's
allegiance to the Cossack ethic was tested. He once went into
battle without cartridges in his gun. On another occasion, when
he tries to establish a friendship with a particular Cossack he is
rounded on fiercely: ' "I see you," he said. "I see the whole of
you. You're trying to live without enemies. That's all you think
about, not having enemies." . . . "You know what comes of this?"
he said, not controlling his breath properly. "Boredom comes of
it. Clear off, damn your eyes!" '

Here is the challenge to Christian and Jewish perspectives. They
are a denial of the manly virtues; invitations to servility and dependence on others to do what has to be done. The denial of enemies
is the denial of ideals which mark off those who do not adhere to
them from those who do. We are called to live like men, proud
and free, not humbling ourselves before gods or men. But we are
called on, not only to live like men but to die like men. Sometimes
we are called on to kill another in order that he may die like a
man. When this test came to Babel, he failed it. He came across
Dolgushov, badly wounded:

He was leaning up against a tree, his boots thrust out apart . . .
His belly had been torn out. The entrails hung over his knees,
and the heartbeats were visible.

'The Poles'll turn up and play their dirty tricks. Here are my
papers. You'll write and tell my mother how things were.'

'No,' I answered, and spurred my horse . . .

'Sneaking off, eh?' he murmured, sliding down. 'Well, sneak
off then, you swine.'

Meeting his friend Afonka, Babel tells him about Dolgushov. The result is the termination of their friendship:

> They spoke briefly; no words reached me. Dolgushov held his papers out to the platoon commander and Afonka hid them away in his boot and shot Dolgushov in the mouth.
>
> 'Afonka,' I said with a wry smile, and rode over to the Cossack. 'I couldn't you see.'
>
> 'Get out of my sight,' he said, growing pale, 'or I'll kill you. You guys in specs have about as much pity for chaps like us as a cat has for a mouse.'
>
> And he cocked his rifle.
>
> I rode away slowly, not turning around, feeling the chill of death in my back.

Here is another example of the Cossack ethic, that suffering must not be allowed to belittle the manly virtues, becoming a direct challenge to the ethic of Christianity and the Jewish Faith. It is clear, therefore, that what tempted Babel away from those perspectives was not seen by him as a form of weakness, waywardness or immorality. No, what tugged at him was itself a powerful moral perspective, a world away from the Faith he had been taught, and from Christ's Sermon on the Mount, but all the more powerful for that very reason.

But was there no pull in the opposite direction? As long as religion was thought to involve a servile loss of manliness, there was not. But were those voices down the centuries, voices which said it was better to suffer wrong than to do wrong; which spoke of a man of sorrows, despised and rejected of men who has borne our griefs and carried our sorrows; which said that the meek shall inherit the earth and that enemies should be loved; — were all those voices the voices of servility? Babel cannot embrace that unqualified view. Other images from churches beckon him. In one church, he has to confess: 'The breath of an invisible order of things glimmered beneath the crumbling ruin of the priest's house, and its soothing seduction ummanned me.'

He is unmanned by the spirituality shown in those who suffer for God and the good. It is no accident that what appeals to Babel is partly the style of people who know how to die. He sees this above all, as Trilling says, in the poor Jews of Poland, so different from the prosperous ones of Odessa. 'In those passionate, angu-

ish-chiselled features there is no fat, no warm pulsing of blood.
The Jews of Volhyma and Galicia move jerkily, in an uncontrolled
and uncouth way; but their capacity for suffering is full of a sombre
greatness, and their unvoiced contempt for the Polish gentry
unbounded.'

Lionel Trilling refers to a revealing image of God Babel discovers
in a church, an image which unites Jewish and Christian traditions
more than Trilling allows for. Trilling says of Babel.

He is captivated by the ecclesiastical painter Pan Apolek, he
who created ecclesiastical scandals by using the publicans and
sinners of the little towns as the models for his saints and
virgins. Yet it is chiefly the Jews who speak to him of the life
beyond violence, and even Pan Apolek's 'heretical and intoxicat-
ing brush' had achieved its masterpiece in his Christ of the
Berestechko church, 'the most extraordinary image of God I had
ever seen in my life', a curly-headed Jew, a bearded figure in a
Polish great-coat of orange, barefooted with torn and bleeding
mouth, running from an angry mob with a hand raised to ward
off a blow.

Babel cannot ignore this greatness in suffering, a greatness
involved not in the glorification of the self, but in dying to the self.
And this spiritual greatness poses questions for the Revolution for
which Babel was fighting, questions put to him by the old Jew
Gedali:

But the Poles, kind sir, shot because they were the Counter-
Revolution. You shoot because you are the Revolution. But
surely the Revolution means joy. And joy does not like orphans
in the house. Good men do good deeds. The Revolution is the
good deed of good men. But good men do not kill . . . Then
how is Gedali to tell which is Revolution and which is Counter-
Revolution?

Babel tells him that the Revolution will open his eyes, but it is
Gedali who threatens to open his by saying that the International
he wants is an International of good people. Babel concludes:
'The Sabbath is coming. Gedali, the founder of an impossible
International, has gone to the synagogue to pray.'

Babel never did resolve the pull of these two images, the way of violence and the way of peace, with their ever-shifting aspects: courage or brutality, spirituality or servility. By 1934 Babel had fallen foul of the masters of the Revolution he had fought for. He was put in a concentration camp in 1937, and died or was killed in 1939 or 1940.

Jewish and Christian spirituality made its mark on Babel, but it did not win him over. Trilling's conclusion is, surely, the right one:

> He makes no pretence that it could ever claim him for his own. But it established itself in his heart as an image, beside the image of the other life that also could not claim him, the Cossack life. The opposition of these two images made his art — but it was not a dialectic that his Russia could permit.

But it is a dialectic which philosophical enquiry must permit. It must bring out what is involved in such opposition, and clarify possible misrepresentations of each other by the parties involved. Religion need not be a form of weakness. As for what Babel saw in the Cossacks, and as for Hemingway's Old Man, it brings no credit on religion to deny that they, too, have their moral perspectives. They may not see God above the sky, but they have addressed life at certain of its limiting horizons, and, in doing so, emerged as heroes of their kind.

Notes

1. Isaac Babel, *After the Battle* in *Collected Stories* (Penguin, 1961).
2. Lionel Trilling, Introduction, ibid., pp. 16–17.
3. Ibid.
4. In *Collected Stories*.
5. Op. cit., p. 27.

16

One Priest, Two Sermons

Hemingway's Old Man, and the ideals of the Cossack life, which Babel observed, showed man faced by some of the extremities of human existence. The character shown by a man in facing death is central to the authors' concerns. The same is true, in different circumstances, in Camus' *The Plague*, in which a city has to face the unheard of threat of the plague. As one might expect, people react differently, but in their midst is Doctor Rieux, with whom the author's sympathies clearly lie. The doctor expresses, in thought and deed, a modest humanism, which gets on with the tasks which have to be done, with compassion and without pretension. There is no reference to supernatural resources in this humanism. Indeed, part of the book explores what religion has to say about such human disasters as the plague. But Camus is not making the story a means to a thesis. If he were, it would not be much of a story. It is in terms of the story itself that questions arise about how religious belief addresses itself to human affliction. Camus is too perceptive an artist to think that it always does so in the same way. There may be radical differences between religious responses, so much so that it is difficult to say that religious belief comes to the same thing in all of them. We begin to see these differences hinted at in Camus' treatment of the two sermons delivered by Father Paneloux in the novel. The content of the second sermon is not explored to any great extent. Camus says enough, however, to make us wonder whether there are religious perspectives and possibilities which, unlike those expressed in the first sermon, would not contradict the virtues of the modest humanism Camus espoused. Whether Camus comes to this conclusion is another matter. As we shall see, his treatment of the sermons reveal unresolved tensions in his exploration of religious belief.

The Plague which came to Oran was thought to be impossible. Discussing the early symptoms, two doctors, Castel and Rieux show why this should be so:

And then, as one of my colleagues said, 'It's unthinkable. Everyone knows it's ceased to appear in Western Europe.' Yes, everyone knew that — except the dead men. Come now, Rieux, you know as well as I do what it is' . . .

'Yes, Castel,' he replied. 'It's hardly credible. But everything points to its being plague.' . . .

'You know,' the old doctor said, 'what they're going to tell us? That it vanished from temperate countries long ago.'

' "Vanished?" What does that word really mean?"[1]

We think, the citizens of Oran thought, that their way of life could not be disturbed fundamentally. Camus asks why this should be so. He gives two answers to this question. First, this confidence was due to the modernity of society and the narrow limits of thought such modernity involves:

Certainly nothing is commoner nowadays than to see people working from morn to night and then proceeding to fritter away at card-tables, in cafes, and in small-talk what time is left for living. Nevertheless, there still exist towns and countries where people have now and again an inkling of something different. In general it doesn't change their lives. Still, they have an intimation, and that's so much to the good. Oran, however, seems to be a town without intimations; in other words, completely modern.

Along with modernity goes a deadly complacency of mind. This is the second reason why Plague was thought to be impossible.

A pestilence isn't a thing made to man's measure; therefore we tell ourselves that pestilence is a mere bogey of the mind, a bad dream that it will pass away. But it doesn't always pass away and, from one bad dream to another, it is men who pass away, and the humanists first of all because they haven't taken their precautions. Our townsfolk were not more to blame than others, they forgot to be modest — that was all — and thought that everything still was possible for them; which presupposed that pestilences were impossible.

This is Camus at his most brilliant in analysis. We need to heed his words today as much as ever. In the name of humanistic liberalism, we still forget to be modest. We do not realise that real freedoms are always freedoms within limits. By forgetting these limits, by thinking 'that everything was still possible', we turn freedom, freedom of expression, for example, into an idle abstraction. But idle abstractions, unfortunately, can have devastating effects. Thinking that every monstrosity, no matter how repulsive, has a right to be expressed, we slowly invite that monstrosity to become normality; a possibility we become accustomed to hearing about. Of course, at any one time it is a matter of careful judgement as to whether what confronts us is this danger or the mere suppression of viewpoints which ought to be heard. But this does not mean that the need for such judgement can be abandoned in the name of licence masquerading as freedom. However varied viewpoints are at any time, there must also be some notion of the 'unthinkable', that which is not entertained as a *possible* viewpoint. The fact that many 'unthinkables' have become thinkable, reaffirms the need for judgement mentioned earlier. But when the notion of the unthinkable is abandoned, then the monster at the gate knows that his day has come. It is ironic that those who protest, march, strike, for unlimited freedoms, are those who create the necessary conditions for the monstrous, the plague. Of course, when the monstrous comes they are horrified, but too late. The liberal humanists are the first against the wall. A regime comes to be which destroys the very freedoms they fought for. Terror comes to power mouthing words of freedom. The mark of its respect for freedom is not whether its route to power was free, but whether, in power, it preserves that same free route by which it can be got rid of. Fortunately, pestilences do come and go. When normality is regained, however, vigilance must not be relaxed. We must always realise that what we have got rid of may return. This is the lesson at the close of Camus' novel:

And indeed, as he listened to the cries of joy rising from the town, Rieux remembered that such joy is always imperilled. He knew what those jubilant crowds did not know but could have learned from books: that the plague bacillus never dies or disappears for good; that it can lie dormant for years and years in furniture and linen-chests; that it bides its time in bedrooms, cellars, trunks, and bookshelves; and that perhaps the day would come when, for the bane and enlightening of men, it roused up its rats again and sent them forth to die in a happy city.'

We do not learn until the end of Camus' story that its narrator has been Doctor Rieux. His perspective on experiencing the plague is one where the need for constant vigilance and sympathy with one's fellowmen are emphasised. At all times, Rieux avoids any hint of knowing superiority. He has been inspired by the example of Tarrou, who has worked tirelessly at his side against the plague until he became its victim. Tarrou does not believe in God, but thinks that men are called to be saints. Rieux's modest humanism is expressed as follows:

Tarrou might seem to have won through to that hardly-come-by peace of which he used to speak; but he found it only in death, too late to turn it to account. If others, however — Rieux could see them in the doorways of houses, passionately embracing and gazing happily at each other in the failing sunset glow — had got what they wanted, this was because they had asked for the one thing that depended on them solely. And . . . it was only right that those whose desires are limited to man and his humble yet formidable love, should enter, if only now and again, into their reward.

These reactions are obviously ones Camus sympathises with. He contrasts them with those of people who wanted to go beyond the humbly human, and his verdict is unequivocal: 'But for those others, who aspired beyond and above the human individual towards something they could not even imagine, there had been no answer.'

The reactions of people to the plague varied, as we would expect, from the heroic to the shabby. In this spectrum, there were those who tried to make sense of the plague in terms of their religious convictions. The most striking example of such an attempt in the novel, is that made by the Jesuit priest, Father Paneloux. But since he turns to God for an answer, Camus' verdict on him must be that he failed to find such an answer. Is this verdict borne out by the text or are there signs that Camus is in some doubt about what to make of this case? As the story shows the encounters between Rieux and Paneloux, we are carried along by them, finding that their questions concerning religion and human suffering become our questions too.

To speak of Paneloux's religious views is no straightforward matter, since he preaches two sermons between which there are important differences. Paneloux's first sermon is preached in the early stages of the plague. People in Oran are not particularly religious, but when they begin to be alarmed by the plague, they think that religion is worth a try; that, at least, it can do no harm. As a result, the cathedral is full for the first sermon, which has a startling beginning: 'Calamity has come on you, my brethren, and, my brethren, you deserved it.'

So far, there is no necessary conflict between these words and Camus' own sympathies. The people had not been vigilant enough. They had allowed evil to creep up on them, the evil they had thought impossible in the twentieth century. Yet, it was this century which witnessed the Nazi Holocaust. So we cannot disclaim all responsibility for the plague. But Paneloux's sermon develops in ways Camus could not condone. For Paneloux, the plague is a heaven-sent punishment for turning from the ways of God. The punishment is not seen as separation from God, a separation involved in sin itself, but as something external to sin which God inflicts as a penalty for it:

The first time this scourge appears in history, it was wielded to strike down the enemies of God. Pharaoh set himself up against the divine will, and the plague beat him to his knees. Thus from the dawn of recorded history the scourge of God has humbled the proud of heart and laid low those who hardened themselves against Him. Ponder this well, my friends, and fall on your knees.

There are contemporary philosophers who argue in this way; who make God's irresistible power the final reason for worshipping him. Here is Peter Geach arguing in this way:

I shall be told . . . that since I am saying not: It is your supreme moral duty to obey God, but simply: It is insane to set about defying an Almighty God, my attitude is plain power-worship. So it is: but it is worship of the Supreme Power, and as such is wholly different from, and does not carry with it, a cringing attitude towards earthly powers. An earthly potentate does not compete with God, even unsuccessfully: he may threaten all manner of afflictions, but only from God's hands can any affliction actually come upon us. If we fully realise this, we shall have such fear of God as destroys all earthly fear: 'I will show you whom you shall fear', said Jesus Christ to his disciples.[2]

To others, this seems to replace a cringing attitude towards earthly powers with a cringing attitude towards a heavenly one. If we listen to Geach, the heavenly power acts in ways too recognisably human and tyrannical: 'Nebuchadnezzar had it forced on his attention that only by God's favour did his wits hold together from one end of the blasphemous sentence to another — and so he saw that there was nothing for him but to bless and glorify the King of Heaven, who is able to abase those who walk in pride.'[3]

Paneloux's congregation begin to kneel as his sermon develops. He warns them that their only hope is to turn to God even at this late hour. Rieux and Tarrou discuss Paneloux's sermon, a sermon which Rieux finds intellectually dishonest: 'Rieux said . . . that if he believed in an all-powerful God he would cease curing the sick and leave that to Him. But no one in the world believed in a God of that sort; no, not even Paneloux, who believed that he believed in such a God. And this was proved by the fact that no one ever threw himself on Providence completely.'

Rieux can never accustom himself to watching people die, seeing many fight for life up to the last moment. All he knows is that as a doctor he has a never-ending struggle to alleviate suffering as best he can. With Tarrou and Paneloux he watches the slow, agonising death of a young child. They are all deeply affected. Paneloux prays to God to spare the child. Remembering the notion of collective responsibility for sin in his sermon, Rieux rounds on him angrily: 'Ah! That child, anyhow was innocent — and you know it as well as I do!'

But the child's death has made its mark on Paneloux too. He tells Rieux that he is working on an essay, *Is a Priest Justified in Consulting a Doctor?* and that he is to preach a second sermon which would contain some of its ideas. By this time, the plague is in its advanced stages. People have lost interest in religion, turning to the occult, superstition and prophecies, to anything that offered hope of a rescue from the plague. Unsurprisingly, there are not so many people in the cathedral to listen to his second sermon as listened to his first.

Father Paneloux still wanted to say that God's will is to be found in all things, but he thought the way he had understood this in his first sermon lacked charity. How could it be of God if it lacked charity? In the first sermon he constantly used 'you', but now he spoke of 'we'. He wanted to face their predicament squarely. How could God's will be in the plague? To put it at its most difficult: how could God's will be in the death of a child? Here, the Christian seems to have his back to the wall when asked for an answer.

He, Father Paneloux, refused to have recourse to simple devices enabling him to scale that wall. Thus he might easily have answered them that the child's sufferings would be compensated for by an eternity of bliss awaiting him. But how could he give that assurance when, to tell the truth, he knew nothing about it? For who would dare to assert that eternal happiness can compensate for a single moment's human suffering? He who asserted that would not be a true Christian, a follower of the Master who knew all the pangs of suffering in his body and in his soul. No, he, Father Paneloux, would keep faith with that great symbol of all suffering, the tortured body on the Cross; he would stand fast, his back to the wall, and face honestly the terrible problem of a child's agony.

But how is that suffering to be faced? Paneloux says that it is not faced by resignation or even humility. The Christian must admit that a humiliation is involved, he must freely assent to it.

'My brothers,' — the preacher's tone showed he was nearing the conclusion of his sermon — 'the love of God is a hard love. It demands total self-surrender, disdain of human personality. And yet it alone can reconcile us to suffering and the deaths of children, it alone can justify them, since we cannot understand them, and we can only make God's will ours.'

The sermon ends there. It does not tell us what self-surrender amounts to, how God's will is to be made our own. These questions were grappled with by Simone Weil in her work. She, like Paneloux, puts aside all compensatory notions of religion. Suffering is not the means to a higher good. Christianity offers a use for suffering, not a remedy for it. We come to see that there is no reason in ourselves why we are visited with ills and misfortunes.

We cease to think of providence as owing us anything. Faced with this phenomenon, existentialists have spoken of 'absurdity' and placed great emphasis on the self and its choices. Faced by the same phenomenon, the Christian speaks of all things being in the hands of God, the gifts of grace. Paneloux mentions, but does not develop, the notion of active fatalism. The Christian is called on to see other human beings and natural objects as gifts of grace, not to be appropriated or dominated by others. He has to die to the self, cease to see himself as the centre of the world. There is no compensation for the death of a child. Yet in the very absence of such compensation, we come to see how God's will can be found in it as it was in the death of Jesus on the Cross.

What are we to make of Camus' treatment of Father Paneloux's second sermon? He is enough of an artist to be able to make it impressive, to see the important differences between it and the first sermon. On the other hand, he cannot develop the ideas in the sermon as Simone Weil did in her work. It is doubtful whether he appreciated them enough to be able to do so. For example, there is a tension between the title he gives to Paneloux's essay, *Is a Priest Justified in Consulting a Doctor?* and the content of the second sermon. The same tension is found in Paneloux's refusal, when he falls ill, to consult a doctor. The essay title and this behaviour smack of fatalism, but Paneloux, in his sermon, makes it quite clear that he is not talking about fatalism:

> It was wrong to say '*This* I understand, but *that* I cannot accept'; we must go straight to the heart of that which is unacceptable, precisely because it is thus that we are constrained to make our choice . . . He made no doubt that the ugly word 'fatalism' would be applied to what he had said. Well, he would not boggle at the word, provided he were allowed to qualify it with the adjective 'active'.

The Danish philosopher, Søren Kierkegaard spoke of this 'active fatalism'. He called it Christian patience, and said that it performed a greater miracle than courage. While courage is the voluntary acceptance of avoidable suffering, patience is the voluntary acceptance of unavoidable suffering. But many will ask how, if something is unavoidable, there can be any question of accepting or not accepting it. It's happened and that's that. Certainly, it's happened, but there is still a question about how it is to be taken up into our lives. Birth, death, suffering, they are all unavoidable, but how are we to live with them? The difference between Paneloux's two sermons is essentially a difference about how the Christian faces up to suffering in his life.

As we have seen, Camus does not develop these thoughts. At times, he suggests the second sermon is not at the heart of religion. He makes a young deacon say to an older priest that he doubts whether Paneloux's forthcoming essay will get the *Imprimatur*. He depicts Rieux listening to the second sermon as follows: 'It crossed Rieux's mind that Father Paneloux was dallying with heresy in speaking thus, but he had no time to follow up the thought.'

This honest remark reflects Camus' relation to the perspective of the second sermon. A harsher version of this reaction can be found in certain philosophical and theological circles today. These circles are acquainted with certain conceptions of religion. Arguments about religion, pro and contra, take place within these conceptions. If someone suggests that these conceptions are inadequate, that they obscure, blind us, and fail to do justice to other religious perspectives, he is likely to be accused of heresy, or of not talking about religion at all. They refuse to admit these religious perspectives into their reflections.

Camus, however, was too open-minded a thinker for this to be true of him. When he speculates on whether Paneloux's second sermon is heretical, that marks a stage in his thinking, rather than a dogmatic refusal on his part to think at all about such possibilities. His open-mindedness is symbolised in the verdict given when Paneloux dies:

> At the hospital Paneloux did not utter a word. He submitted passively to the treatment given him, but never let go of the crucifix. However, his case continued doubtful, and Rieux could not feel sure how to diagnose it . . . Even at the height of his fever Paneloux's eyes kept their blank serenity and when, next morning, he was found dead, his body drooping over the bedside, they betrayed nothing. Against his name the index-card recorded: 'Doubtful case.'

Perhaps the conviction that religious belief is meaningless had become a 'doubtful case' for Camus. Around, or shortly after, the time he was writing *The Plague*, Camus became acquainted with the work of Simone Weil. He recognised a kindred spirit in her, and, by the end of his life, had become intensely interested in her work. His untimely death makes it futile to speculate whether he would have come to a full appreciation of the religious perspectives she talked of, perspectives so different from the conceptions of religion he so rightly attacked. He might have come to give a fuller account of something he already saw, with an artist's instinct, had to be given a place in his reflections, namely, why a priest came to see the necessity of preaching a second sermon.

Notes

1. All quotations from Albert Camus, *The Plague* (Penguin, 1965).
2. Peter Geach, 'The Moral Law and the Law of God' in *God and the Soul* (Routledge & Kegan Paul, 1969), p. 127.
3. Ibid., pp. 126–7.

Part IV
Under God's Heaven

*Who hath believed our report? and to whom
is the arm of the Lord revealed?*

17

Who's Who

To determine what is, and what is not, of God, is of fundamental importance for any serious believer. But this concern with *what* is of God, can easily become a curiosity concerning *who* is of God; a kind of 'who's who' in the realm of the spirit. Believers may bring with them, into religion, the concern with who's who which operates so strongly elsewhere. In religion, it takes the worst form of all: spiritual pride. The proud person thanks God that he is not as other men are. Depictions of such pride in literature often take a comic form. We are shown comic pride before a fall; a fall which may lead to revelation.

Although she is not the author we are mainly concerned with in this essay let us first note Flannery O'Connor's marvellous treatment of comic pride in her powerful short story, *Revelation*.[1] Mrs Turpin, a respectable Southern white lady, knows who's who in the sight of God. God's order is reflected in the social order in the South. She does not over-estimate her own position on the social scale, but she does not under-estimate it either. She knows the details of every rung, and the identity of the people on them. She thanks God for creating her a respectable woman.

Sometimes, her categories give her trouble. After all, people of good breeding sometimes lose their money, and the common get rich. Even blacks own cattle and cadillacs. Nevertheless, she struggles to hold on to her sense of who's who. The severest blow to her pride occurs when a sullen college girl, irked by her self-satisfied respectability, tells her: 'Go back where you came from, you old wart hog from hell.'

She can't get the girl's words out of her mind. They spark off a comic, but recognisable, theological speculation in Mrs Turpin. How could she be both saved and a wart hog from hell? It would have been different had God created her a nigger or white trash, but he hadn't. He had created her, and her husband, Claud, respectable, with a little of everything, and the good sense to use it properly. But the girl's words still pursue her. Worse, she feels

that there is a message in them, a message from God she does
not want to hear. Back on the farm, hosing down the hogs, she
begins to protest against God for sending such a message to her;
a protest which culminates in furious anger: ' "Go on," she yelled,
"call me a hog! Call me a hog again. From hell. Call me a wart
hog from hell. Put that bottom rail on top. There'll still be a top
and a bottom!" ' Her anger explodes into a question for God:

> A final surge of fury shook her and she roared, 'Who do you
> think you are.'
> The colour of everything, field and crimson sky, burned for
> a moment with a transparent intensity. The question carried
> over the pasture and across the highway and the cotton field
> and returned to her clearly like an answer from beyond the
> wood.

Who do you think you are? In the returning echo, she finds God's
question to her; a question which leads to the final revelation:

> There was only a purple streak in the sky, cutting through a
> field of crimson and leading, like an extension of the highway,
> into the descending dusk. She raised her hands from the side
> of the pen in a gesture hieratic and profound. A visionary light
> settled in her eyes. She saw the streak as a vast swinging bridge
> extending upward from the earth through a field of living fire.
> Upon it a vast horde of souls were rumbling toward heaven.
> There were whole companies of white-trash, clean for the first
> time in their lives, and bands of black niggers in white robes,
> and battalions of freaks and lunatics shouting and clapping and
> leaping like frogs. And bringing up the end of the procession
> was a tribe of people whom she recognized at once as those
> who, like herself and Claud, had always had a little of every-
> thing and the God-given wit to use it right. She leaned forward
> to observe them closer. They were marching behind the others
> with great dignity, accountable as they always had been for
> good order and common sense and respectable behaviour. They
> alone were on key. Yet she could see by their shocked and
> altered faces that even their virtues were burned away. She
> lowered her hands and gripped the rail of the hog pen, her eyes
> small but fixed unblinkingly on what lay ahead. In a moment
> the vision faded but she remained where she was, immobile.

At length she got down and turned off the faucet and made her slow way on the darkening path to the house. In the woods around her the invisible cricket choruses had struck up, but what she heard were the voices of the souls climbing upward into the starry field and shouting hallelujah.

Here, as in so many of her stories, Flannery O'Connor lets the comic carry us along until, with a surprising, but prepared for, turn, the comic yields a deeper revelation. That revelation, however, is mediated through the concrete detail of the story; it is never an abstract proposition. Mrs Turpin comes to a religious sense of the mystery of other people, but it is a sense which finds itself through the manners of her community. Flannery O'Connor says:

There are two qualities that make fiction. One is the sense of mystery and the other is the sense of manners. You get the manners from the texture of existence that surrounds you. The great advantage of being a Southern writer is that we don't have to go anywhere to look for manners; bad or good, we've got them in abundance. We in the South live in a society that is rich in contradiction, rich in irony, rich in contrast, and particularly rich in its speech.[2]

She deplores the kind of regional writing which trades on the term 'Southern', but she goes on to insist:

An idiom characterises a society, and when you ignore the idiom, you are very likely ignoring the whole social fabric that could make a meaningful character. You can't cut characters off from their society and say much about them as individuals. You can't say anything meaningful about the mystery of a personality unless you put that personality in a believable and significant social context. And the best way to do this is through the character's own language.[3]

And what a language Flannery O'Connor had at her disposal in creating Mrs Turpin! The South was still permeated, albeit in distorted forms, with the language of theology and the Bible. She once said that even if the South is not Christ-centred, it is certainly Christ-haunted.

But, now what if the South we were talking about was not the Deep South in America, but the South of England in the 1950s of this century? No one would be tempted to speak of it as Christ-centred or Christ-haunted. Further, if we said that we would be concerned with youngish middle-class people, quite well educated and often associated with High Anglicanism, we would hesitate to attribute to this social milieu an idiom rich in religion or theology. Yet, it was in the context of this social fabric that Barbara Pym wrote her novel, *A Glass of Blessings*, published in 1958; a novel which also depicts the fall of a comic pride.[4]

In many ways, it would be hard to think of two novelists more different from each other than Flannery O'Connor and Barbara Pym. One works through the religious distortions found in freaks, lunatics, bogus prophets, to offer large and startling revelations to an unbelieving world. The other, the most English of writers, deals in the minutiae of the manners of a narrow community, manners which appear to border on the trivial. Yet, both are masters of the idiom of the communities they write about, and, for that reason, can create believable characters. Further, in Wilmet Forsyth, Barbara Pym too succeeds in portraying, by comic means, a character who believes she has mastered who's who in her relations with other people. The texture of existence which surrounds the two characters is, of course, very different. The possibilities for Mrs Turpin are far richer than those open to Wilmet Forsyth. Where one comes to a dramatic revelation, the other comes to a half-realised sense of religious possibilities. Yet, placed as we are, far nearer the world of Wilmet than that of Mrs Turpin, attention to Barbara Pym's sparkling miniature is well worthwhile.

Speaking of Barbara Pym's six novels, published between 1950 and 1961, and of the world they open up to us, Philip Larkin says:

> Their narratives have the air of being picked up almost at random; the characters have usually been living for some time in the circumstances in which we meet them, and yet some small incident — new tenants in the flat below, a new curate . . . serves to set off a chain of modest happenings among inter-related groups of characters, watched or even recounted by a protagonist who tempers an ironic perception of life's absurdities with a keen awareness of its ability to bruise . . . The moral of it all seems to be, as the vicar says 'in too casual a tone to

sound priggish', that 'We must accept people as we find them and do the best we can.'[5]

But this is precisely what Wilmet Forsyth cannot do. She has preconceived ideas of who's who: ideas concerning the natural endowment of style and sophistication. In some strange way, some people are predetermined to possess such endowments and others to lack them. Wilmet possesses them, while her dowdy acquaintance, Mary Beamish, does not. When Wilmet's mother-in-law regrets that Mary is tied to her sick, ageing mother, Wilmet replies: 'I know . . . But Mary is somehow the kind of person to be put upon. I suppose there must always be people like that. And after all, what would she have done if she hadn't devoted her life to her mother and good works? Married and had children? That's what people always say, isn't it?' The invoking of these alternatives by Wilmet is ironic, since Mary's dowdiness makes marriage extremely unlikely:

Obviously . . . it was Mary and people like her who bought the trying electric blue or dingy olive green dress which had been reduced because nobody could wear it . . . She tried a few dresses which fitted quite well but were uninteresting. Then I asked the saleswoman to bring something black. I wondered why I was taking all this trouble over Mary Beamish, for when one came to think of it what did it matter what she wore? She might just as well buy a dress as much like her old blue as possible, for all the difference it would make to her life.

How different is Wilmet's conception of herself! When a male admirer compliments her, she reacts: 'I was pleased at his compliment for I always take trouble with my clothes, and being tall and dark I usually manage to achieve some kind of distinction. Today I was in pale coffee brown with touches of black and coral jewellery'.

Like people, churches either possess or lack style. Having moved to London, Wilmet attends St Luke's because the church in her immediate neighbourhood is unbearably Low. What is true of people and churches, is also true of places. Wilmet declines to travel on London's trolley buses: 'I had noticed them sometimes going to places that seemed impossibly remote and even romantically inviting, but I had never been bold enough to risk the almost certain disillusionment waiting at the other end.'

The title of Barbara Pym's novel is taken from a poem by the seventeenth-century poet, George Herbert:

> When God at first made man,
> Having a glass of blessings standing by;
> Let us (said He) pour on him all we can:
> Let the world's riches, which dispersed lie,
> Contract into a span.

Wilmet looks out from her privileged position and perceives, accurately, she thinks, those on whom the glass of blessings has bestowed its contents. She also notes those devoid of these blessings and feels sorry for them. Among the latter are her husband Rodney and her friend Rowena's husband, Harry. She and her friend had been Wrens and their husbands dashing army majors when they first met. But Rodney and Harry have become dowdy and boringly reliable. Wilmet welcomes the attentions of the notoriously unreliable, but handsome, Piers Longridge, who, after failing to do well at Oxford or Cambridge, she can't remember which, has flitted from job to job. She is certain he needs her and finds it natural that it should be so. Yet, it is reliable old Harry who tries to hold her hand when she visits Rowena. She thinks him a silly old thing, but wonders whether he has always admired her. She allows him to flirt with her over lunch: 'Did I mind — did Rowena mind — did any of us mind? After all, it made no difference to our fundamental relationships — or did it?'

When Piers Longridge asks her to spend an evening with him, she has to refuse because she has arranged a dinner party. At Christmas, among her presents, she discovers a heart-shaped little box with an inscription inside it:

> If you will not when you may
> When you will you shall have nay.

She wonders why Piers has sent the present and what the words mean. Her life is complicated by the arrival of a handsome priest, Father Ransome, at St Luke's. He has lodgings with Mary Beamish. When her mother becomes ill, Mary tells Wilmet that Marius has been a great comfort to her:

Marius? I thought, and then realized that she must mean Father Ransome. I wondered in what way he was being a comfort — in practical ways or simply by the exercise of his charm? Then it occurred to me that he probably would not use his charm on Mary, whom he regarded as a fine person — that, presumably, was reserved for people like me who were less fine, the kind of woman who would expect it. The idea depressed me, as did my sophistication and inability to accept even a pleasant smile from a clergyman at its face value.

But her depression does not last long. She is soon trying to help those less fortunate and sophisticated than herself. She is horrified to discover that Mary Beamish after her mother's death, contemplates entering a convent. She also tries to keep secret the kleptomanic tendencies of Bason, a man for whom her husband arranged a job in the clergy house.

Of course, Wilmet is not sophisticated at all, as her comic naivety reveals all too well. But she is rescued, not simply from naivety, but from pride. Barbara Pym shows this by a series of modest disclosures. The disclosures cannot be anything but modest, because the language and idiom at her disposal would make any attempt at a large statement pretentious in the extreme. Yet, the revelation which comes to Wilmet, though limited, is effective within the limits of her situation. It is a believable revelation because it does not bypass the context in which she is placed, but speaks directly to it.

Wilmet discovers that the heart-shaped box was not sent by Piers, but by silly old Harry. Worse, the news is given to her by Harry's wife Rowena who had been fully aware all along of her husband's attraction to her. She finds out too that her husband has got Bason the job at the clergy house, not in ignorance of his kleptomanic tendencies, but precisely to help him over them. Father Thames is well aware of the fact too, tolerating the disappearance of precious objects from his room, confident of their eventual return. When Mary Beamish decides not to stay in the convent, responding to Father Ransome's appeals for help in his difficulties and doubts concerning the relation of Anglicanism to Rome, Wilmet is confident that they will not marry.

For a moment a wild idea came into my mind that Marius and Mary — the names sounded odd and yet right together — might marry, but I dismissed it almost before it had time to show itself, for obviously if he went over to Rome he would want to go on being a priest and therefore couldn't marry anybody. And even if he stayed where he was and decided to marry, he would choose somebody younger and more attractive than Mary. Besides, women did not come out of convents to marry people — it would be a complete reversal of the old procedure. All the same I wondered if it ever *had* been done.

She does not have to wonder for long. Father Ransome marries dowdy Mary Beamish. Even Wilmet's conception of her relation-ship with Piers is misconceived. Immaculately dressed, she goes to meet him in his flat. She compares herself with inelegant women, and wonders what sort of future they can possibly have. But her own immediate future has a shock in store for her. She discovers that Piers is a homosexual, sharing his flat with a male model, called Keith. So far from loving her, Piers pities her as one of those who, through no fault of their own, are incapable of loving their fellow human beings. When she leaves the flat, her world has fallen apart.

I felt battered and somehow rather foolish, very different from the carefree girl who had set out across the park to meet Piers. But I was not a girl. I was a married woman, and if I felt wretched it was no more than I deserved for having let my thoughts stray to another man. And the ironical thing was that it was Keith, that rather absurd little figure, who had brought about the change I had noticed in Piers and which I had attri-buted to my own charms and loving care.

But it is the absurd Keith, fingering her lined curtains in her flat on a later visit, who reveals that he and Piers had discussed her in precisely the way she had reflected on other people in her thoughts. Two further revelations await her. To her amazement, her mother-in-law announces her intention to marry Professor Root. She wants Wilmet and her husband out of her house so that, with her intended, she can look forward to sharing her seventies and eighties. These new plans prompt Wilmet's hus-band, the dowdy Rodney, to confess that he has taken a woman in his department out to dinner once or twice. Wilmet has to realise that she too has changed over the years and that her husband has not found in her all she has assumed, so confidently, she still had to give.

Perhaps Wilmet's world is not completely overthrown, like that of Mrs Turpin, but it has taken quite a blow. According to Larkin, 'we leave her, half realizing that love must be earned rather than idly pursued'. That is a just comment on her romanticism, but it does not get to the essence of the matter. As with Mrs Turpin, we have witnessed, in Wilmet, the fall of comic pride. Rowena, Harry, Mary, Father Ransome, Father Thames, Rodney, her mother-in-law, Piers and even Keith, all of whom she saw centred on herself, have, in their different ways, from the trivial to the important, made their arrangements, and settled their affairs, without reference to, or consultation with, her.

Through these cumulative revelations, Wilmet Forsyth begins to recognise that life's blessings are gifts of grace; that people cannot be summed up in neat categories. Like Mrs Turpin, she has to give up her sense of who's who. She has to wait on other people; something she has never done. For her, that means being faithful in the little, the small things, which make up her social surroundings.

Barbara Pym died in 1980. Through the swinging 1960s, her novels were virtually ignored. She was without a publisher for 16 years, until a change in her fortunes occurred in 1977 when both Philip Larkin and Lord David Cecil chose her as one of the most underrated novelists of the century. The 1960s, with its weakness for large, pretentious, pseudo philosophies, and its desire for immediacy, instant solutions, was hardly a time to appreciate a novel which showed the importance of faithfulness to the ordinary decencies of the daily round. Wilmet had dismissed many of these decencies as boring trivialities. Father Ransome once said to her: 'it's the trivial things that matter isn't it?'

Wilmet begins to see that life's blessings are in God's hands. People have no reason to boast when they possess them, and no reason to be condescending towards those who lack them. When Mary, blissfully happy at the thought of spending the rest of her life with Father Ransome, tells Wilmet that she sees life as a glass of blessings, Wilmet is tempted to respond in her old, accustomed way. She begins to wonder how they will respond to poverty once old Mrs Beamish's money has run out. But she has learned a lesson and checks her impulse.

'But Mary would be happy whether they had money or not. I turned over in my mind her description of life as being a glass of blessings, and that naturally led me to think about myself. I had as much as Mary had — there was no reason why my own life should not be a glass of blessings too. Perhaps it always had been without my realising it.'

Notes

1. All quotations from Flannery O'Connor's *Revelation* in *The Complete Stories* (Farrar, Straus & Giroux, 1981).
2. Flannery O'Connor, 'Writing Short Stories' in *Mystery and Manners* (Farrar, Straus & Giroux, 1969), p. 103.
3. Ibid., p. 104.
4. All quotations from Barbara Pym, *A Glass of Blessings* (London: Penguin, 1980).
5. Philip Larkin, 'The World of Barbara Pym' in *Required Writing* (Faber & Faber, 1983). pp. 240–1.

18

Displaced Persons

Christians, it has been said, are to be *in* the world, but not *of* the world — displaced persons, one might say. This is precisely what Mark Twain did say in 1908, in a little note called, 'Something about Repentance', in which he argued that our use of the notion involves 'a misassociation of words'.

> We get the notion early, and keep it always, that we repent of bad deeds only; whereas we do a formidably large business in repenting of good deeds which we have done. Often when we repent of a sin, we do it perfunctorily from principle, coldly and from the head; but when we repent of a good deed the repentance comes hot and bitter and straight from the heart.[1]

Mark Twain has no doubt that what he is speaking of is quite familiar to his readers:

> I am quite sure that the average man is built just as I am; otherwise I should not be making this revelation of my inside. I say the average man and stop there; for I am quite certain that there are people who do not repent of their good deeds when the return they get for them is treachery and ingratitude. I think that these few ought to be in heaven; they are in the way here.[2]

Twain has no doubt, either, that he is not one of these displaced persons. He is sure that he has committed millions of sins which he has, probably, repented of. Apart from the recent ones, and a few scattered amongst the others, he cannot remember them. Where his good deeds are concerned, things are very different:

> In my time I have done eleven good deeds. I remember all of them, four with crystal clearness. These four I repent of whenever I think of them — and it is not seldomer than fifty-two times a year. I repent of them in the same old original furious

way, undiminished, always. If I wake up away in the night,
they are there, waiting and ready; and they keep me company
till the morning. I have not committed any sin that has lasted
me like this save one; and have not repented of any sin with
the unmodifying earnestness and sincerity with which I have
repented of these four gracious and beautiful good deeds.[3]

What will the Christians, the displaced persons, make of all
this? Not much, Twain thinks: 'Possibly you who are reading these
paragraphs are of those few who have got mislaid and ought to
be in heaven. In that case you will not understand what I have
been saying and will have no sympathy with it; but your neighbour will, if he is fifty years old.'[4]

But what if one wants to talk about these few who, according
to Twain, are in the way down here and ought to be in heaven?
If Twain is right, this will be a formidable undertaking. I do not
have in mind testifying as though I were one of the few, or
persuading anyone to join them. I'm simply referring to the lesser
task of trying to give to the many just some idea of what the
few are up to. If, as Twain thinks, these few will have difficulty
understanding him, is it not even more likely that the majority
will have difficulty in understanding the few — the few said to
be *in* the world, but not of it? Still, an attempt has to be made,
but, here, it will be made, not by extolling the virtues of the few,
but by indicating some of the difficulties they have to face in
attempting to obey heaven's dictates here on earth.

Whether we see cynicism or scepticism in Twain's remarks, or
whether we detect his tongue firmly in his cheek, his refreshing
honesty cannot be denied. Further, it must be emphasised, he
does not repent of his good deeds because the world has not
rewarded him. Some philosophers and theologians, in their eager-
ness to commend the Gospel of the few to the many, have actually
suggested that the many have miscalculated the world's rewards.
If only they calculated properly, it is said, they would see, after
all, that it is the way of the few which leads to these rewards. To
come to God, you do not have to stop putting number one first,
because worshipping God is really the best way of furthering the
interests of number one. So if you want to look out for the future,
worshipping God's the thing. No, Twain is not guilty of *that*
vulgarity. He knows that obeying God's call involves renouncing
worldliness. So does obeying the demands of moral decency.

No, it is not this renunciation that worries Twain, but a renunciation of a far more drastic kind. He repents of his four gracious and
beautiful good deeds, not because they have not been rewarded by
the world, but because they have not been given *moral* recognition.
They have been repaid by treachery and ingratitude. Twain is not
referring to deeds done *in order* to receive moral praise. That would
be an instance of what the Danish philosopher, Søren Kierkegaard,
called egocentric service of the good. The call to renounce that
desire for moral reputation and respectability, is as easy to understand as the renunciation of worldliness. The acknowledgement
Twain has in mind is that involved in the ordinary decencies of
life. Gratitude is commonly expressed for good deeds, and apologies are commonly received for bad ones. When these expressions
are withheld, the average person feels offended, and rightly so,
we want to say. How often have we heard it said, 'He couldn't
even say "Thank you" ', or 'He didn't even apologise'. These
expectations, minimal though they are, go deep with us. Simone
Weil has shown why:

> Every time that we put forth some effort and the equivalent of
> this effort does not come back to us in the form of some visible
> fruit, we have a sense of false balance and emptiness which
> makes us think we have been cheated. The effort of suffering
> from some offence causes us to expect the punishment or apolo-
> gies of the offender, the effort of doing good makes us expect
> the gratitude of the person we have helped.[5]

Twain made the effort to do some good, and was repaid with
treachery and ingratitude. He, too, felt empty, cheated, and he
repented of his good deeds when his expectations for ordinary
moral responses, the common decencies, were not fulfilled.
Simone Weil goes on to say that the Christian is called on to
renounce these expectations, these moral claims. Twain understands that call, but cannot respond to it. He views the few who
can as objects of wonder, displaced persons, who ought to be in
heaven.

The believer's love of the good, his love of God, is not to be
deflected, even by the lack of these moral returns, returns which
are, for all of us, so natural a part of our normal expectations. Of
course, some saints apart perhaps, in practice a believer's faith
will be deflected, tempted, tried, again and again. What we are

concerned with here is the character of a certain kind of love of God, together with the deep difficulties such a love has to face.

We have seen, then, two ways in which a Christian may be disappointed by his treatment in this world. First, he may have expected the world to smile on him. Second, he may have expected gratitude to be shown for his moral endeavours, and apologies offered for the wrongs he suffers. But gratitude and apologies may not be forthcoming. The Christian's Faith of which I speak asks him to rise above the wounds inflicted by these disappointments.

Yet, deep-going through these expectations are, they are expectations relating to what a Christian may expect *for himself*: good fortune, thanks, apologies. But there are other expectations which sorely try his faith: expectations which have to do, not with himself, but with others. The Christian I have in mind does not love his neighbour *in order* to love God. He loves God *in* loving his neighbour. That love involves self-sacrifice. But what if self-sacrifice, in obedience to God, does not bestow the fruits of that sacrifice on its intended object? Worse, what if the self-sacrifice actually increases the misery and wretchedness of the loved one? What then? Can the Christian say, 'Well, I played *my* part. I sacrificed'? No, for if indeed he loves the neighbour, his concern will not be focused on his own endeavours, but on the effects they have had on his neighbour. If misery and wretchedness ensue, he may feel that the sacrifice is mocked by the outcome. This is not a case of goodness not being rewarded by the world, or not being acknowledged morally, but of the good playing a part in the creation of evil. Can Christians hold on to their faith even in these circumstances? There is, of course, no general answer. Some do, and some do not. Those who can still love God, even in these circumstances, may well be looked upon, even more than the few Twain had in mind, as displaced persons, the mislaid ones who ought to be in heaven.

Edith Wharton, in a wonderful short novel, *Bunner Sisters*, published in 1916, explores the character of Ann Eliza Bunner, whose faith is undermined in precisely the circumstances I have depicted. Edith Wharton, who was born in 1862, and who died in 1937, a contemporary of Henry James, is a very underrated writer. She is best known for three novels, *The Age of Innocence*, *The House of Mirth* and *The Custom of the Country*. Virago Press are to be congratulated for making more of her work available. Unfortunately, some of the politicised prefaces of these publications, if followed, would distance, and mask from, us, the depth and power in Edith Wharton's work.

In the introduction to the collection which contains *Bunner Sisters*, Marilyn French says of Edith Wharton's novellas:

> They were all written within and against the literary context of women's fiction in the decades around the turn of the century. That context was a celebration of the 'cult of domesticity', a focus on women and women's worlds which exalted the joys of motherhood, wifehood, and love . . . Among its themes was women's self-sacrifice, glorified as an immolation of the self on the altar of the well-being of others and resulting in the triumph of nobility and morality.[6]

On this reading, Ann Eliza Bunner is simply a victim of conditioning, self-deception, and romantic illusions about the nobility of self-sacrifice. Edith Wharton's purpose is taken to be the ruthless exposure of these illusions and self-deceptions. In *Bunner Sisters*, according to Marilyn French, 'the "virtue" of self-sacrifice is . . . desecrated, stripped of whatever moral exaltation, nobility, or grandeur it possesses'.[7]

When Marilyn French refers to the virtue of self-sacrifice, she places the word 'virtue' in inverted commas. Perhaps she thinks that the whole notion of self-sacrifice is confused in some way. Our purpose, here, is not to extol the virtue, but to try to understand it. Unless one endeavours to see how self-sacrifice *can* be regarded as a virtue, it is hard to see how one could understand what Edith Wharton is doing in *Bunner Sisters* at all. It is only in the context of what self-sacrificing *can* mean, that Ann Eliza Bunner's loss of faith can be appreciated. If Edith Wharton had given us a character, too good to be true, indulging in romantic conceptions of self-sacrifice, Ann Eliza's plight would indeed be that of someone whose fond illusions are exposed for what they are. In her character, Edith Wharton has given us something far subtler and more complex. Ann Eliza's sacrificial deeds are of a different character at different times. They are tempted, tried and invaded by impurities in familiar ways. These intrusions, however, do not expose an inherently pseudo virtue. On the contrary, the faith which is finally undermined was a genuine one. It is the very depth and genuineness of the faith which gives to the story of its demise its arresting power.

Ann Eliza Bunner and her younger sister, Evelina, keep a shop in a shabby New York basement; a shop in which they sell artificial flowers, bonnets and homemade preserves.

The Bunner sisters were proud of the neatness of their shop and content with its humble prosperity. It was not what they had once imagined it would be, but though it presented but a shrunken image of their earlier ambitions it enabled them to pay their rent and keep themselves alive and out of debt; and it was long since their hopes had soared higher.[8]

As Marilyn French says:
'Ann Eliza Bunner . . . is "well-trained in the arts of renunciation". She has, it appears raised her younger sister and has always sacrificed her needs to Evelina's. Evelina takes for granted that she will pour the first cup of tea for herself, and be given the larger piece of pie.'[9]

More demandingly, although badly needing a pair of new shoes, Ann Eliza buys Evelina a clock for her birthday. The clock has been bought from Herman Ramy, a German who has opened a little shop in their square. Ann Eliza had always stayed at home, deferring to Evelina's desire to go to market, but the discovery of Herman Ramy's shop has created a strange excitement in her. A habitual churchgoer, like her sister, Ann Eliza never felt that providence had intended that Evelina, unlike herself, should be confined to this cramped existence. 'But now she began to transfer to herself a portion of the sympathy she had so long bestowed on Evelina. She had at last recognised her right to set up some lost opportunities of her own; and once that dangerous precedent was established, they began to crowd upon her memory.'

The clock breaks down. Ann Eliza is elated at the prospect of seeing Herman Ramy again. However, while she is ministering to an invalid neighbour, Evelina goes instead of her to the shop. To her dismay, she sees that Evelina is interested in Ramy too. Before long he is visiting them regularly. When a neighbour suggests that wedding bells will ring soon for her younger sister, Ann Eliza is alarmed at her own reactions:

Evelina's cheeks were pink, and her blue eyes glittered; but it seemed to Ann Eliza that the coquettish tilt of her head regrettably emphasised the weakness of her receding chin. It was the first time that Ann Eliza had ever seen a flaw in her sister's beauty, and her involuntary criticism startled her like a secret disloyalty.

Evelina is insensitively unaware of her elder sister's emotions. Typically at her evening prayers, Ann Eliza wonders how she could ever have thought that Ramy could be interested in her: 'Grief held up its torch to the frail fabric of Ann Eliza's illusions, and with a firm heart she watched them shrivel into ashes; then, rising from her knees full of the chill joy of renunciation, she laid a kiss on the crimping pins of the sleeping Evelina and crept under the bedspread at her side.'

To her amazement, when Herman Ramy does propose, it is to her, and not to Evelina. She renounces this glimmer of hope of future happiness to stay with Evelina, but she is sustained in doing so by indulging in a sense of the grandeur of renunciation.

She knew the crucial moment in her life had passed, and she was glad she had not fallen below her own ideals. It had been a wonderful experience, full of undreamed-of fear and fascination; and in spite of the tears on her cheeks she was not sorry to have known it. Two facts, however, took the edge from its perfection: that it had happened in the shop, and that she had not had on black silk. She passed the next hour in a state of dream ecstasy. Something had entered into her life of which no subsequent impoverishment would rob it.

But she is wrong. The world's impoverishments can destroy such romanticism all too easily. Ann Eliza's love for her sister, however, has never been just this, and in the destruction of her indulgence, the deeper love is tested. To her dismay, Ann Eliza notices that Ramy is paying more and more attention to her sister. When their engagement is announced, she tries to warn Evelina against the obvious self-interest she observes in Ramy's proposal. The advice is cruelly rejected. Ann Eliza's genuine love for her sister enables her to feel glad for her when she marries Ramy. At least, she hopes, she will still be able to look after her. But this is denied her when the newly-weds announce their departure for St Louis where, it is said, better opportunities await them. Her love for Evelina is sorely tested. She feels like a mother towards her.

Well, this was what happened to mothers. They bore it, Ann
Eliza mused; so why not she? Ah, but they had their own chance
first, she had had no chance at all. And now this life which she
had made her own was going from her forever; had gone,
already, in the inner and deeper sense, and was soon to vanish
in even its outward nearness, its surface-communion of voice
and eye. At that moment even the thought of Evelina's happiness refused her its consolatory ray; or its light, if she saw it,
was too remote to warn her. The thirst for a personal and
inalienable tie, for pangs and problems of her own, was parch-
ing Ann Eliza's soul: it seemed to her that she could never again
gather strength to look her loneliness in the face.

But gather strength she does, even to the extent of giving her
own savings to help finance the departure she dreads. After the
departure, the business declines rapidly, and Ann Eliza has to
endure great hardship. Evelina's letters soon stop and Ann Eliza
loses all contact with her. Her worries for her sister's safety grow
as time goes by. On hearing that Ramy has been discharged from
his job she tries, unsuccessfully, to find her sister. The effort
exhausts her and she becomes ill. A neighbour looks after her: 'As
far as she could remember, it was the first time in her life that she
had been taken care of instead of taking care, and there was a
momentary relief in the surrender.'
Ann Eliza's worries for her sister increase when she discovers
that Ramy lost his job because of an addiction to opium. When,
suddenly, Evelina does return, she says that she has been to hell
and back. She had lost her baby, been abused and deserted for
another woman. She half-condemns Ann Eliza for introducing her
to Ramy in the first place. She is critical of the decline in the
business and in their home. Insensitive, as always, to what Ann
Eliza has gone through, Evelina says, 'You don't know what life's
like — you don't know anything about it — setting here safe all
the while in this peaceful place.'
It is not this rebuke, however, which undermines Ann Eliza's
faith, but, rather, the plight of the sister she loves. 'She felt she
could no longer trust in the goodness of God, and that if he was
not good he was not God, and there was only a black abyss above
the roof of Bunner Sisters.'
When Evelina says she is dispirited, Ann Eliza finds that she
cannot rebuke her, religiously, as she would have in the past.

Evelina has come home to die, but, even during her terminal illness, Ann Eliza is denied the close relationship with her she longs for so much. To her horror, she discovers that Evelina has become a Catholic. She feels cut off from her. The priest who visits Evelina tells her that she will see her baby again, thus bringing her a comfort Ann Eliza cannot provide. 'The funeral took place three days later. Evelina was buried in Calvary Cemetery, the priest assuming the whole care of the necessary arrangements, while Ann Eliza, a passive spectator, beheld with stony indifference this last negation of her past.'

No doubt, strong arguments can be advanced to show that Ann Eliza spoiled Evelina; that her early sacrifices did more harm than good; that Ann Eliza had a perfect right to a life of her own and lacked a proper self-respect. Yet, given all these limitations, within them, surely, a rare self-sacrificial love is found, a love of such a kind that one reader, at least, would feel he had no right to judge Ann Eliza — no right at all.

In *The Age of Innocence*, as in *Bunner Sisters*, Edith Wharton explores the phenomenon of a buried life. In both cases, critics cry 'A buried life is a wasted one'. The big difference between the works, is that Newland Archer and Countess Olenska are *sustained* by the notion of a buried life, whereas Ann Eliza's faith is undermined. What undermines it? Not the absence of the world's rewards — that goes without saying. Not the absence of moral recognition which agitated Twain — that goes without saying too. No, what undermines it is something deeper:

> Self-effacement for the good of others had always seemed to her both natural and necessary, but then she had taken it for granted that it implied the securing of that good. Now she perceived that to refuse the gifts of life does not assure their transmission to those for whom they have been surrendered; and her familiar heaven was unpeopled.

For Ann Eliza, God should see to it, somehow or other, that the fruits of self-sacrifice are guaranteed transmission to their intended beneficiary. But what if Christianity means what it says — that God *is* love; no more, and no less? Then that love has no power external to itself to guarantee its success. The securing of the good which Ann Eliza seeks is in the hands of love, in the hands of God, but love always involves the possibility of its rejection. When its fruits are tasted, believers, no doubt, rejoice. But these fruits are not guaranteed. There is a fellowship of suffering as well as of joy, and the one who is said to be able to save, was also a man of sorrows, and acquainted with grief. It is to the worship of a God such as this that Christians are called — called to be displaced persons.

Notes

1. Mark Twain, 'Something about Repentance', in *Letters from the Earth* (Perennial Library, Harper & Row, 1962), p. 135.
2. Ibid.
3. Ibid,, pp. 135–6.
4. Ibid., p. 136.
5. Simone Weil, 'Concerning the "Our Father" ' in *Waiting on God* (Fontana, 1959), p. 173.
6. Marilyn French, Introduction in Edith Wharton, *Madame de Treymes* (Virago, 1984), p. viii.
7. Ibid., p. xiv.
8. All quotations from Edith Wharton's *Bunner Sisters* in *Madame de Treymes*.
9. Op. cit., p. xiv.

19

Beyond the Call of Duty

At the end of the previous essay, I spoke of a Christianity which sometimes involves 'a fellowship of suffering'. But what a dangerous phrase that is! Whenever one writes of it, however haltingly, one must ask oneself whether one has the right to do so. Also, in the previous essay, we saw that Christian love has no power to guarantee the realisation of its fruits. We saw the implications of this fact for Edith Wharton's character Ann Eliza. But the truth has to stand the test of far more than fiction. It has to stand the test of facts, no matter how terrible those facts may be. The test must be passed without deception, and without any falsification of the facts in question. Many have thought this to be impossible. In our century, this is certainly not surprising in view of what the century has witnessed — the horrors of the Holocaust. Given such testimony of human suffering, is it possible to talk of God's absolute goodness and love? That is the question I shall discuss in this chapter.

Suddenly, in 1942, all foreign Jews were expelled from the little town of Sighet in Transylvania. Among those witnessing the expulsion was a young 12-year-old boy, called Elie Wiesel. He was particularly saddened by the departure of Moché the Beadle, who was instructing him in the teachings of the cabbala. After a few days, however, the natural anxieties of the Jewish community were eased. They were told that the deportees had arrived in Galicia, were working there, and were satisfied with their lot. Life at Sighet returned to normal. Several months went by. Then Moché the Beadle reappeared in their midst:

He told his story and that of his companions. The train full of deportees had crossed the Hungarian frontier and on Polish territory had been taken in charge by the Gestapo. There it had stopped. The Jews had to get out and climb into lorries. The lorries drove toward a forest. The Jews were made to get out. They were made to dig huge graves. And when they had finished their work, the Gestapo began theirs. Without passion, without haste, they slaughtered their prisoners. Each one had to go up to the hole and present his neck. Babies were thrown into the air and the machine gunners used them as targets. This was in the forest of Galicia, near Kolomaye. How had Moché the Beadle escaped? Miraculously. He was wounded in the leg and taken for dead . . .

Through long days and nights, he went from one Jewish house to another, telling the story of Malka, the young girl who had taken three days to die, and of Tobias, the tailor, who had begged to be killed before his sons . . . [1]

We all know now, of course, that this is an account of an atrocity perpetrated during the Nazi Holocaust. But what was the reaction of the Jews of Sighet?

People refused not only to believe his stories, but even to listen to them.
    'He's just trying to make us pity him. What an imagination he has!' they said. Or even: 'Poor fellow. He's gone mad.'

Elie Wiesel, one of the most distinguished novelists and historians of the Holocaust, has been telling these stories ever since. Why did the Jews of Sighet refuse to believe what they heard, a refusal which prevented them from escaping from the terrible fate that awaited them? Strangely enough, much of the answer resides in the fact that the terrible story they were told was beyond the call of duty. When we say that actions are beyond the call of duty, we usually refer to actions which achieve more than duty demands. We think of saints and heroes. But the Holocaust is beyond the call of duty in a very different sense. The absolute evil of it seems dumb to duty's call; it seems to be beyond its reach. We know what our duties are, and we know the lame excuses we often provide when we do not fulfil them. When the call of duty is unheeded, we have a range of words by which we can condemn the omission such as ungrateful, unkind, mean, spiteful, disregarding. In this sense, both praise and condemnation fall within the call of duty; within the exercise of our normal moral vocabulary. Had Moché the Beadle spoken of similar immoral deeds, the Jews of Sighet would have believed him. But this! It was unthinkable, unimaginable; only a madman could suggest such things. Because he told a story so monstrous, that it fell outside the normality of immorality, the story told by Moché the Beadle fell outside the bounds of the believable at the same time. And so the response was not condemnation and horror, but pity; pity for Moché the Beadle who, it seemed, had gone mad!

But that is not all. By 1942, the facts about Auschwitz were known in London, Stockholm, Switzerland and America. But the Jews in Hungary were not told. 'In March-April 1944 we still believed that Auschwitz is the name of a peaceful railway station somewhere in Poland. We never could have imagined that hundreds and thousands of men and women and children could be massacred and reduced to ash and the world would keep silent. We couldn't have believed it.' Some people have asked why the Jews went so passively to their destination; why they didn't fight or resist. Wiesel responds: 'Who are those who ask these questions? How do they dare, really? I don't. When I think of these people, abandoned, betrayed, forgotten, forlorn, deceived, who am I to judge them? Who am I to question their motivation? What does that mean; resist? How could they resist? With what?'[2]

Absolute evil beyond the call of duty, who could be expected to believe it? Absolute evil, having become known to some, is not proclaimed. Who could believe that? But this incredulity was not simply a Jewish phenomenon. It was a far more pervasive twentieth-century characteristic. Surely, at this stage of man's development, progress, rather than absolute evil, was the dominant thought. After all, in 1944, the Jews of Sighet had every reason to be heartened by news from the Russian front. Victory was certain; it was simply a matter of time. Time was running out for Hitler:

> People said: 'The Russian army's making gigantic strides forward . . . Hitler won't be able to do us any harm, even if he wants to.'
>
> Yes, we even doubted that he wanted to exterminate us.
>
> Was he going to wipe out a whole people? Could he exterminate a population scattered throughout so many countries? So many millions? What methods could he use? And in the middle of the twentieth century!

François Mauriac, the French novelist, recalling the Occupation, tells of his reaction when his wife told him of the trainloads of Jewish children at Austerlitz station:

At that time we knew nothing of Nazi methods of extermination. And who could have imagined them! Yet the way these lambs had been torn from their mothers in itself exceeded anything we had so far thought possible. I believe on that day I touched for the first time upon the mystery of iniquity whose revelation was to mark the end of one era and the beginning of another. The dream which Western man conceived in the eighteenth century, whose dawn he thought he saw in 1789, and which, until August 2, 1914, had grown stronger with the progress of enlightenment and the discoveries of science — this dream vanished finally for me before those trainloads of little children. And yet I was still thousands of miles away from thinking that they were to be fuel for the gas chamber and the crematory.[3]

In his stories, this is what Elie Wiesel proclaims again and again: not the possibility, but the actuality of absolute evil in the Holocaust; an evil beyond the call of duty. In his early work, *Night*, from which we have been quoting, Wiesel depicts the fate of the Jews of Sighet in their journey from one concentration camp to another. He shows that, in being subjected to an evil beyond the call of duty, many Jews found that the ordinary duties they would not have questioned in normal circumstances, no longer had a hold on them. They found themselves, through affliction, at a degraded place beyond the call of these duties.

In the long march from Buna to Buchenwald, Wiesel watches men die without appealing for help, without fuss, in the snow. Sons leave their fathers' bodies without tears. Rabbi Eliahou searches desperately for his son from whom he has been separated on the road. Wiesel has seen the old man limping, and his young son go ahead of him. A terrible thought crossed his mind: the son, believing the end was near, had wanted to lose his father, to increase his own chances of survival:

> And, in spite of myself, a prayer rose in my heart, to that God in whom I no longer believed.
> My God, Lord of the Universe, give me strength never to do what Rabbi Eliahou's son has done.'

They break their journey in a barracks where they are kept for three days without food. The weak are selected and shot. They continue the journey to Buchenwald by train, packed into cattle wagons. When the train stops, the dead are thrown out to be left, unburied, in the snow. The living rejoice. When the train stops near some German workmen, they throw pieces of bread into the wagons, watching the living skeletons fight over them. Some of the bread comes into Wiesel's wagon. He sees an old man manage to get some, only to be attacked by a younger man:

> Felled to the ground, stunned with blows, the old man cried: 'Meir. Meir, my boy! Don't you recognise me? I'm your father . . . you're hurting me . . . you're killing your father! I've got some bread . . . for you too . . . for you too . . .'
> He collapsed. His fist was still clenched around a small piece. He tried to carry it to his mouth. But the other one threw himself upon him and snatched it. The old man again whispered something, let out a rattle, and died amid the general indifference. His son searched him, took the bread, and began to devour it. He was not able to get very far. Two men had seen and hurled themselves upon him. Others joined in. When they withdrew, next to me there were two corpses, side by side, the father and the son.
> I was fifteen years old.

Of the hundred in Wiesel's wagon, 12 survived the journey to Buchenwald, including his father and himself. His father's health declines rapidly. He is ashamed at his own reluctance to give him his soup ration. His father's neighbours in the dormitory hit him because, although he has dysentry, he is too weak to get out of bed to relieve himself. Wiesel is given unequivocal advice by the head of the camp; advice which negated, asked him to place himself beyond, all the duties he had been instructed in as a child:

> Listen to me, boy. Don't forget that you're in a concentration camp. Here, every man has to fight for himself and not think of anyone else. Even of his father. Here, there are no fathers, no brothers, no friends. Everyone lives and dies for himself alone. I'll give you a sound piece of advice — don't give your ration of bread and soup to your old father. There's nothing you can do for him. And you're killing yourself. Instead, you ought to be having his ration.

His father's cries, in his delirious state, annoy an SS officer who beats him. The young boy hears his father cry out for him, but he does not move, fearing the blows. When he goes to bed that night, his father is still alive.

> I awoke on January 29 at dawn. In my father's place lay another invalid. They must have taken him away before dawn and carried him to the crematory. He may still have been breathing.
>
> There were no prayers at his grave. No candles were lit to his memory. His last word was my name. A summons, to which I did not respond.
>
> I did not weep and it pained me that I could not weep. But I had no more tears. And, in the depths of my being, in the recesses of my weakened conscience, could I have searched it, I might perhaps have found something like — free at last!

The survivors at Buchenwald, Wiesel among them, were saved from extermination by a siren warning, and the decision of the resistance movement to act. In hospital, Wiesel is able to see himself in a mirror for the first time since the days of the ghetto in Sighet: 'From the depths of the mirror, a corpse gazed back at me.

The look in his eyes, as they stared into mine, has never left me.'

As one might expect, the behaviour of people in concentration camps varied considerably. There were responses which evoke awe and wonder in those who hear of them. These are not the responses recorded in *Night*. Wiesel testifies to the effect of extreme affliction on people's ordinary moral sensibilities; to the way they became alienated from them. The reader is moved to profound pity. He wishes to pass no judgement. It would be perverse of him to do so. If he made a judgement, he, too, would be judged. Wiesel forces us to remember the absolute evil that occurred, and the illusory conviction that such things can never happen.

The contact with absolute evil has another effect on Wiesel: it puts faith in God beyond him:

> Never shall I forget that night, the first night in camp, which has turned my life into one long night, seven times cursed and seven times sealed. Never shall I forget that smoke. Never shall

I forget the little faces of the children, whose bodies I saw turned into wreaths of smoke beneath a silent blue sky.

Never shall I forget those flames which consumed my faith forever.

Never shall I forget that nocturnal silence which deprived me, from all eternity, of the desire to live. Never shall I forget those moments which murdered my God and my soul and turned my dreams to dust. Never shall I forget these things, even if I am condemned to live as long as God Himself. Never.

He witnesses the hanging of a young child at Buna.

The SS seemed more preoccupied, more disturbed than usual. To hang a young boy in front of thousands of spectators was no light matter. The head of the camp read the verdict. All eyes were on the child. He was lividly pale, almost calm, biting his lips. The gallows threw its shadows over him.

This time the Lagerkapo refused to act as executioner. Three SS replaced him.

The three victims mounted together onto the chairs.

The three necks were placed at the same moment within the nooses.

'Long live liberty!' cried the two adults.

But the child was silent.

'Where is God? Where is He?' someone behind me asked.

At a sign from the head of the camp, the three chairs tipped over.

Total silence throughout the camp. On the horizon, the sun was setting.

'Bare your heads!' yelled the head of the camp. His voice was raucous. We were weeping.

'Cover your heads!'

Then the march past began. The two adults were no longer alive. Their tongues hung swollen, blue-tinged. But the third rope was still moving; being so light, the child was still alive . . .

For more than half an hour he stayed there, struggling between life and death, dying in slow agony under our eyes. And we had to look him full in the face. He was still alive when I passed in front of him. His tongue was still red, his eyes were not yet glazed.

Behind me, I heard the same man asking:

'Where is God now?'

And I heard a voice within me answer him:

'Where is He? Here He is — He is hanging on this gallows . . .'

That night the soup tasted of corpses.

As a result of contact with such affliction, as a result of witnessing absolute evil, many lose their faith in God, and many did not. Again, would any believer want to pass judgement? Again, were he to do so, would not he, himself, be judged?

Our concern is rather different. Faced by the Holocaust Wiesel does more than note that many did lose their faith. He also suggests, in *Night*, at least, that faith, because of its nature, *must* be lost in such circumstances. True, in other works, he carries on conversations with God. This is partly because he cannot imagine the Jewish people without such questioning conversations. It is also because the alternative to faith, an optimistic, humanistic ethic, is rendered even less plausible by the Holocaust.

What kind of God is murdered by the Holocaust, for Wiesel? A God who has elected the Jewish people to prosper; who has promised to deliver them from harm. The only one, Wiesel says, who kept his promises to the Jews, was Hitler! He will not compromise one jot on the recognition of absolute evil in the Holocaust. In this, he is perfectly right. He is perfectly right, too, in rejecting attempts to explain this absolute evil in terms other than itself. He does not want it familiarised by our explanatory devices, psychological, psychoanalytic, sociological or economic. He wants to confront the mystery of evil and keep intact the only appropriate response: not understanding, but horror.

A kind of religion offers its explanations too; explanations which Wiesel rejects, quite rightly, along with the others. Theodicies are supposed to explain God's ways to men; to show how evil is the means to a higher good and, therefore, not so evil as might have been thought at first. These vulgarities, unfortunately, are still all too evident in theology and the philosophy of religion. Similar strategies abound. 'There are explanations of absolute evil', we are told, 'but only God understands them. Accept the Holocaust on trust!' But if there *is* a justifying explanation of it, that would make it all the more monstrous. During the Holocaust, some said that God was testing his people's love! The very thought is incredible. An averagely decent father would not even contem-

plate such a demonic experiment. Wiesel rejects all these explanations. But with their departure, all possibility of religious faith
seems to depart as well. He will not contemplate any talk of the
Holocaust as a triumph of faith.

> No. I think the word 'triumph', unfortunately does not apply
> to anything relevant to the Holocaust. There was no triumph. I
> think Man was defeated there. The Jew in some way came out
> in a better way, because he is used to suffering and because of
> historic situations that he has known. It happened that he was
> not the executioner, but the victim. And in those times it was
> better to be victim than executioner. But no one triumphed. It
> was triumph for nobody — for man or for God either. Therefore
> we have this strange, strange feeling of helplessness . . . But
> something went wrong with creation. Maybe the angel of Death,
> to use a cabbalistic expression, substituted himself for God
> then.[4]

No doubt 'triumph' is the wrong word, but it does not follow
that no one could want to speak of God as present even in situations such as this. To witness absolute evil, and to see it as such,
is to feel at the same time that an absolute good is being outraged,
desecrated. Wiesel says that in the Holocaust it was better to
be victim than executioner. That conviction is found down the
centuries. Socrates said it was better to suffer wrong than to do
wrong. The absolute good does not triumph when violated by
absolute wrong: it suffers. It can offer no explanation, no end to
which the evil is a means. On such matters, it is dumb; it simply
is what it is in its suffering. For the religious believers I have in
mind, God and absolute good are one. If absolute good can suffer,
so can God. In Christianity, there is a suffering God; a God who
can be crucified. But we do not have to look outside the Jewish
Faith to find a belief that the divine is present in suffering. The
presence of the divine does not explain away the suffering, or
justify it, in any way. The divine itself suffers. When Isaiah speaks
of this suffering, who can resist hearing, after reading the eloquent
testimony of Elie Wiesel, echoes of those reactions to the Holocaust
that continue to haunt him?

> Who hath believed our report? and to whom is the arm of the
> Lord revealed?

For he shall grow up before him as a tender plant, and as a root out of a dry ground: he hath no form nor comeliness; and when we shall see him, there is no beauty that we should desire him.

He is despised and rejected of men; a man of sorrows, and acquainted with grief: and we hid as it were our faces from him; he was despised, and we esteemed him not.

Surely he hath borne our griefs, and carried our sorrows: yet we did esteem him stricken, smitten of God, and afflicted.

But he was wounded for our transgressions, he was bruised for our iniquities: the chastisement of our peace was upon him; and with his stripes we are healed.

All we like sheep have gone astray; we have turned every one to his own way; and the Lord hath laid on him the iniquity of us all.

He was oppressed, and he was afflicted, yet he opened not his mouth: he is brought as a lamb to the slaughter, and as a sheep before her shearers is dumb, so he opened not his mouth.

He was taken from prison and from judgement: and who shall declare his generation? for he was cut off out of the land of the living: for the transgressions of my people was he stricken . . .

Therefore will I divide him a portion with the great, and he shall divide the spoil with the strong; because he hath poured out his soul unto death; and he was numbered with the transgressors; and he bare the sin of many, and made intercession for the transgressors.

Like the stories Elie Wiesel insists shall be told, stories so strange that, at first, no one believed their report, here, too, is a strange story — a story of a suffering servant, a suffering God. There are some who believe it.

Notes

1. All quotations from Elie Wiesel's *Night* in *Night, Dawn, The Accident* (Robson Books, 1974).
2. Elie Wiesel, 'What is a Jew?', interview of Elie Wiesel by Harry James Cargas in Harry James Cargas, (ed.), *Responses to Elie Wiesel* (Persea Books, 1978), p. 153.
3. François Mauriac, 'Foreword' in *Night, Dawn, The Accident*, pp. 7–8.
4. 'What is a Jew?', p. 154.

New York Notebook.

P242 Feeling of absence of God - affliction - Darkness is care - Totality of all that is formerly thought of god

Divineness inside care - affliction soul of man - presence of god is a ... removing he presence it. Sin being the

God given a faculty - Joy is the soul. Mystical Truth is one.

Refs & Vob 25th, 256. Suffering vost Man. 260. Faith and it is believing that God is Love / Reality is Love and nothing else. Embrace Christ in space (Non neumatical) only this way does love be... impotent.

263 when a man 80s not consent to obey God. Then there is no spirit in him.

Sea Time. 264 Pray for Spiritual Death - Christ living in him.

N.B. Parable of Kternal Now - Payment is God. He is without degree

268. There ought to be an appropriate and special parable & Link with God every activity in...

Life & every sense on Jain. For everything in life the right & be a prison? G8 a prison.

Every worldly activity - meaning in when God created it?

269. A conviction can become a fact by a miracle. - With God. all things are possible meaning...

story of Christ - point of no return. Service 271. Negative or positive of is the - Supernatural virtues

be imposed for a certain time.

1 Kings XIX - the Lord was not in the fire, and after the fire a still small voice.

About a story. The Nightingale - the Holy Spirit. Saviour, luck? & a temple in heart?

In having a Folk tale we live at once... through everything that is expressed that is the spiritual domain & which... State reflex. - Approach & Effect of the word is by...

3 Asc in states - idiot - naive - philosopher of the Theatre - has... Can be represented in the soul as in the universe. Fire and authentic God to completely exist

Uply revere - if I remember by some God & a human being.

The thought of fear gives a color of eternity & the events of life. - Detachment makes it possible to

P 199.

Sanctity is the only way out from time. Very fixes us to eternity 205. Virtue is not why or wherefore. Her reason is beyond you. Ask no more but apply yourself to haul[?]ing your infinity 206. There who have arrived at the absolute express themselves only by identities — the good is the good. list.

To be detached from the fruits of action — soul needs an architectonic depth.

P 208. The purpose... We is to conduct a meditative to the soul.

(i.e. not one Dimensional. p 209.)

20

Revealing the Hidden

As we have already seen in previous essays, many critics of religion have often wondered how, with all the evil in the world, people can believe in a loving God. Some philosophers have gone so far as to say that the presence of evil makes belief in such a God unintelligible.

Yet, when critics speak in this way, they often seem not to realise that the difficulties they mention are not unknown to believers. So far from being unknown, many religious believers have faced these very same difficulties, and worked through them in their relationship to God. Some find they can believe untroubled by doubts. But, for others, struggle is part of their faith.

Among these others, is the Welsh poet-priest, R. S. Thomas. In his work, we find an impressive struggle to mediate religious sense in verse. Born in 1913, ordained in the Church in Wales in 1937, R. S. Thomas found difficulties awaiting him when he took up his first country living in Manafon in mid-Wales in 1942: 'I was brought up hard against this community and I really began to learn what human nature, rural human nature was like. And I must say that I found nothing that I'd been told in theological college was of any help at all in these circumstances.'[1]

The difficulties the priest has to face are centred on the peasant figure, Iago Prytherch and his life of unrelenting toil. If the Gospel of Jesus Christ is to speak, it ought to be able to speak to Iago Prytherch:

A Peasant
Iago Prytherch his name, though, be it allowed,
Just an ordinary man of the bald Welsh hills,
Who pens a few sheep in a gap of cloud.
Docking mangels, chipping the green skin
From the yellow bones with a half-witted grin
Of satisfaction, or churning the crude earth
To a stiff sea of clods that glint in the wind —

So are his days spent, his spittled mirth
Rarer than the sun that cracks the cheeks
Of the gaunt sky perhaps once in a week.
And then at night see him fixed in his chair
Motionless, except when he leans to gob in the fire.
There is something frightening in the vacancy of his mind.
His clothes, sour of years of sweat
And animal contact, shock the refined,
But affected, sense with their stark naturalness.
Yet this is your prototype, who, season by season
Against siege of rain and the wind's attrition,
Preserves his stock, an impregnable fortress
Not to be stormed even in death's confusion.
Remember him, then, for he, too, is a winner of wars,
Enduring like a tree under the curious stars.[2]

A Peasant is, justifiably, one of R. S. Thomas' best known poems.
It is full of tension, of mood and counter-mood. At first we may
think that the poet is belabouring the peasant. He speaks of 'the
vacancy of his mind'. Yet, this is not meant to contrast unflatter-
ingly with superior intellectuals. Not at all. True, the peasant
shocks the refined intellectuals, but their sense is described as
affected. And the peasant is described as 'an impregnable fortress',
who is not to be stormed, even by death which confuses so many.
Could as much be said of the intellectuals? The poet asks us to
remember the peasant, for he, too, is 'a winner of wars'. He
'endures like a tree', and yet, he endures under curious stars. The
stars, the heavens, which, for the psalmist, declared the glory of
God, are curious about Iago Prytherch. What sense is to be made
of his unrelenting toil? Endurance for endurance's sake; a refusal
to be broken — that's understandable enough. But what God can
break in on this world? How can the Gospel speak to it? In the
poem *Soil*, the poet gives us a picture of the peasant's world:

A field with tall hedges and a young
Moon in the branches and one star
Declining westward set the scene
Where he works slowly astride the rows
Of red mangolds and green swedes
Plying mechanically his cold blade.

This is his world, the hedge defines
The mind's limits; only the sky
Is boundless, and he never looks up;
His gaze is deep in the dark soil,
As are his feet. The soil is all;
His hands fondle it, and his bones
Are formed out of it with the swedes.
And if sometimes the knife errs,
Burying itself in his shocked flesh,
Then out of the wound the blood seeps home
To the warm soil from which it came.[3]

If the hedge defines the mind's limits, how does that mind find a place for God? The boundless sky might tell of God, but, hedged in as he is, he never looks up. The whole movement of the poem is a downward one, down to the soil. How, then, can there be an ascent to God? Or how can a God come down to this world?

And so the poet is confronted by the peasant. There are moods when the poet is irritated by him, by his stubbornness and slowness, his indifference to learning. And yet, he comes back to him again and again — he cannot turn away from the peasant's challenge. In *A Priest to his People*, the poet makes this plain:

I have taxed your ignorance of rhyme and sonnet,
Your want of deference to the printer's skill,
But I know, as I listen, that your speech has in it
The source of all poetry, clear as a rill
Bubbling from your lips; and what brushwork could equal
The artistry of your dwelling on the bare hill?
You will forgive, then, my initial hatred,
My first intolerance of your uncouth ways,
You who are indifferent to all that I can offer,
Caring not whether I blame or praise,
With your pigs and your sheep and your sons
                              and holly-cheeked daughters
You will still continue to unwind your days
In a crude tapestry under the jealous heavens
To affront, bewilder, yet compel my gaze.[4]

The peasants compel the poet's gaze. They exact from him, as they should from any religious believer, a fundamental respect.

But this respect for sheer endurance constitutes a threat to religion, for what if endurance is sufficient; what if endurance is all? R. S. Thomas is fully aware of the threat:

> Well, I came out of a kind of bourgeois environment which, especially in modern times, is protected; it's cushioned from some of the harsher realities; and this muck and blood and hardness, the rain and the spittle and the phlegm of farm life was, of course, a shock to begin with and one felt that this was something not quite part of the order of things. But, as one experienced it and saw how definitely part of their lives this was, sympathy grew in oneself and compassion and admiration; and since you've got in these communities people who've probably been like this over the centuries, the very fact that they endure at all – that they make a go of it at all – suggests that they have got some hard core within them. One has to face this as a priest, this sort of attack, as it were, from their side.[5]

But how does he face it as a priest? Not by any simplistic answers. He knows there is no instant uplift, no short-cuts to salvation.

> *Flat* Yesterday a sinner
> today fetching my soul
> from the divine laundry
> to wear it in the march past
> tomorrow of the multitude
> of white robes no man
> can number?
> Too simple.
> There are girls, reversions,
> the purse's incontinence.
> Truth has its off-days,
> too . . .[6]

R. S. Thomas not only rejects instant salvation. He also rejects tired theodicies which try to justify God's way to men; theodicies which try to argue that every evil is the means to some higher good. If God's nature is to be determined by some kind of report on how decent people fare in the world, R. S. Thomas is in little doubt about the kind of God who will emerge.

The Island   And God said, I will build a church here
              And cause this people to worship me,
              And afflict them with poverty and sickness
              In return for centuries of hard work
              And patience. And its walls shall be hard as
              Their hearts, and its windows let in the light
              Grudgingly, as their minds do, and the priest's
              words be drowned
              By the wind's caterwauling. All this I will do,
              Said God, and watch the bitterness in their eyes
              Grow, and their lips suppurate with
              Their prayers. And their women shall bring forth
              On my altars, and I will choose the best
              Of them to be thrown back into the sea.
              And that was only on one island.[7]

Such a God would be the poet's Devil. If this is the god who is to break through, R. S. Thomas would reject him. But where does this leave him, faced, as he is, with the undeniable fact of human suffering? The poet-priest has to admit that he feels speechless; feels that God is hidden from him. This is how he feels as he comes out into the darkness after visiting a seriously ill pensioner, *Evans*.

       It was not the dark filling my eyes
       And mouth that appalled me; not even the drip
       Of rain like blood from the one tree
       Weather-tortured. It was the dark
       Silting the veins of that sick man
       I left stranded upon the vast
       And lonely shore of his bleak bed.[8]

Many philosophers, if they were listening to all this would say, 'But, of course, this is no more than you should expect. Of course the sense of religion is hidden. That's because God is hidden. We have no proof of his existence; no verification, even in principle, of it. Until God's existence can be verified, of course the sense of religion is hidden — it is indeed a mystery to reason and common-sense.' Are these philosophers right? Should the believer be expected to produce his God? The philosophers' demand is ironic, because anything that the believer could produce would not be

God. God is not a being among beings; not an additional fact to
those facts already known. God is not hidden, in this sense, and
therefore could not be produced either, as a magician produces a
rabbit out of his hat. R. S. Thomas in the poem, *Somewhere*, gently
mocks these philosophical requests for verification:

> Something to bring back to show
> you have been there: a lock of God's
> hair, stolen from him while he was
> asleep; a photograph of the garden
> of the spirit[9]

And in the poem, *Waiting*, he exposes the confusions involved in
such expectations:

> Face to face? Ah, no
> God; such language falsifies
> the relation. Nor side by side,
> nor near you, nor anywhere
> in time and space.[10]

And, yet, in his poetry, R. S. Thomas does celebrate a genuinely
religious sense of a hidden God, a Deus absconditus. How does
this belief in a hidden God express itself in his poetry? How does
it reveal a hidden God? Or, better, how does one reveal the
hidden?

The prophet Isaiah tells us, 'Vere tu es Deus absconditus —
Verily thou art a hidden God'. Often, when we speak of revealing
the hidden, once the hidden has been revealed, then, it is no
longer hidden. The hidden solution of a puzzle, once revealed, is
no longer hidden. The hidden answer to a detective mystery, once
revealed, is no longer hidden. The hidden figure behind the bush,
or the hidden snake entwined in it, once revealed is no longer
hidden. The unconscious motive, the implicit pattern, once
revealed, is no longer hidden. Is that what Isaiah meant when he
said, Verily, thou art a hidden God? Is that the kind of hidden
God in R. S. Thomas' poetry? No, in these religious contexts,
when we come to accept a revelation of the hidden God, what is
revealed is revealed *as hidden*. The hiddenness is part of what we
mean by God. The French philosopher Simone Weil said, 'God
decided to hide himself so that we might have an idea of what he

is like'.[11] I think R. S. Thomas, after a long journey in verse, comes to the meaning of these words. This is not to say that doubts and struggles do not recur — they do. But there is also this revelation in verse of the sense of waiting on a hidden God.

In 1976 R. S. Thomas delivered the annual literature lecture in the National Eisteddfod at Cardigan. His title was *Abercuawg*. The lecture began as follows:

Where is Abercuawg? I'm not certain that this is the right way of asking the question. I'm half afraid that the answer to that is that it does not exist at all. And as a Welshman I do not see any meaning in my life if there is no such place as Abercuawg, a town or village where the cuckoos sing . . . The fact that we travel to the locality of Machynlleth to search for the location of Abercuawg and say, 'No, that is not it', means nothing. This is not an occasion for disappointment and hopelessness, but a way of getting to know better, through its absence, the nature of the place we are looking for.[12]

Abercuawg cannot be another place alongside all the other places. It gives a sense to all places through not being identified with any one of them. God, like Abercuawg, comes into the believer's world as the sense which the givenness of things has for him. In relation to the natural world, that sense is given in a love of its beauty, a love which, Simone Weil says, is an implicit form of the love of God. Grace in nature is more than natural grace.

But how is this love of the beauty of the world to include acceptance of its harshness? There seems to be no correlation between loving God and the course of the lives of those who worship him. This being so, there seems to be an amoral arbitrariness in the divine will. Commenting on this arbitrariness, ironically, in *De Rerum Natura*, Lucretius pointed out that, in the end, it results in the irrelevance of the gods to human life. He demonstrates this irrelevance in asking why, according to the gods, they send thunderbolts to earth:

But if Jupiter and other gods shake the shining regions of heaven with appalling din, if they cast fire whither it may be the pleasure of each one, why do they not see to it that those who have not refrained from some abominable crime, shall be struck and breathe out sulphurous flames from breast pierced through, a sharp lesson to mankind? Why rather does one with no base guilt on his conscience roll in flames all innocent, suddenly involved in a tornado from heaven and taken off by fire? Why again do they aim at deserts and waste their labour? Or are they then practising their hands and strengthening their muscles? And why do they suffer the Father's bolt to be blunted against the earth? Why does he himself allow this, instead of saving it for his enemies? Why again does Jupiter never cast a bolt on the earth and send his thunder when the heaven is clear on all sides? Does he wait until clouds have come up, to descend into them himself, that he may be nearby to direct hence the blow of his bolt?[13]

That, then, is Lucretius' challenge: why doesn't Jupiter thunder from a clear sky? Horace, however, takes up this challenge. He confesses that he had thought in this way himself, but now has had reason to revise his views. He has come to see that Lucretius' question excludes certain religious possibilities:

> I, a chary and infrequent worshipper of the gods, what time I wandered, the votary of a foolish wisdom, am now compelled to spread my sails for the voyage back, and to retrace the course I had abandoned. For though it is the clouds that Jove is wont to cleave with his flashing bolts, this time he drove his thundering steeds and flying car through a sky serene — his steeds and car, whereby the lifeless earth and wandering streams were shaken . . .

What has led Horace to change his mind?

> . . . . Power the god does have. He can interchange the lowest and the highest: the mighty he abases and exalts the lowly. From one man Fortune with shrill whirring of her wings swiftly snatches away the crown; on another she delights to place it.[14]

Everything in the King's reign was sunny and serene, but, suddenly, he loses his crown — Jupiter thundered from a clear sky. Such possibilities can never be eradicated. We cannot imagine human life without them. They are the primary data out of which grows the conviction and confession that our lives are in the hands of the gods. To deny this is said to be hubris, the kind of hubris that led Oedipus to deny so vehemently that he *could* ever be cursed among men.[15]

There are similar conceptions in the Judaeo-Christian tradition. There, too, from an indifferent sky the rain falls on the just and the unjust. But from this very indifference comes the conception that we are creatures who are dependent on grace, having no claims against providence. The impartiality of the skies is beyond our 'Whys?' and 'Wherefores?'. Believers are purged of the idea that anything is theirs by right. The relentless change of the seasons which, for Larkin, showed nothing, here reveals that the self is not the centre of the world. Here is Thomas' expression of this religious conviction:

> Is there blessing? Light's peculiar grace
> In cold splendour robes this tortured place
> For strange marriage. Voices in the wind
> Weave a garland where a mortal sinned.
> Winter rots you; who is there to blame?
> The new grass shall purge you in its flame.[16]

Nature's contingencies, graces of nature, we might say, are seen as expressions of God's will. It is important, however, to note the way our beliefs are formed in such contexts. We do not *first* have an idea of God, abstractly defined, which we then try to reconcile to such contingencies as their explanation. Rather, it is in reacting to such contingencies that believers are led to speak of human life as being in the hands of the God.

Belief in a God of grace manifests itself, not only in the reactions of human beings to nature, but also in their reactions to each other. Peter was confident that he would never deny Christ. Whatever others might do, it was unthinkable that *he* would deny him. Yet, he denied any knowledge of him, not once, but three times. Jupiter, one might say, thundered from a clear sky. To get to the essence of Peter's denial, Simone Weil said we should re-examine its popular location. Peter did not deny Christ when he broke his promise, but when he made it. He thought of himself as self-sufficient and, in so doing, denied that he was a creature in need of grace. We think we can rely on a certain relationship, we think the worst is over, we think someone had everything to live for, and then Jupiter thunders from a clear sky.

Realising that we and others are creatures of grace is internally related to seeing others as God's creatures, as beings not to be made subject to our own designs. Offences against them are spiritual offences. That is why a man who says he loves God but hates his brother is called a liar. Believers are not told to love others in order to love God, but that God is loved *in* loving others.

God's love is his omnipotence. He has no other kind of omnipotence. That is why, in face of requests for certain kinds of help, the skies are indifferent, silent. Many philosophers and theologians have shouted their speculations into space, determined to explain providence in terms of their theodicies. Their answers, in a century which has witnessed the Holocaust, has brought religion into deserved disrepute. They have failed to see that the notion of God's will does not transcend, but is born of an appreciation of what is inexplicable in human life. In thinking otherwise, they have darkened sanctities with their theodicies. When we realise that theodicies attempt to provide reasons where none are to be found, we realise, too, that there are situations in which love and goodness are necessarily silent in face of atrocity. They do not compensate; they suffer. At the very heart of Christianity is a God who was crucified, whose silence before his executioners marks the parameters of Love's domain. This is what is realised by R. S. Thomas' priest:

> To one kneeling down no word came,
> Only the wind's song saddening the lips
> Of the grave saints, rigid in glass;
> Or the dry whisper of unseen wings,
> Bats not angels in the high roof.
>
> Was he balked by silence? He kneeled long,
> And saw love in a dark crown
> Of thorns blazing, and a winter tree,
> Golden with fruit of a man's body.[17]

Notes

1. 'R. S. Thomas: Priest and Poet', transcript of John Ormond's film for BBC television, broadcast on 2 April 1972, in *Poetry Wales*, Spring 1972, p. 49.

2. 'A Peasant' in R. S. Thomas, *Selected Poems 1946–1963* (Granada, 1983).
3. In *Selected Poems*.
4. In R. S. Thomas, *Song at the Year's Turning* (Rupert Hart-Davis, 1955).
5. In 'R. S. Thomas: Priest and Poet', p. 50.
6. In R. S. Thomas, *Between Here and Now*, (Macmillan, 1981).
7. In R. S. Thomas, *Later Poems 1972–1982* (Macmillan, 1983).
8. In *Selected Poems*.
9. In *Later Poems*.
10. In *Later Poems*.
11. Simone Weil, *Lectures on Philosophy*, tr. H. S. Price, introduction by Peter Winch (Cambridge University Press, 1978), pp. 171–2.
12. See 'Abercuawg' in Sandra Anstey (ed.), *R. S. Thomas Selected Prose*, introduction by Ned Thomas, (Poetry of Wales Press, 1983).
13. Lucretius, *De Rerum Natura*, Book VI, trans. W. H. D. Rouse (Loeb Classical Library, 1943), pp. 472–3.
14. Horace, *Odes*, Book I, Ode XXXIV, *The Poet's Conversion* in *The Odes and Epodes*, trans. C. E. Bennett (Loeb Classical Library, 1919), p. 91.
15. See D. Z. Phillips, 'What the Complex did to Oedipus' in *Through a Darkening Glass* (University of Notre Dame Press and Basil Blackwell, 1982).
16. In *Selected Poems*.
17. In *Selected Poems*.

21

A Realism of Distances

Ee-oo-ii! Eee-OO-ii!

That sound is the sound of peacocks as they begin to roost at evening time at Andalusia, which was the O'Connor family farm in Milledgeville, Georgia, and the home of the American short-story writer, novelist and essayist, Flannery O'Connor. She was born in Savannah, Georgia in 1925, but moved to Milledgeville when she was 12. She graduated in 1945 from Georgia State College for Women, now Georgia College, already knowing that what she wanted to do was to write. She went North to study at the University of Iowa's School for Writers, but, in 1951, was stricken with lupus, then an incurable disease. She returned to Milledgeville to live with her mother and died there, 13 years later, at the age of 39. In that short time, Flannery O'Connor's literary achievements were outstanding. As a result, we now have two novels, 31 short stories, and collections of her essays, letters and reviews. Regrettably, however, it must be said that her work is still not as well known as it might be on this side of the Atlantic.

In her essay on peacocks called 'The King of the Birds', Flannery O'Connor says of the peacocks' cry:

> He appears to receive through his feet some shock from the centre of the earth, which travels upward through him and is released: *Eee-roo-ii! Eee-oo-ii!* To the melancholy this sound is melancholy and to the hysterical it is hysterical. To me it has always sounded like a cheer from an invisible parade . . . at short intervals during the day and night, the cock, lowering its neck and throwing back its head, will give out with seven or eight screams in succession as if this message were the one on earth which needed most urgently to be heard.[1]

What is it in Flannery O'Connor's fiction that many find so arresting, and others recoil from as though they were being reminded of something they did not wish to know? Flannery

212

O'Connor wrote as a Catholic writer, and at the centre of her fiction is the conviction that this world is a place of exile and that, for the most part, man lives at a distance from his true home. Her task, as she saw it, was to show the realism of this sense of distance. What is this invisible parade she believed in, and the urgent message concerning it which she heard in the peacocks' cry? Caroline Gordon says of Flannery O'Connor:

> She came to the conclusion that the fiction writer — the 'good fiction writer' is a 'realist of distances'. His protagonist, no matter how forthrightly he is portrayed in his mundane surroundings, is always involved in a supernatural experience. The chief concern of the fiction writer, she held is 'with mystery as it is incarnated to human life'.[2]

We resist mystery because we tend to give the primary place to explanation. But religion brings to our attention, the limits of human existence, limits for which no further explanations can be found. Religion, *in this context*, asks us to die to the understanding. What confronts us is not put right by the understanding. In religion, meeting what confronts us is a form of acceptance in terms of the grace of God. As we saw in the last essay, such acceptance can arise from contemplating the fact that the rain falls on the just and the unjust. Everything is ours, not by right, but by the grace of God. This is what Job came to realise. The theodicies, the explanations, offered by his so-called comforters, are seen as a kind of hubris which invades the heavens. Putting these aside, for Job, is a matter of letting wonder take the place of explanation. He is asked a number of questions by God which are meant to evoke this wonder: he is asked whether the rain has a father, whether he knows the treasures of the snow, and to reflect on the laying of the foundations of the earth: 'When the morning stars sang together and all the sons of God shouted for joy' (*Job*:38:7). This wonder at creation is also Job's redemption. It is what enables him to say, 'The Lord gave, and the Lord hath taken away; blessed be the name of the Lord' (Job 1:21).

But the celebration of mystery and grace in Christianity is realised, not only in our relations to the external world, but in our relations to other human beings. Here, too, Flannery O'Connor wanted to reveal religious mysteries which may come to us at the limits of explanation. The mysteries she reveals are not like detective mysteries. They can be solved. They are not philosophical mysteries. They can be dissolved. Flannery O'Connor's mysteries are revealed *as mysteries*. The notion of God's grace is not meant to explain contingencies in our relations with each other. On the contrary, the very notion of divine grace grows out of contemplating these very contingencies.

To talk of mystery, in this way, brought Flannery O'Connor up against the tendency to think that everything can be understood. We find it hard to accept good and evil as primary data. We want to explain them in terms of conditions held to be more fundamental than themselves: psychological, sociological or economic. Flannery O'Connor was under no illusion about the power of the resistance to mystery: 'Since the eighteenth century, the popular spirit of each succeeding age has tended more and more to the view that the ills and misfortunes of life will eventually fall before the scientific advances of man, a belief that is still going strong even though this is the first generation to face total extinction because of these advances.'³

As if these difficulties were not enough, Flannery O'Connor had to combat tendencies within religious circles themselves to etherealise faith; to create an unbridgeable gap between the mundane and mystery. In her novels and stories she combats, again and again, the Manichean heresy: the belief that all matter is evil and that spirituality consists in approaching the infinite directly without the mediation of matter. Such attempts at pseudo-directness make the operation of grace a matter of instant uplift. It is no surprise that those in flight from grace seek instant answers elsewhere. Flannery O'Connor, on the other hand, shows the distance between man and God realistically, by showing grace and mystery at work in human life. As Sister Kathleen Feeley has said:

> To make the mystery of man's Redemption transparent in fiction, Flannery O'Connor grounded her work in reality. She portrayed the visible world by accurate description, making it real — as she said herself — 'through what can be seen, heard, smelt, tasted and touched'. She captured people, places and events in the rural South and, through her art, used them to suggest the life of all mankind. For her, reality did not lead to mystery; it included it. The unseen was as real to her as the visible universe.⁴

In one of Flannery O'Connor's favourite short stories, *The Artificial Nigger*, she explores a relationship between an old man and his grandson, a relationship which is to change when mystery and grace enter into it. When we first meet Mr Head, there is little to suggest that mystery or grace mean anything to him. On the contrary, he is a self-sufficient man, wise in the ways of the world. '. . . age was a choice blessing and that only with years does a man enter into that calm understanding of life that makes him a suitable guide for the young. This, at least had been his experience.'

This calm understanding is to be put to the test, since he and his grandson, Nelson, are to take a journey from the country to the city. In the grandfather's view, the journey is to be a moral lesson for the young boy. He had been born in the city and was boastful about it. He needed to be taught a lesson, to realise the distance he had to travel between immaturity and maturity, ignorance and knowledge, pride and humility. Since he was born there, Nelson insists that this will be his second visit to the city, although he cannot remember anything about it. Mr Head seems confident that he has the maturity and knowledge required to take the boy on this journey which is both geographical and moral. Once he has shown the boy the city, he is confident he will be content to stay at home.

Yet, appearances are deceptive. Neither Mr Head nor Nelson are as confident as they seem to be. They have good reason not to be. Mr Head would like to give the impression that the city, the way of the world, is something he knows all about and has mastered. It is now time to show this to his grandson. Yet, early on in the story, there are signs that all is not well. Mr Head had vowed to wake before Nelson to prepare for their early start. He did not need an alarm clock to wake him: 'His physical reactions, like his moral ones, were guided by his will and strong character'. Yet, Nelson beats him to it and has already made the breakfast when he wakes. Nelson asks if he is sure that he won't get lost in the city. Mr Head replies, 'Have you ever seen me lost?' Actually, he does not know his way around the city. He is apprehensive about wandering far from the railway station; he won't enter large stores because last time he had done so, he couldn't find his way out again. In fact he and Nelson walk in circles and when they find themselves outside the railway station yet again, Nelson's suspicions grow, but Mr Head denies that he is lost.

But Nelson's bravado is not what it seems either. The city which
he claims to remember with such pride, is far more alien to him
than he will admit. As they near the city he has his secret fears:
'He realised the old man would be his only support in the strange
place they were approaching. He would be entirely alone in the
world if he was ever lost from his grandfather.' Grandfather and
grandson are in a common condition, but one which they will
not admit to each other and only partially and grudgingly to
themselves.

In Mr Head's talk of the city to the young boy, the sign, above
all others, that things aren't good there is, to use his own words,
the presence of niggers. The boy had never seen one, the last
having been chased from the county 12 years earlier. He boasts
that he will recognise one when he sees one, but is ashamed and
angry when he fails to do so on the train, thinking that the term
'nigger' only applied to people who were very black. At Nelson's
failure, Mr Head comments to a fellow-traveller: 'He's never seen
anything before . . . Ignorant as the day he was born, but I mean
for him to get his fill once and for all.'

Nelson's journey from ignorance to knowledge is going to be
one in which he learns who's who in the world. On the train, Mr
Head shows him some people with very black skins, the way he
can put-down the rudeness of the black waiters, the roped off
areas where black people had to sit in the dining car, the black
shoe-polishers in the city. When Nelson annoys him by claiming
to remember where he was born as they inadvertently wander
into a black neighbourhood, Mr Head replies: 'This is where you
were born — right here with all the niggers.'[5]

When they get out of the black neighbourhood, Mr Head is
convinced they are travelling in the right direction because the
people are white now. But to get out of the black neighbourhood,
Mr Head makes Nelson ask a black woman for directions. She
teases Nelson, and he finds himself desiring her.

He stood drinking in every detail of her. His eyes travelled up
from her great knees to her forehead and then made a triangular
path from the glistening sweat on her neck down and across
her tremendous bosom and over her bare arm to where her
fingers lay hidden in her hair. He suddenly wanted her to reach
down and pick him up and draw him against her and then he
wanted to feel her breath on his face. He wanted to look down

and down into her eyes while she held him tighter and tighter.
He had never had such a feeling before. He felt as if he were
reeling through a pitchblack tunnel.

As Sister Kathleen Feeley says:

> This encounter drains all pride from Nelson; in some obscure
> way, he realises what Mr Head has not learned in sixty years:
> that one's moral reactions cannot always be 'guided by his will
> and strong character', as Mr Head asserts. His face 'burning
> with shame', Nelson takes the old man's hand. His trembling
> mouth could have told his grandfather that he had seen enough,
> even before he voiced his capitulation: 'I only said I was born
> here and I never had nothing to do with that. I want to go
> home.'[6]

The boy has started the journey from pride to humility, but his
grandfather has not. On the contrary, he still wants to teach the
boy a lesson. When Nelson falls asleep, he moves about 20 feet
away from him. When he wakes, he will realise his true dependence on his maturity To the old man's dismay, Nelson panics
when he wakes and begins to run, making it difficult for his
grandfather to keep up with him. Nelson collides with a woman,
upsetting her groceries and injuring her ankle. She is angrily
claiming compensation and threatening to call the police. When
Mr Head arrives, Nelson clings to him desperately. The woman
turns her demands on Mr Head. He denies all knowledge of
Nelson:

> 'This is not my boy', he said. 'I never saw him before.'
> He felt Nelson's fingers fall out of his flesh
> The women dropped back, staring at him in horror, as if they
> were so repulsed by a man who would deny his own image and
> likeness that they could not bear to lay hands on him. Mr Head
> walked on, through a space they silently cleared, and left Nelson
> behind. Ahead of him he saw nothing but a hollow tunnel that
> had once been a street.

Mr Head's denial of Nelson echoes, of course, Peter's denial of
Christ. Both Peter and Mr Head had gloried in their own self-
sufficiency; had said that no matter what happened in the city,

they could be relied on, would never let anyone down. But for them, it might be said, Jupiter thundered from a clear sky. Simone Weil has said that the essence of Peter's denial is not in the breaking of the promise, but in the making of it. In making their promises, Peter and Mr Head are saying that they do not need the grace of God. After his denial, Peter wept. Mr Head, still lost in the city, is brought to a confession too. He is forced to turn his back on his self-sufficiency; to ask a passer-by to point him in a homeward direction: 'He waved both arms like someone shipwrecked on a desert island. 'I'm lost!' he called 'I'm lost and can't find my way and me and this boy have got to catch this train, and I can't find the station. Oh Gawd I'm lost! Oh help me Gawd I'm lost!'

So Mr Head and Nelson have made their respective confessions. They've confessed their need. But where do they go from there? Nelson has new feelings of anger and hatred which he cannot cope with. He cannot forgive his grandfather's denial of him. Neither can Mr Head see how his grandson can forgive him, although he needs that forgiveness desperately.

They are brought together through the grace and mercy which is mediated through a plaster statue of a black man. Flannery O'Connor tells us in a letter where the title of the story, *The Artificial Nigger* came from:

Well, I never had heard the phrase before, but my mother was out trying to buy a cow, and she rode up the country a-piece. She had the address of a man who was supposed to have a cow for sale, but she couldn't find it, so she stopped in a small town and asked the countryman on the side of the road where the house was, and he said, 'Well, you go into this town and you can't miss it 'cause it's the only house in town with an artificial nigger in front of it'. So I decided I would have to find a story to fit that.

On their way to the railway station, Mr Head and Nelson come across such a statue. 'It was not possible to tell if the artificial Negro were meant to be young or old; he looked too miserable to be either. He was meant to look happy because his mouth was stretched up at the corners but the chipped eye and the angle he was cocked at gave him a wild look of misery instead.' Grandfather and grandson are drawn together before the statue:

The two of them stood there with their necks forward at almost the same angle and their shoulders curved in almost exactly the same way and their hands trembling identically in their pockets. Mr Head looked like an ancient child and Nelson like a miniature old man. They stood gazing at the artificial Negro as if they were faced with some great mystery, some monument to another's victory that brought them together in their common defeat. They could both feel it dissolving their differences like an action of mercy. Mr Head had never known before what mercy felt like because he had been too good to deserve any, but he felt he knew now.

Still, something of the old desire to be wise remains; the desire to appear wise to the boy. But when he tries to speak in the old way, he finds new revelatory words forcing their way to his lips. They forge a new unity between the boy and himself:

He looked at Nelson and understood that he must say something to the child to show that he was still wise and in the look the boy returned he saw a hungry need for that assurance. Nelson's eyes seemed to implore him to explain once and for all the mystery of existence.

Mr Head opened his lips to make a lofty statement and heard himself say, 'They ain't got enough real ones here. They got to have an artificial one.'

After a second, the boy nodded with a strange shivering about his mouth, and said, 'Let's go home before we get ourselves lost again'.

In the very degradation of the black man in the statue, in the representation of that which Mr Head had taught Nelson to regard as the lowest in life, that which mature wisdom would lead one to avoid and disown, in this very source, a need in all men is to be discovered — the need to acknowledge a common humanity and a common limitation, standing in need of grace and forgiveness. The revelation which comes from the statue of the despised and the rejected echoes, once again, the grace which is mediated in the despised and rejected Saviour of Christianity.

The two travellers come home, the train from the city disappearing like Eden's serpent into the woods. As for Mr Head, he sees the distance from God at which he had been living his life. He had settled for the seen in his assessment of people and places:

> He had never thought himself a great sinner before but he saw now that his true depravity had been hidden from him lest it cause him despair. He realised that he was forgiven for sins from the beginning of time, when he had conceived in his own heart the sin of Adam, until the present, when he had denied poor Nelson. He saw that no sin was too monstrous for him to claim as his own, and since God loved in proportion as He forgave, he felt ready at that instant to enter Paradise.

As for Nelson, although he still looks at his grandfather with a mixture of fatigue and suspicion, when he sees the city train disappear, he says, 'I'm glad I've went once but I'll never go back again!' Back home again, grandfather and grandson, old and young, I like to think they heard, as never before, the cry of the peacock, urgent, but, at the same time, a cheer for an invisible parade. *Eee-oo-ii! Eee-oo-ii!*

An invisible parade! The possibility of such a notion is far removed from the starting point of these essays. There, belief in God was thought to commit us to 'a somewhere over the rainbow'. It was said that we need to empty such a heaven, and by so doing make the sky a friendlier place, a part of labour and a part of pain, not a dividing and indifferent blue — make it a human sky. For others, it was not so. The sky remains endless, showing nothing. How can an indifferent sky tell of God? Why doesn't Jupiter thunder from a clear sky? Yet, as we have seen, for believers, that indifferent sky becomes an impartial one with a religious aspect, making it possible for them to see themselves as creatures under God's heaven. This experience, which, as we have seen, comes to the grandfather and his grandson in Flannery O'Connor's story, also came to the poet R. S. Thomas in *The Moor:*

> . . . I walked on
> Simple and poor, while the air crumbled
> And broke on me generously as bread.

I do not find the majority of philosophers of religion discussing these possibilities of religious belief. The journey by which we have arrived at them has been both literary and philosophical:

from 'a somewhere over the rainbow' to a sacramental sky. It is a journey, I believe, which must be undertaken by anyone seriously interested in the issues which confront philosophy and religion today.

Notes

1. In Flannery O'Connor, *Mystery and Manners* (Farrar, Straus & Giroux, 1969), pp. 14–5.
2. Caroline Gordon, forewood to *Flannery O'Connor: Voice of the Peacock* by Kathleen Feeley (Fordham University Press, 1982), p. xi.
3. Flannery O'Connor, 'The Grotesque in Southern Fiction' in *Mystery and Manners*, p. 41.
4. Kathleen Feeley, *Flannery O'Connor: Voice of the Peacock*, (Fordham University Press), pp. 5–6.
5. In Flannery O'Connor, *The Complete Stories* (Farrar, Straus & Giroux, 1981).
6. Kathleen Feeley, op. cit., p,. 122.

Index of Names

Index of Subjects